YEARS

SIMON &
SCHUSTER

ALSO BY HILLARY RODHAM CLINTON

State of Terror
(with Louise Penny)

The Book of Gutsy Women:
Favorite Stories of Courage and Resilience
(with Chelsea Clinton)

What Happened

Stronger Together
(with Tim Kaine)

Hard Choices: A Memoir

Living History

It Takes a Village: And Other Lessons
Children Teach Us

SOMETHING LOST, SOMETHING GAINED

Reflections on Life, Love, and Liberty

HILLARY RODHAM CLINTON

Simon & Schuster

NEW YORK   LONDON   TORONTO
SYDNEY   NEW DELHI

1230 Avenue of the Americas
New York, NY 10020

First Simon & Schuster hardcover edition September 2024

SIMON & SCHUSTER and colophon are registered trademarks of Simon & Schuster, LLC

"Both Sides Now" written by Joni Mitchell. Published by Crazy Crow Music (SOCAN). By Arrangement with Reservoir Media Music (ASCAP).

The letter dated June 5, 1994, from John F. Kennedy, Jr. to President and Secretary Clinton, is quoted with permission from Caroline Kennedy.

Excerpt from the composition "Keep Marching" from the Broadway musical *Suffs*. Music and Lyrics by Shaina Taub. © 2023 Shaina Taub.

"The Hill We Climb" Copyright © 2021 by Amanda Gorman. Used by permission of the author.

"Silence" written by Anasuya Sengupta.

Simon & Schuster: Celebrating 100 Years of Publishing in 2024

For information about special discounts for bulk purchases, please contact Simon & Schuster Special Sales at 1-866-506-1949 or business@simonandschuster.com.

The Simon & Schuster Speakers Bureau can bring authors to your live event. For more information or to book an event, contact the Simon & Schuster Speakers Bureau at 1-866-248-3049 or visit our website at www.simonspeakers.com.

Interior design by Paul Dippolito

Jacket photograph © Annie Leibovitz
Hairstylist: Sally Hershberger
Makeup: Rebecca Restrepo
Stylist: Tabitha Simmons

Manufactured in the United States of America

1   3   5   7   9   10   8   6   4   2

Library of Congress Cataloging-in-Publication Data is available.

ISBN 978-1-6680-1723-4
ISBN 978-1-6680-1725-8 (ebook)

For my grandchildren
Charlotte, Aidan and
Jasper with love and
hope for the future you
and your generation
deserve.

Let us, then, be up and doing,
  With a heart for any fate;
Still achieving, still pursuing,
  Learn to labor and to wait.

—Henry Wadsworth Longfellow
"A Psalm of Life"

CONTENTS

SOMETHING LOST, SOMETHING GAINED

She held court like a queen. As I watched Joni Mitchell at the Grammys in 2024—singing from a lavish armchair that looked like a golden throne and, as one critic put it, "wielding a cane like a scepter"—the word that kept coming to mind was "regal." Mitchell was eighty years old, and in 2015, she had suffered a debilitating brain aneurysm that left her virtually unable to speak, let alone sing. Yet she fought back, and now here she was, performing her spellbinding song "Both Sides Now." Many of the music world's biggest stars listened in rapt attention. At home, I too was on the edge of my seat.

I've been a Joni Mitchell fan since the 1960s. There were two wonderful early versions of "Both Sides Now," one from Mitchell, who wrote the song, and a cover by the great Judy Collins. I thought both were terrific, although at that point I had more questions than answers about life and I didn't really know what it meant to be in love. It was still a few years before I would meet the tall, red-bearded law student who couldn't stop talking about Arkansas. But I was the right age to be captivated by a song about how the passage of time can bring a new perspective on life and love.

It was a heady, anguished, exhilarating time to be a college student. The Vietnam War was raging. Protests for peace, civil rights, and social justice were swelling. The innocence and illusions of childhood were falling away. "Tears and fears and feeling proud," as the song goes. Like so many in my generation, my eyes had been opened to a darker side of American life, to injustice, corruption, assassinations, and war. At Wellesley College and then Yale Law School, I joined protests and marches, read everything I could get my hands on, and stayed up late into the night discussing the fate of the world with my classmates. Some days it felt as if looking "at life from both sides now" gave me enormous clarity—about right and wrong and what it would take to make progress; other days, it just felt confusing. When Mitchell sang, "I really don't know life at all," she was speaking for many of us. The mix of emotions she captured felt so specific to our time and place, but also timeless. Most young people leaving behind adolescence and grappling with adulthood have felt some version of it.

Later, Mitchell came to occupy a special place in my family's life. In 1978, I was walking down the King's Road in the Chelsea neighborhood of London with Bill (who looked less like a Viking but was still quite excited about Arkansas), when we heard Judy Collins's cover of Mitchell's "Chelsea Morning" wafting from one of the storefronts. Bill started singing along. "If we ever have a daughter, we should name her Chelsea," he said. Two years later we did.

We had our share of "dreams and schemes and circus crowds." Then one day I looked up and I was seventy-six. There was Joni Mitchell again, singing on my television, her voice deeper and world-weary but unmistakably hers. The old words took on new meaning. Gone was the twentysomething shaking off the rose-colored glasses of a love affair and the illusions of adolescence, and in her place was a matriarch reflecting on the hard-earned wisdom of a long, eventful life.

> *Oh, but now old friends, they're acting strange*
> *And they shake their heads and they tell me that I've changed*
> *Well, something's lost, but something's gained*
> *In living every day.*

It felt like I was listening with new ears, almost as if I were hearing the song for the first time.

Personally and professionally I've come through so many highs and lows, times when I felt on top of the world and others when I was in a deep, dark hole. After all these years, I really have looked at life and love "from both sides now." How do you tally up and reckon with the losses and gains of a life? Or of a nation and a world? These are questions with often incomplete, unsatisfying, or missing answers.

Old wounds still hurt, but I have a new sense of proportion. Time will do that. I look back on things that used to feel monumental, existential even, with clearer, calmer eyes. Rivals like the Bushes and the Obamas have become friends. The cut-and-parry of politics matters less, but the check-and-balance of democracy matters more. And little moments now loom large. Hugging my daughter, holding my husband's hand, making my grandchildren laugh with a silly knock-knock joke, going for long walks and afternoon swims. Glorious grandmother days with "ice cream castles in the air / And feather canyons everywhere."

But loss is also an ever-present companion. "So many things I would have done / But clouds got in my way."

On the afternoon of Thursday, May 30, 2024, I was sitting at the desk in my little home office in Washington editing this book. I had the sound turned off on my phone so I could concentrate. But when I picked it up to check the time, I saw the breaking news alert that Donald Trump had been convicted of thirty-four felonies related to election fraud in 2016. I put down my pen, took a deep breath, and felt tears in my eyes. There was a jolt of disbelief that he had been held accountable for interfering in the election. A pang of vindication. It was now beyond a reasonable doubt that Trump had committed serious crimes in order to win. He was exactly who we thought he was. But with vindication also came sorrow, because nothing can change what happened or the damage done since, and it's far from clear that his conviction will be enough to prevent him from returning to power. Sorrow because our country deserves better than this disgrace.

That's not all. Since 2016, people have asked me, "Will you ever be able to move on?" Move on? I wish. History has its hold on me, on all of us. As Faulkner wrote, "The past is never dead. It's not even past." I live with it every day. And every day I make an effort to turn my eyes to the future instead.

I closed the breaking news alert and exchanged a few funny tweets and memes with friends over text. "Did you know Donald Trump is the first actor from the movie *Home Alone 2* to be convicted of 34 felonies?" I laughed, picked up my pen, and got back to work. That evening I had to appear at an event for women's rights. I started my remarks by asking, "Anything going on today?" The audience roared with a kind of catharsis.

People also ask if I reveled in schadenfreude when Trump was impeached (twice), defeated, indicted in four different cases, and now convicted of thirty-four felonies. *Schadenfreude* is one of those long German words with a very specific meaning: "Finding joy in the troubles of others." Not particularly admirable, but quite human. Scholars like Tiffany Watt Smith have traced similar concepts across cultures and languages. The French call it *joie maligne*. In Japan they say, "The misfortunes of others taste like honey."

Whenever Trump suffers some new humiliation, memes pop up on social media with me laughing, sipping champagne, or flashing a knowing smile. My favorite is the photo taken by the great Barb Kinney of President Obama and me backstage at the 2016 Democratic National Convention. We're sitting in two black chairs pulled close together. Barack, usually restrained and self-controlled, is doubled over with laughter. I've just shared something so funny I could barely get through it. I wish I could remember what it was. Fortunately, countless internet users have come up with their own captions, many of them about Trump. Like: "And then he said, 'No one has more respect for women than I do.' "

It would be funnier if it weren't so awful.

Was there even a tiny bit of schadenfreude when I heard about the verdict in New York? I won't say no. But the truth is that I felt more relief than pleasure seeing the rule of law prevail, even briefly.

And surprise. During the trial, I had tried not to pay much attention. Trump has spent his entire life avoiding accountability; I didn't think this time would be different. And the whole thing was just so sordid and painful. There was the national disgrace—not so much the spectacle of a former president on trial but the fact that this criminal was president in the first place. There was also the opening of old wounds. Prosecutors made the case that Trump "orchestrated a criminal scheme to corrupt the 2016 presidential election." Pundits seeking to distract from these damning allegations claimed these were mere bookkeeping errors—victimless crimes. But there were victims. A fraud was committed against the American people, against all of us.

Trump committed election fraud because he was convinced that a late-breaking scandal would have sunk his campaign. Was he right? Did his criminal conspiracy tip the outcome? Here's what I can tell you: the 2016 election was decided by 77,744 votes out of a total 136 million cast. If news about Trump's affair with porn star Stormy Daniels had caused just forty thousand people across Wisconsin, Michigan, and Pennsylvania to change their minds, I would have won. It's no wonder that on election night, one of the lawyers who had negotiated the hush money cover-up deal texted his counterpart: "What have we done?"

Even now, just thinking about that moment makes fury well up in my chest. I'm glad the crimes have been exposed and the truth is known. But as long as he remains within striking distance of the White House, the dominant emotion I feel is dread—plus determination to do all I can to stop him.

People often say to me, "You warned us, and I wish we had listened." What am I supposed to say to that? Yes, I did warn you. Yes, I said Trump was a con man, a Russian puppet, and a threat to democracy. I warned that he would end abortion rights, inflame our divisions, and botch every crisis he faced. I take no pleasure in being right. In fact, I hate it.

In Greek mythology, there was a woman named Cassandra who was blessed by being able to see the future but cursed to never be believed. She tried to warn the Trojans that Greek invaders were hiding in the giant horse they were pulling inside their gates, but no one listened. In 2016, that's how it felt. I tried to raise the alarm in every way I could, but the media and many in the political establishment dismissed me as overwrought, even hysterical. They didn't take Trump seriously. Or literally. They thought I was trying to distract from the real issue: my emails. And they were convinced I would win, so it didn't matter.

At a recent event, a retired senior FBI official came up to me and apologized for the way the bureau mishandled the investigation into my emails. He wanted me to know how sorry he was that he hadn't stopped Jim Comey, the FBI director who trashed me in public and foolishly announced that he was reopening the investigation just days before the election. I stared at him for a minute, trying to contain my anger. You're sorry? Now? Finally, I said, "I would have been a great president," and walked away.

Cassandra wasn't drinking champagne as Troy burned. She was miserable.

People sometimes ask if I'll ever run for president again. I will admit that I was tempted during Trump's disastrous presidency. I knew I could do a better job for America. I never doubted my capability, and I still had the desire to do it—what politicos call "the fire in the belly." Third time's the charm, right? But I knew in my head that the answer, in my case, was no. I had my shot. It was time to pass the baton and move on.

It took a while for my heart to catch up. How do you give up on a dream, especially one so big, one that you came so close to reaching? It wasn't easy accepting that I would never serve as president. It started with keeping busy, trying new things, cultivating new dreams. President Joe Biden's success in governing helped close the gap between my head and my heart. So did seeing Kamala Harris become the first woman vice president. She and I have had long talks about the challenges facing women at the highest levels of public life, and I admire how she's persevered and become an important partner for the president.

Harris is chronically underestimated, as are so many women in politics. I was impressed by her record as attorney general in California, where she took on drug traffickers and predatory lenders, and as a U.S. Senator. Her sharp questioning of Trump's odious Supreme Court nominees was particularly memorable. So it was no surprise that after those same justices helped overturn *Roe v. Wade*, Harris became the Biden administration's most passionate and effective advocate for restoring women's reproductive rights.

While it still pains me that I couldn't break that highest, hardest glass ceiling, I'm proud that my two presidential campaigns paved the way for women like Harris, Kirsten Gillibrand, Amy Klobuchar, and Elizabeth Warren to run, and for Harris to serve as vice president. I still believe we will have a woman president one day. I hope it's sooner than many expect.

There are other losses that pain me, too. I miss my parents, my brother Tony, dear friends and colleagues. I miss loved ones still here physically but lost in the past because of Alzheimer's and dementia.

I miss a time when truth mattered. I miss fact-based debates about policies to solve problems and improve lives. I miss the clear separation of church and state, once sacrosanct, now breached by culture warriors and Christian nationalists. I miss elections where everyone respects the will of the people, without constant attacks by sore losers and wannabe dictators.

I don't feel *old*. Yes, I have more aches and pains than I used to. I go to more funerals than I'd like. But I also read more novels and see more Broadway shows. Somehow, I've become a novelist myself— and a Broadway producer and a Hollywood filmmaker; I even took clown lessons with Chelsea at the Moulin Rouge in Paris, red nose and all. Never thought I'd ever do that!

More important, my curiosity about the world and the thrill I get from rolling up my sleeves and diving into new problems have not diminished with age; if anything, they've deepened. That's why I relish speaking out against election deniers and democracy doubters and talking with guests on my podcast who challenge my thinking, inspire me to work harder, or just make me laugh. It's why last year I went to the salt flats of Gujarat, to meet Indian women who harvest salt under a broiling sun, to learn how they're coping with the extreme heat caused by climate change. It's why I gladly respond to requests for help from people around the world, from Afghanistan to Arkansas.

Once, I wasted energy worrying what critics might say or how the media would respond; now I have an easier time brushing all that aside and just doing what feels right and important. Time and so many battles won and lost have given me a thicker skin and a stiffer spine.

Jane Fonda has a great way of looking at the process of aging. She says people used to think about aging as an arc: "You're born, you peak at midlife, and then you decline into decrepitude." But that's outdated, especially in a time when we can live healthy, productive lives for decades longer than previous generations. Now, Jane says, we should see aging as a staircase: "You gain well-being, spirit, soul, wisdom, the ability to be truly intimate, and a life with intention."

It's like the great athletes and actors who find new strengths as they age. Like Serena Williams playing smarter, not just harder, or LeBron James earning so many more assists in his later seasons, or Meryl Streep fearlessly embracing getting older in her life and roles.

That's the kind of aging I want to do.

When Bill turned seventy, it struck him that he had now lived longer than any man in his family going back three generations. He had always secretly believed he would die young. And when he started having heart trouble, he became more sure of it. Yet somehow he was still here.

We started talking a lot about what it means to have more

yesterdays than tomorrows. Putting it like that really focuses the mind. We both have a profound sense of gratitude for all the blessings we've received in our lives—and a sense of responsibility. It is clearer than ever that we have to use our remaining tomorrows to try to give our grandchildren—and all kids—a better world. Every day matters more if there are fewer of them ahead. What are we going to do with the time we have left? How can we make, in the words of Mary Oliver, our "one wild and precious life" count?

When you're young, you live every day in the present tense. When you're old, it's tempting to live in the past, even an imagined past. These days, I find myself thinking mostly about the future—and how important it is to live, in Longfellow's phrase, "with a heart for any fate."

I've spent my life working to build a better, fairer, freer world, and I've lived long enough to see astounding progress. My family didn't own a television set until I was five, yet I can now FaceTime with my grandchildren from across the globe. My mother was born before women had the right to vote and was able to proudly cast a ballot for me for president. I came of age in a world where women couldn't have bank accounts in their own name and went on to become the first woman to win a presidential primary, the nomination of a major party, and the national popular vote. I grew up in a time of segregation, yet I had the great honor to serve as secretary of state for our first Black president. I hope the years ahead will bring even more exciting advances for America and the world. But, to borrow a line I love from the Tony Award–winning musical *Suffs*, "progress is possible, not guaranteed." We have to work for it. Fight for it. Earn it. And right now, so much of what we've gained is in danger of being lost.

The January 6 insurrection scared me, and it should scare you, too. Our democracy is under assault from within and without. Abortion rights are already eliminated or severely restricted in more than half the states in our country. Voting rights are hanging by a thread. If Republicans take control of the government in the next election, I have no doubt they'll try to tear up the social safety net we've spent generations building—big cuts to Medicaid, Medicare, and Social Security and gutting Obamacare. Anything that helps hardworking people get ahead and live a decent life will be on the chopping block. Instead of pulling together to take on generational challenges like climate change and economic inequality, it feels like we're spinning further apart. Technology, especially social media, is making us more lonely and more divided—and it's having a particularly devastating impact on our kids. Sometimes it seems as if common sense itself is in danger of disappearing. How else to explain the calls to poison control centers from people who drank bleach during the pandemic?

Yet despite all our problems, I remain "an optimist who worries a lot," to borrow a phrase from my friend Madeleine Albright. I still believe there's nothing wrong with America that can't be fixed by what's right with America. Our country is bigger than the trolls and tyrants. Still, if you're not worried, you're not paying attention. If you *are* paying attention, then keep setting goals and planning to make the most of all the tomorrows you have ahead. Let's earn our optimism.

This country was built by men and women who believed in service, community, and working together for the greater good—pioneers who stuck together in wagon trains, farmers who pitched in on barn raisings and quilting bees, immigrants who joined volunteer fire departments, enslaved people who risked their lives to serve on the Underground Railroad and help others escape to freedom. When the French writer Alexis de Tocqueville visited America in the 1830s, he called this our "habits of the heart." The sense that we're all in it together made our democratic experiment possible—and it may be the only thing that can save us still.

Winning elections at every level is essential. We have to defeat the demagogues and election deniers so convincingly that there's no room for dirty tricks. We have to strengthen voting rights and fight back against disinformation. But ultimately, winning the next election is not enough. We must work together to restitch our unraveling social fabric and to rebuild Americans' trust in one another, our democracy, and our shared future. There's so much to lose—but even more to gain if we keep going together.

"Tears and fears and feeling proud." That's what it was like writing this book. Once again Joni nailed it. I had several false starts and fell down more rabbit holes than Alice. But in the end, I found what I was looking for. This book reflects the mix of anxiety and optimism I feel in this strange, perilous moment. It's a love letter to life, family, and democracy.

This book is a snapshot of how I see the world right now. My editor suggested that it should feel like sitting with me at a dinner party, so it's both political and personal. It's about the fight for democracy and also about being a friend, wife, mother, and grandmother. It's about getting older—and, I hope, a little wiser. You should feel free to read it straight through or jump around, the way a good conversation does.

Despite spending decades in the public eye—or perhaps *because* of it—sharing my most personal reflections does not come naturally. Through all my years of public service, the "service" part has always come easier to me than the "public" part. I'd generally rather write about policy and politics. Make an argument. Have a debate. But I've discovered that it can be liberating to open up. I hope that combining the two—the broccoli and the ice cream, if you will—makes for a rewarding meal. You will find both in this book.

These days, I find myself thinking about the past with new perspective. I write about that. But more than anything, I find myself thinking about the future. I write about that, too. This book reflects the time in which it was written, in the spring and early summer of 2024, as it became clear Donald Trump would be the Republican presidential nominee, and so it explains my passionate, deeply felt conviction that allowing him to take power again would be catastrophic for our country and the world. If he gets back to the White House, we'll have more inflation and less freedom. It won't just be a rerun of his first term. Since losing in 2020, Trump has become even more unhinged and dangerous. He wants us to fear the future and fear one another. He'd take us backward, with abortion bans, tax cuts for billionaires, and sweetheart deals for polluters at home and dictators abroad. He'd rerun the same trickle-down economics playbook that has failed previous Republican presidents—including him. It's not a coincidence that ten of the past eleven recessions have hit during Republican administrations. Trump presided over a significant net drop in jobs. And of all the net new jobs created in America since 1989, just 4 percent came under Republican administrations. Democratic administrations, including Biden-Harris, have inherited economic crises, gotten the country back on its feet, and helped create 96 percent of all the new jobs. It's like clockwork: They break it, we fix it. With the Supreme Court granting him immunity from prosecution for official acts, there's virtually no limit on the crimes he could commit and the damage he could do to our democracy.

I also explain why I think that electing Democrats is so crucial in this difficult time. Republicans have nominated a convicted criminal who only cares about himself. Democrats have led America's comeback and at every level are fighting for the American people. That's an easy choice. Can you tell I feel strongly about this?

But this book is not just about one election. The issues you'll find in these pages, from the battle between democracy and autocracy to the fight for women's rights and civil rights, the climate crisis, and the economic concerns of working families, all will continue to be vital no matter who wins in November. The work won't stop. The fight will go on. And so must we.

I believe that if you want to keep going, you have to keep learning. You have to stay open to new experiences and new ideas. You'll read about some of the ways I've been doing that. My students at Columbia University challenge me to see the world through their eyes and their passions. The women organizing resistance to cruel abortion bans in many states are upending long-standing assumptions about what is possible in politics. Ukrainian soldiers, citizens, and leaders are teaching all of us about the resilience of democracy.

I'm still learning from those closest to me. After nearly a half century of marriage, I discover new joys every day just from loving, talking, and laughing with my husband. Chelsea continues to delight and amaze me with her courage, from taking on bullies and liars wherever they emerge, including the fact-based battles she wages against vaccine deniers, to the global work she does to help bring health care to those in need. She tells her wonderful children she wants them to be brave and kind, both of which she is.

I'm still learning from my faith and the way it challenges me every day in this season of my life. As we are reassured in Isaiah 46:4, "I will be your God throughout your lifetime, until your hair is white with age. I made you and I will carry you along and save you."

The years since the 2016 election have been ones of challenge and change for me, our country, and the world. I have followed the tumult from my home and from the inside of the maelstrom, looking for ways to help stop the tides of disunion and disinformation. I've kept busy supporting candidates and causes who represent my values, speaking out against threats to women and democracy. I've found new ways to pursue my interests, from the classroom to the theater. Everyone has to find their own approach to aging, but for me, remaining in the fight is who I am and who I'll always be.

Joni Mitchell's right. Something's lost, but something's gained. There's more life to live. I can't wait.

INSURRECTION

On the afternoon of January 6, 2021, I came home from a walk near our house in Chappaqua, New York, and found Bill and Chelsea transfixed in front of the television in our breakfast room. Bill was sitting at the glass table with his head in his hands and a sadness about him that I hadn't seen in a long time. Chelsea was standing by the table, watching in shock and disbelief.

"What's happened?" I asked, with a sinking feeling in my heart.

Bill and Chelsea both looked at me and started trying to explain the inexplicable. There was chaos at the Capitol. Nobody on cable news had a great handle on what was going on, but it looked as if a mob of Trump supporters was attacking police officers and forcing its way into the Capitol to disrupt the official certification of the 2020 election results. Trump himself had just given a speech to a crowd on the Ellipse outside the White House, urging his followers to "walk down Pennsylvania Avenue" and "fight like hell," otherwise "you're not going to have a country anymore."

His claims of widespread voter fraud had already been exposed as a lie, plain and simple. There was no evidence. None. Every court had rejected his fantasies. Honest state and local elections officials—both Republicans and Democrats—had resisted his intimidation campaign. Yet he refused to admit he had lost, fair and square. Instead, he whipped his followers into a frenzy with the lie that somehow Vice President Mike Pence could single-handedly overturn the election results. The arsonist in chief had poured on the gasoline and lit the match. Now he stood back and watched from inside the White House as the conflagration ignited.

I sat down next to Bill and stared at the violent images in horror. I had served for eight years as a U.S. senator for New York. Every day, I'd walked the halls of the Capitol now filled with insurrectionists hunting members of Congress and the vice president. One of my happiest memories was taking the oath of office on the Senate floor on January 3, 2001, with Bill, Chelsea, and my mother beaming from the gallery above. I swore to "support and defend the Constitution of the United States against all enemies, foreign and domestic." Now, two decades later, those enemies were swarming that same Senate chamber.

I remember finding my desk on the Senate floor for the first time and feeling the weight of civic responsibility and the thrill of serving our great democracy. Now a shirtless rioter in face paint and a horned hat was rifling through papers left by fleeing senators. He became known as the QAnon Shaman and left a note that warned, "It's only a matter of time, justice is coming."

I thought about the fear we all felt during the evacuation of the Capitol on September 11, 2001. I had raced there as soon as I heard the news of the terrorist attacks on New York's World Trade Center and then made sure my staff moved safely to a nearby town house on Capitol Hill after the evacuation. It was a terrible, disorienting, crushing day. Our country was under attack, and no one knew when or from where the next blow would come. Now, twenty years later, we were under attack again. I prayed for the senators, representatives, and staff trying to escape the mob and wondered how things possibly could have gotten this bad.

As we watched, I thought about my three grandchildren. They, along with their parents, had moved in with us in March 2020 during the COVID-19 pandemic. It was the only silver lining of the dark cloud that hung over the whole world. The six- and four-year-olds came over from the guesthouse to see us all the time, showing up in our bedroom early in the morning and asking Bill and me to make breakfast or play. They often came over in the afternoon for tea and cookies with me in the kitchen, time I treasured. How could we explain to them what was happening? Could we honestly tell them everything was going to be okay?

Later, one of my closest aides called to say that his brother Jon, a D.C. police officer on bicycle duty that day, had been urgently called to join the fight at the Capitol. Showing up with no protection other than a bike helmet, he'd joined his colleagues trying to hold the line outside. Soon he was pressed back by the surging mob, punched and pummeled through the rotunda, and then blinded with bear spray on the stairs up to the Senate chamber. Jon had been adopted from overseas as a baby and felt pride and gratitude for being an American. It was part of why he had joined the police force. Now there he was in the heart of American democracy, bleeding for the country that took him in.

I thought about all the brave officers I'd known over the years and trusted with my life, and the attacks on the Capitol Police made me furious. I looked at the Trump flags waving amid the chaos on the television screen and thought about all the times some sanctimonious right-winger had lectured about how they "backed the blue" and believed in "law and order." Where were they now? Were they in the crowd waving those flags? Attacking police officers with clubs and firing pepper spray in their faces?

This was no ordinary riot. It was not a protest that got out of hand. As we've learned, it was a coordinated assault on our democracy with the goal of reversing the election and keeping Trump in power. As one hard-core Trumpist from Michigan explained later: "We weren't there to steal things. We weren't there to do damage. We were just there to overthrow the government."

I had feared something like this might happen, had warned about it as far back as 2016. In our third debate in that campaign, Trump had refused to commit to accepting the results of the election. If he lost, he would claim it was rigged. Violence was a staple of his rhetoric. Hostility to democracy and the rule of law was a core element of his "strongman" brand. (It's no surprise, but deeply concerning, that during his June 2024 debate with President Biden he once again refused to commit to accepting the election results). I had conceded on national television and attended Trump's inauguration, despite serious concerns about Russian interference, just as Al Gore had conceded in 2000 when the Supreme Court stopped the recount in Florida—a recount he seemed likely to win. In 2020, by contrast, without any basis other than he had lost, Trump refused to concede and whipped up the Big Lie to incite his followers to reject the outcome. All of that led predictably to the insurrection on January 6. When you start viewing the other party as traitors, criminals, or otherwise illegitimate—for example, if you spread the lie for years that our first Black president wasn't actually born in the United States, or if you lead "Lock her up!" chants at your campaign rallies—politics becomes a blood sport. Soon enough, actual blood gets spilled.

Of the many awful images from the Capitol that day, one that caught my eye and sent a chill through my heart was the picture of a Trumpist defiantly carrying a Confederate flag through the halls of Congress. The man was eventually sentenced to three years in prison for his role in the insurrection, including using his flagpole to attack Eugene Goodman, the heroic Capitol Police officer who famously managed to divert the mob away from fleeing senators. The judge noted that using a Confederate flag to assault a Black police officer was particularly hateful.

The prominent presence of that racist flag was a reminder that this violent spasm was not an isolated incident and that Trump is not an aberration but an apotheosis. The image encapsulated a long legacy of hate. It reflected the Republican Party's strategy, starting in the 1960s, of embracing white supremacy in order to wield power. It captured the GOP's increasing radicalization over recent decades, including rejecting core democratic principles such as accepting electoral defeat and condemning violence and extremist groups. Trump didn't invent any of that, but he took it to the next level.

A few months after January 6, while filming the Apple TV+ series *Gutsy* with Chelsea, I met two women who knew all too well the consequences of whipping up hateful rhetoric and racist violence. Down in Virginia, I sat on a covered porch with Dawn Collins and Susan Bro. Rolling thunder threatened rain that never came, while Susan tried to teach Dawn and me to crochet (I've never figured it out). Dawn and Susan were brought together by a terrible bond. Dawn's son, Richard Collins III, was twenty-three years old and a newly promoted lieutenant in the Army when he was fatally stabbed at the University of Maryland, for no reason but his race, by a member of a white supremacist group while he was waiting with friends for an Uber. Susan's daughter, Heather Heyer, was killed while protesting the 2017 white supremacist rally in Charlottesville, Virginia, when a neo-Nazi deliberately plowed his car into the crowd, fatally injuring her. Losing a child is the worst thing that can happen to a parent. If they had given in to despair and bitterness, no one could have faulted them.

But instead, over tangled purple yarn and glasses of white wine, both mothers told me how they spend their days: combatting hate and doing everything they can to make sure other parents don't face the same horror. Dawn and her husband fought for stronger hate crime laws in Maryland, launched a scholarship foundation in their son's name, and lead programs designed to break down racial barriers. Susan started a foundation in her daughter's name to advocate for stronger hate crime legislation around the country and the anti-racist causes that Heather believed in so deeply. Dawn told me that every chance Susan gets to speak about her daughter, she makes sure the world knows about Richard, too.

Somehow, when their lives were touched by senseless hate, Susan and Dawn found love and purpose. It gives me hope that they choose to honor Richard's and Heather's memories by working for a better world. "What else would I do right now?" Susan said. "We're moms,"

Dawn added. "We didn't ask for this. But now that it has come to my door, we have to buck up and do what we have to do."

Sadly, I've known too many moms like Dawn and Susan who've lost children to racist violence. During my 2016 campaign, I became close with a remarkable group of women known as Mothers of the Movement. Among them was Sybrina Fulton, whose seventeen-year-old son, Trayvon Martin, was shot and killed while taking a walk to buy Skittles at a convenience store near Orlando, Florida, in 2012. He was unarmed—just a Black kid wearing a hoodie in America. Lucy McBath's son, Jordan Davis, was shot in Jacksonville, Florida, while listening to music in a car that a white man thought was too loud and too "thug." There are so many stories like this, so many grieving parents. Yet like Dawn and Susan, these mothers were able to turn their mourning into a mission. Lucy even ran for Congress and won.

Mothers like Dawn, Susan, Sybrina, and Lucy already knew what many other Americans woke up to on January 6: Racist rhetoric can lead to violent action.

What can we do about it? I wanted to understand how normal people get drawn into a life of hate and violence—and how they can pull themselves free. So I went to see Shannon Foley Martinez, a former white supremacist who now works to deprogram and rehabilitate people leaving hate groups. Shannon took Chelsea and me (and a small film crew) canoeing near her home in Athens, Georgia. It wasn't lost on me as we paddled along that we weren't far from the site of the last documented mass lynching in America, Moore's Ford Bridge, where a mob of twenty armed white men shot and killed two Black couples in 1946. One of the women killed was seven months pregnant. To this day no one has been held accountable for their murders.

Back in the 1990s, from the time she was fifteen until she was twenty, Shannon was active in the violent white supremacy movement. She attended Klan rallies, tagged public property with swastikas, assaulted people of color, tear-gassed a gay nightclub, and underwent paramilitary training to prepare for the race war her neo-Nazi leaders promised was imminent. Her comrades were white supremacists like the fanatics who years later carried torches through Charlottesville chanting "Jews will not replace us!" and like many of the insurrectionists who stormed the Capitol on January 6.

Then, remarkably, she managed to get herself out and change her life. Now Shannon helps people escape violent extremism. She's seen how the dangerous, hateful movement has metastasized. The rise of social media allowed white power leaders to more easily reach and radicalize thousands of new recruits. Hate-fueled memes and videos circulate online, evading detection in the dark corners of the internet with coded hashtags and innuendo. Things only got worse when Trump publicly and proudly fanned the flames of racial resentment from the campaign trail and then the White House, emboldening white supremacists to emerge from the shadows.

I saw firsthand how fast conspiracy theories could spread and radicalization could take hold. During the 2016 campaign, a shocking number of people became convinced that I am a murderer, a terrorist sympathizer, and the evil mastermind behind a child-sex-abuse ring. Alex Jones, the right-wing talk-show host, posted a video about "all the children Hillary Clinton has personally murdered and chopped up and raped."

This was not the first time that I was the subject of wild conspiracy theories or partisan rage that veered into mania. In the 1990s, supermarket tabloids used to splash headlines such as "Hillary Clinton Adopts Alien Baby" across their front pages. I was even burned in effigy by a crowd in Kentucky furious that I had proposed taxing cigarettes to help fund universal health care for all Americans. The president of the Kentucky Association of Tobacco Supporters chanted "Burn, baby, burn" as he poured gasoline on a scarecrow in a dress labeled I'M HILLARY. By 2016, I fully expected to play a starring role in the fever dreams of extremists at the margins of American politics.

But something had changed. The margins infected the mainstream. Social media gave conspiracy theories far wider reach than ever before. Fox News and other right-wing media outlets gave repeated outlandish lies "credibility." And before Trump, we'd never had a presidential candidate—and then an actual president—who used the biggest bully pulpit in the world to be an actual bully and traffic in this kind of trash. The results were tragic but predictable. In early December 2016, a twenty-eight-year-old man from North Carolina fired an assault rifle inside a pizza restaurant in Washington, D.C., because he had read online that it was the headquarters of my supposed child-sex ring. Thankfully, no one was harmed. But the pizzeria attack foreshadowed the violence to come: QAnon followers and militia members storming the Capitol on January 6, 2021; mass shooters leaving behind manifestos riddled with misogyny, racism, anti-Semitism, and other conspiracy theories promoted in far-right (and far-left) echo chambers.

Shannon is doing what she can to fight back. She rescues people she meets online, at white supremacist rallies, or through concerned loved ones. When she's trying to deprogram white supremacists, her approach is not to try to change their politics but to help them address their trauma and move away from resorting to violence. "I've found you can't argue people out of their deeply entrenched worldview. They just entrench further," Shannon says. So she asks a lot of questions and patiently listens. What drew them to the white power movement? How is it serving their life? Why are they afraid of leaving? What might their lives look like without hate? These connections can take a long time to develop, and even longer to lead to de-radicalization. Disengagement, she says, is a process—not an event.

That's how I found myself in a canoe with Shannon and a young woman she's mentoring named Samantha, who recently left the white power movement with Shannon's help. Samantha was introduced to white supremacist groups by an abusive ex-boyfriend, an organizer of the 2017 Unite the Right rally in Charlottesville, where Susan's daughter was killed and whom Samantha would later testify against. Samantha helped me better understand how people like her are recruited into and radicalized by white supremacist groups. Most people, she acknowledged, are not initially comfortable with racist slurs or Nazi rhetoric, so recruiters lightheartedly introduce offensive humor to appear less violent than they really are. But the more time members spend online in alt-right chat rooms and channels, the more they get used to the ugliness of the ideology. When you stop being shocked, you start being radicalized.

It would have been so much easier for Shannon to have left this dark chapter in her life in the rearview mirror and never look back. It's not like she has extra time on her hands: Shannon bartends thirty hours each week and cares for her eight children. But she feels a powerful responsibility to make amends for her past.

I wondered whether Shannon's thoughtful, empathetic approach could offer lessons not just for rescuing radicalized individuals but for healing our wounded country. What will it take to pull us out of the madness? Is there any way to drain the fever swamps so we can stand together on firmer, higher ground?

I also marveled at the empathy Shannon managed to summon for even the most (yes, let's say it) *deplorable* bigots. She has known the worst of the worst and still finds room in her heart for them as human beings, still believes it's worth the effort, the emotional labor, to reach out to them.

I've struggled with this myself. In 2016, I famously described half of Trump supporters as "the basket of deplorables." I was talking about the people who are drawn to Trump's racism, sexism, homophobia, xenophobia, Islamophobia—you name it. The people for whom his bigotry is a feature, not a bug. It was an unfortunate choice of words and bad politics, but it also got at an important truth. Just look at everything that has happened in the years since, from Charlottesville to January 6. The masks have come off, and if anything, "deplorable" is too kind a word for the hate and violent extremism we've seen from some Trump supporters.

In 2022, an editor at a major American newspaper reached out to ask if I would write an op-ed reflecting on my "basket of deplorables" comment six years on. A gunman in Buffalo, New York, had just massacred Black shoppers at a supermarket, reportedly influenced by the racist "great replacement" theory, which had been promoted aggressively by Tucker Carlson on Fox News and embraced by many Republican leaders. The *New York Times* had published a meticulous investigation that found that on more than four hundred episodes of his top-rated cable news show, Carlson explicitly pushed the incendiary claim that immigrants and people of color are displacing whites. The newspaper editor said that he and his colleagues spent a half hour at their editorial meeting talking about this report, and "the notion that the most racist show on cable news is also the most popular stuck with a lot of us." Several editors, he said, brought up my "deplorables" comment and "how prescient" I had been. Did I want to write an op-ed about it?

It was tempting. In 2016, I warned about the rising influence of the alt-right and the threat to democracy from a political movement that endorses violence and refuses to accept basic norms of decency and pluralism. I was largely mocked or dismissed by many in the mainstream media stuck in a "both sides" straitjacket. Now they finally wanted to listen, but they were still intent on exploring this threat primarily through the lens of a six-year-old political controversy. I found that approach emblematic of the media's shortsightedness and declined the offer.

I do wish that back in 2016 people had heard the rest of my comments and not just the word "deplorables." I also talked about the other half of Trump supporters, "people who feel that the government has let them down, the economy has let them down, nobody cares about them, nobody worries about what happens to their lives and their futures, and they're just desperate for change." And, I emphasized, "those are people we have to understand and empathize with as well." That's especially true because many are living with unresolved trauma in their lives.

Empathy for people you agree with is easy. Empathy for someone you deeply, passionately disagree with is hard but necessary. What Shannon does, feeling empathy for Nazis and Klansmen, is damn near superhuman. As a Christian, I aspire to this kind of radical empathy but often fall short. Talking about the "deplorables" in 2016, I said, "Some of those folks, they are irredeemable." Part of me would still say this is objectively true. Just look at the lack of remorse from many of the January 6 insurrectionists who've been convicted of sedition and other crimes. But another part of me wants to believe something else. I'd like to believe there's goodness in everyone and a chance at redemption, no matter how remote.

Shannon is remarkably optimistic for someone who spends so much time with Nazis. "Hopeless people," she told me, are "easily controlled and manipulated. But hopeful people can move mountains." It isn't easy to keep hold of that hope, but Shannon doesn't think there's any other choice. Our country has "mountains that need moving," she said, so "I feel an obligation to hope." As a small emblem of that hope, Shannon covered her tattoo of a white power symbol with a beautiful tattoo of a heron, looking free and ready to soar.

Democracy has been under attack and in retreat all over the world in recent years, but often in subtler, less violent ways than we saw on January 6. Authoritarian politicians like Viktor Orbán in Hungary, Nicolás Maduro in Venezuela, and Vladimir Putin in Russia cloak their power grabs behind the veneer of electoral legitimacy. They get elected and then use the power of the state to dismantle the institutions of democracy. I can't tell you how many times as secretary of state I had to explain to some foreign leader that winning an election was not enough if he turned around and ruled like a dictator.

It was heartbreaking to watch once vibrant and hopeful democracies like Hungary slowly slide backward toward authoritarianism. I remember the exuberant early days after the fall of communism, when

Hungarians were celebrating their new freedoms and looking ahead to a bright democratic future. In 1996, I spent a glorious summer afternoon walking through the narrow streets of old Budapest in a straw hat, watching people laugh and shop and enjoy the wide-open possibilities of their liberated country. I also met with women and children from the country's largest minority group, the Roma, who have faced centuries of discrimination. We all hoped that Hungary's new democracy would bring acceptance and opportunity for the country's minorities.

Orbán actually helped lead the opposition to Soviet rule and promoted democracy. And when he served as prime minister the first time, from 1998 to 2002, he was a conservative but not yet a demagogue. He even brought Hungary into NATO. But when he returned to power eight years later, things took a darker turn. Orbán whipped up hatred of immigrants, Jews, Roma, and LGBTQ+ people. He called for women to return to their homes and produce more children for their country. He consolidated power, rewrote the constitution, manipulated elections, attacked the independent media, and cracked down on dissent.

When I visited Budapest as secretary of state in 2011, I warned Orbán in private that this was a dangerous path and then publicly urged him to protect the free press, independent courts, and constitutional checks and balances. Orbán wasn't listening. He had grown arrogant, contemptuous, addicted to power.

There wasn't any single dramatic moment you could point to—no burning of the Reichstag, no tanks rolling through Tiananmen Square, no January 6—but Hungarian democracy eroded under the relentless pressure Orbán deployed. It's become essentially a one-party state, with opponents marginalized, propaganda on the airwaves, corruption in the ministries, a thumb on the scale in the courts, and, above all, an unconstrained leader with an insatiable taste for power and no attachment to democratic norms or values. Minorities are persecuted. Migrants are scapegoated. Civil society has largely been crushed.

With a record like that, it's not surprising that Orbán became an ally of Vladimir Putin and an icon for right-wing extremists in the United States. In March 2024, Orbán visited Trump at Mar-a-Lago and endorsed his campaign for president. Trump, who makes no secret of his admiration for dictators and tyrants the world over, praised the Hungarian leader. "There's nobody that's better, smarter or a better leader than Viktor Orbán," Trump raved. "He's fantastic." I have no doubt Trump would love to replicate Orbán's authoritarian tactics here in the United States.

"Fascism," as Yale history professor Timothy Snyder put it, "is might over right, conspiracy over reality, fiction over fact, pain over law, blood over love, doom over hope." It's a threat that Madeleine Albright, who passed away in 2022, knew well. As a girl, she fled first the Nazis and then the Communists—a refugee twice over by the age of eleven. Madeleine grew up to be a fierce champion of democracy. As my husband's secretary of state, she stood up to dictators like Serbia's Slobodan Milošević. She was also my traveling companion and guide on trips to her native Czech Republic, Hungary, and other former Soviet bloc countries. In recent years, she became increasingly alarmed by democratic backsliding around the world, including here at home.

In 2018, she sounded the alarm in a prescient book, *Fascism: A Warning*, which drew on her firsthand experience with authoritarianism and described Trump as the first president in the modern era "whose statements and actions are so at odds with democratic ideals." After the January 6 insurrection, Madeleine imagined Abraham Lincoln weeping. "My family came to America after fleeing a coup, so I know that freedom is fragile," she wrote. "But I never thought I would see such an assault on democracy be cheered on from the Oval Office."

I've spent more than half a century in the crucible of politics. I've seen the best and worst of it. And at the end of the day, I still believe deeply in American democracy because I believe in the basic decency of the

American people. I believe that if you dig deep enough, through all the mud of politics, eventually you hit something hard and true: a foundation of fundamental values and aspirations that still binds most of us together as Americans.

This is a lesson I learned a long time ago and never forgot. In the summer of 1972, I went door-to-door in the Rio Grande Valley of Texas trying to register new voters for the election between President Richard Nixon and Senator George McGovern. The communities I visited were tight-knit, hardworking, and understandably wary of a twenty-four-year-old blond girl from Chicago who spoke no Spanish. Yet many families opened their homes to me. Mothers and grandmothers who worked long hours for not much money invited me to sit at the kitchen table, drink very strong coffee, and talk. So did college students studying late into the night and union workers up early in the morning. Some of the people I met were immigrants, and some were among the original inhabitants of the area, with ancestors stretching back generations in the valley. Some didn't know they were eligible to vote or didn't see why they should. But for many of the people I registered, politics wasn't a game; it was about making life better for their families. Democracy wasn't a concept in a civics textbook; it was a promise that had inspired them or their parents to leave behind everything they knew to build a new future in a new land. America wasn't just a place on a map; it was a dream that was worth working and fighting—and, yes, voting—for.

One of my guides both to the area and to the struggle to realize America's promise was Franklin Garcia, a Mexican American labor organizer and civil rights activist. He drove me around South Texas and introduced me to people and places I never would have found on my own. When I went door-to-door, Franklin often came along, vouching for me to skeptical Texans. He would offer to come inside, assure our hosts that I was someone to be trusted, and translate conversations where necessary. When a man told us he'd never voted before, Franklin helped me explain in specific terms how voting could lead to better jobs and schools, clean water, and housing. When a woman said she was scared to register even though she was a citizen, Franklin seconded my points about how important it was to set an example for her children and how we all have to participate for the community and our country to thrive. McGovern lost that election in a landslide, but I gained a better understanding of American democracy that has lasted me a lifetime.

On January 6, insurrectionists erected a gallows near the west front of the Capitol and chanted "Hang Mike Pence." Like the Confederate flag they carried inside, it was a throwback to America's ugly past and a preview of what the future could hold. But we don't have to accept that fate.

Just two weeks later, with the bloodthirsty cries of the mob still ringing in my ears, I went to the Capitol to attend Joe Biden's inauguration and show support for the peaceful transfer of power. Trump didn't show up. That same morning, from her home in Georgia, Shannon Foley Martinez recorded a video appealing to followers of QAnon who might be "grappling with a sense of confusion, betrayal, shame, embarrassment, and anger." This was a chance to move forward.

From the Capitol dais, the brilliant poet Amanda Gorman, only twenty-two but wise beyond her years, read from her poem "The Hill We Climb":

> We've seen a force that would shatter our nation, rather than share it,
> Would destroy our country if it meant delaying democracy.
> And this effort very nearly succeeded.
> But while democracy can be periodically delayed,
> It can never be permanently defeated.

They were stirring, much-needed words to hear just two weeks after the attack. Listening, I hoped the people who stormed our seat of government would be held accountable under the law, Republican elected officials would stand with their Democratic colleagues to re-pudiate Trump and his enablers, and the country would move on.

Sadly, that's not what happened. Yes, hundreds of insurrectionists have been tried and convicted. But after a brief moment of hesitation, Republicans rallied around Trump and his alternative-reality narra-tive. Healing, moving on, growing stronger together? Not a chance.

President Biden called the 2020 campaign a battle for the soul of America. Today the battle continues, fiercer than ever.

ONE IS SILVER AND
THE OTHER'S GOLD

Labor Day 2022. We were all a little wobbly that Monday morning—Ann, Bonnie, Judy, Patsy, Allida, and I—as we stepped aboard a vintage wooden motorboat in the waters of Lake Geneva, Wisconsin. We were on the last leg of a nonstop three-day extravaganza celebrating Ann's seventy-fifth birthday. There were cocktails and brunches, a costume dance party and a sunset dinner cruise. And, because Ann and I are mission-driven kindred spirits, there were also informative and inspiring conversations led by and about women who stepped up to lead. Our final-day excursion was meant to give us a look at the property on Williams Bay where Ann is building the eight-acre Women's Leadership Center that has been her passion project for several years. Given the choice between sleeping in or rallying at sunrise, we rallied. We zipped up fleece jackets in the morning chill and shoved off. Our friend was making her dream come true, and we were there to cheer her on.

I was seven years old when I first met Ann in our shared hometown of Park Ridge, Illinois, about sixty miles southeast of Lake Geneva. Ann was the tall, smart girl with brown hair who went to a different elementary school but connected with me in ballet class at the Dorothy Lykle Dance Studio and in Sunday school and confirmation classes at First United Methodist Church, just a six-block walk from my home. As teenagers, Ann, Judy, and I bused together to summer church camp on the shores of Lake Geneva and did all the camp things that make for gauzy childhood memories. We swam off the little dock at the sandy beach. We sat cross-legged on the floor of the candlelit lodge to sing hymns (yes, "Kumbaya" was one) and ponder with our youth minister, the Reverend Don Jones, all the pressing questions of an idealistic youth: God, justice, peace, and civil rights. In our cabin at night, stacked up in bunk beds and waiting for sleep to come, we whispered our secrets and our dreams, which included living lives of service—the "do all the good you can" ethos of Methodism founder John Wesley—that Reverend Jones was helping us to imagine.

Now, some sixty years later, we were back at that lake, back together—along with three other high school friends, Bonnie, Patsy, and Hardye, and Allida, a historian and Memphis native who seamlessly fit right into our gang almost a decade earlier, when she supported my 2008 presidential campaign and interviewed many of my longtime friends. Summer 2022 proved difficult for Hardye, who was in treatment for lung cancer. When she woke on Sunday feeling ill, she skipped the rest of the weekend itinerary to head home to Chicago. On the boat that Monday morning, the rest of us worried over how frail Hardye seemed. We commiserated about our aging bodies and reminisced about old times, feeling blessed to still have one another. Then something so familiar caught my eye. "There's our dock!" I yelled, fumbling for my phone to get a photo of the nondescript speck on shore. (It hadn't yet occurred to me that we could ask the boat captain, Ann's friend Charles, to pull us closer for a good look.) While Ann, Judy, and I giddily snapped pictures, I asked Ann, "Do you remember the Prell?" She laughed. "How could I forget?" Prell was the iconic shampoo of our teen years. At the end of a camp day of sports, singing, swimming, and sunning, we girls would lather up our hair with Prell and jump off the dock to rinse the shampoo out in the lake. I shudder now to think of the environmental implications, but we thought ourselves hilariously practical back then.

Our memories of days past were framed that Labor Day weekend by Ann's plans for nurturing the women leaders and explorers of to-morrow. She had dubbed the three-day celebration "Close Encounters of a New Kind," a shout-out to her favorite movie, Steven Spielberg's *Close Encounters of the Third Kind*. Ann had cleverly mined the 1977 science-fiction classic for a party theme—the film's "We Are Not Alone" tagline was printed on rainbow cards that decorated the table settings—and an excuse to have us dress up in futuristic, space-themed costumes. Our birthday girl was stunning in a red jumpsuit just like those in the movie. The ever-sunny Patsy, a retired speech and language pathologist, dressed as the center of our solar system. Bonnie, the stylish artist of our pack and designer of some of my fa-vorite pieces of jewelry, dressed as an astronaut—albeit one acces-sorized with a perfectly cut blazer. And me? In a flowy purple robe decorated with gold stars, I guess you could say I was dressed as an interplanetary wizard. (Ann decided I looked like Harry Potter's Pro-fessor McGonagall—close enough!) Singing along with a fabulous cover band, we danced in a circle to vintage hits like Stevie Wonder's "Signed, Sealed, Delivered (I'm Yours)" like we were sixteen again.

We are not alone. The double entendre resonated with me—and not just because, like Ann, I've always been fascinated by the possi-bility of other life-forms in the universe. (When I was thirteen, and excited about President John F. Kennedy's space mission, I wrote NASA to inquire about being an astronaut. They passed. *No girls al-lowed,* they wrote.) It resonated because there on the dance floor, en-circled by just a few of the women who have blessed my life with their friendship, my heart was full. I saw once again how, throughout the wild ride of my life—whether it was on steep uphills or even steeper downfalls, in front of energizing crowds or soul-sucking critics—I have never been alone.

Bill was in the middle of a press conference with White House re-porters in December 1997 when he took a question about his former advisors and allies, George Stephanopoulos and Dick Morris, who were publicly writing off Bill's second term as a lame-duck snooze. Bill jokingly replied that, as President Harry Truman famously said, "if you want a friend in Washington you need to get a dog," and then announced that we had decided to name our new chocolate Lab puppy Buddy, after Bill's favorite uncle who had recently died.

Politics, especially in the nation's capital, can be a lonely, back-stabbing business. Sure, you have a huge contacts file of people you identify as friends—supporters, donors, advisors, and celebrities—who are generous with their time and talents and will always take your call. But it's an emotionally fraught irony of public life that, even in a crowded room of these well-intentioned friends, you can feel lonely. In that room, you're a symbol, a vessel for others' aspirations, activism, and investments. I don't say this with any regret. It's just reality. It's what people like Bill and me sign up for when we step up to lead change-making. In that crowded room, you're genuinely grateful for the people who support you. You feel real affection for them (most of them, anyway). But in that room, you're "on." Always on. Projecting confidence, optimism, and impeccable affability. It's the complex, flawed—and sometimes just plain exhausted—human being inside who is left feeling unseen. And, from time to time, even lonely.

In an interview with *Essence* three years before her death in 2014, Maya Angelou described once being asked by another magazine to do a photo shoot for its special issue on friendship. "The editor wanted me to bring Oprah," Maya said, going on to explain why she objected. "I have 30 years on Oprah. She calls me her friend, her mother, all that. I am very close to her in a motherly way." Maya told the editor she would instead be photographed with the three dear women—none of them famous—whom she called her "sister friends." "Most people really don't become friends. They become deep and serious acquaintances." Sister friends are different. They know your spirit. Your values coincide. They see the real you and love you anyway.

This is the story of *my* sister friends. From my childhood and young adulthood. From my hippie days at Wellesley College and Yale Law School, and my earliest days of building a career and family. Friends whose bonds were forged in the white-hot crucible of presidential politics. And some I found only recently, when a lot of us who are older might give up on making new friends. I cannot fit in these pages all the stories of all the women dear to me. But I hope to capture, in these few snapshots, the special magic of girlfriends that's possible at any age—and no matter who you are—if your heart is open and generous and willing to do the work of meaningful friendship.

Decades ago, when I was preparing to move our family from the Arkansas governor's mansion to the White House, several people warned me against inviting new people into my life. *The power and fame that attach to the White House attract opportunists and sycophants,* I was told. *Trust no one.* Beginning a friendship is a trust fall. You make yourself vulnerable, tip backward, and trust that the other person will be at your back to catch you before you fall. I had already encountered a fair share of ulterior motives in Arkansas politics and fully expected even more in the nation's capital. But it seemed an unnatural way to live, shutting yourself off. And so I kept making friends all along—in the White House, among the hardworking and fun-loving women staffers known as Hillaryland, and on the campaign trail. There, I happily found that high-stakes politics, starting with Bill's 1992 campaign for president and going through my races for the Senate and White House, introduced me to amazing women who, over our time in the trenches together, became lasting friends.

Women who campaigned for and with me, raised money, won over voters, and gave public talks about me even though they were afraid at first. Women whose homes I've stayed in, whose breakfast tables have seen me in my robe and slippers, and with whom I've traveled the world, long after the campaigns ended. We remain involved in each other's lives and each other's causes. I cannot imagine my life any other way.

Old friends, new friends, sister friends. Together, these special women are one big reason, even before our beloved dog Buddy (and then Seamus and Tally and Maisie), I was never lacking for loving support, nor shy about giving it.

Even in Washington, D.C.

Cheryl, Patsy, and I first met in the first-grade Sunday school class taught by my mother, Dorothy, at First United Methodist Church of Park Ridge. Cheryl, who is now a writer (and author of a wise guide to grandparenting, *Good to Be Grand: Making the Most of Your Grandchild's First Year*), once confessed to me that it was only my mother who made an impression: "I don't remember you at all from Sunday school," she said, "but your mother was fantastic!" The following year, when I was in second grade at Eugene Field Elementary School, I joined a Brownie troop with another eight-year-old named Sukie. In the school cafeteria, the moms who volunteered as troop leaders, with Sukie's mother, Pixie, at the helm, taught us the words to the famous Girl Scout song: "Make new friends, but keep the old. One is silver, and the other's gold." (I still sing those lines to Sukie whenever I see her now.) Sukie would come to my house to play and marvel at how our thick, floor-length drapes made our living room look like the inside of Disney's Cinderella castle. It was the highest compliment to my father and his small drapery business.

Sixth grade (1958–59) was the game changer for all of us. That was the year when a boy named Dennis and I traded dog tags. It was the fad back then to wear a personalized aluminum dog tag on a bead chain, and if a boy liked you—*like* liked you—he asked you to trade tags and tie a knot in your chain to signify that you were "spoken for." And so it happened that sixth grade was also when Sukie found out how fast I could run. I had always been sporty—softball, swimming, tennis, ice skating—but when someone noticed the knot in my chain one morning before the first bell, I took off running before anyone could get a look at Dennis's name on the tag. Sukie, who made her career in administration at NASA, still laughs about it: "You took off like a bullet!" Judy, a retired teacher who was, so many years later, in the Lake Geneva motorboat with us, laughs about it, too. By high school, Dennis had eyes only for her. They married in 1969. So, she ended up with his dog tag.

Even more monumentally, sixth grade was when a magnetic girl named Voda—but we called her Betsy—moved with her family to Park Ridge. She landed in Mrs. King's classroom with Sukie and me. "Voda . . ." Sukie wondered, sounding out the new girl's exotic name. "Could that be Russian?" (Turns out it meant "water" in Slavic languages.) We were dazzled. Big eyes, brown curly hair. Smart, funny, kind, and mischievous, Betsy quickly became one of Mrs. King's favorites. And mine. Betsy and I were joined at the hip in class, on the playground, and in and out of each other's houses. We would walk to the Pickwick Theatre on Saturday afternoons, once sitting mesmerized through *Lover Come Back*, starring Doris Day and Rock Hudson, three times in a single day. After the movies we'd order olive burgers from the nearby Pickwick Restaurant, which I loved so much I later took ABC's Barbara Walters there for an interview while I was promoting my book *Living History*. When vanity struck (which was often enough) and I didn't want to wear the Coke-bottle glasses I needed to correct my terrible nearsightedness, it was Betsy who led me through the school corridors or around town like a Seeing Eye friend.

With our bigger friend group, we delighted in birthday parties and sleepovers. The girls would tease me—and still do!—for being asleep already whenever the slumber-party fun turned to practicing hairstyles, which would be a lifelong conundrum for me (the hairstyling, not the sleeping). One time, Sukie staged a "surprise kidnap breakfast," where she conspired with all our mothers for permission to come to our houses on a Saturday morning, wake us up, and whisk each of us off to her house for pancakes. The catch: We couldn't change out of our sleep clothes; we could only brush our teeth. I'd gone to bed with rollers in my hair, and so, with an embarrassed shriek, off I went to breakfast in pajamas and curlers.

It was Betsy who nudged me to take chances and follow the call to activism that I felt deep inside. The day after the 1960 presidential election between Nixon and Kennedy, our junior high social studies teacher, Mr. Kenvin, came to school with bruises, telling us that he'd been beaten at a polling place in Chicago when he tried to monitor the poll workers. That got Betsy and me riled up. We went to the pay phone outside the school cafeteria and called the mayor's office, asking to speak to Mayor Daley about what had happened to Mr. Kenvin. The very nice woman who answered said she would be sure to give the mayor our message. About a week later, Betsy, always the instigator, showed me a full-page newspaper ad looking for volunteers to fact-check voter rolls in Chicago by going door-to-door. We told our parents we were going to the movies and then hopped a bus to downtown Chicago to the Drake Hotel, where we were handed sheets of voter information and then assigned to two strangers with cars—Betsy to one, me to the other. We were dropped off in different Chicago precincts to knock on doors, alone, and verify that people were really living where they were registered. Did I mention we were thirteen years old? Only by the grace of God did the two of us make it back to the Drake that day, having done our duty to democracy and Mr. Kenvin. Our parents were not impressed and grounded us both.

After high school, adulthood inevitably scattered us. Many in our circle went to college and settled back in Illinois. Our friend Kathleen took to the skies as an airline stewardess (the correct term at the time) for Continental and flew many times accompanying young American soldiers back and forth from service in Vietnam. I was the only one to cross the Allegheny River for college and then stay on the East Coast. I spent four wonderful years at Wellesley College, a world-class women's college in Massachusetts. After attending a large public high school, I savored the chance to study with young women who, like me, cared about getting a great education, even if I didn't know yet what I would do with it. The greatest gift of those four years, though, was bonding with women who would become lifelong friends. Together we've celebrated weddings, babies, new jobs, promotions, and retirements. The women of Wellesley have been generous with their friendship and support through all my campaigns—some expat classmates even rounded up American voters overseas—and my nonprofit work. Every five years, we hold a reunion on campus (except for our twenty-fifth, which I was delighted to host at the White House), and I attended our fifty-fifth in 2024. Each time, I am impressed by and grateful for my classmates whose friendships have sustained me over the years.

Back in the day, while I shared new adventures with new friends on Wellesley's faraway campus, Betsy was the glue that held our hometown crew together. She was our ringleader, the one who tracked every birthday and milestone and would gather the gang for pizza or a drink whenever I was back home in Illinois. Every five years, on the occasion of our high school reunions, Cheryl and Ann alternated hosting a pre-party for that core group of us Park Ridge girls (and the lone guy in our pack, Ricky, whom I've known since we walked home from kindergarten together). Over time, those gatherings expanded to include husbands. Betsy and hers, Tom, drove almost seven hundred miles through the night to stand beside me as Bill and I wed in 1975 in Fayetteville, Arkansas. Then came children. And, eventually, one Arkansas governor.

As Bill climbed higher in elective politics—state attorney general, governor, president—my girlfriends found every way they could to help. Kathleen threw a hometown fundraiser, gathering some of our 1992 campaign's earliest donations, some of which were as high as $500, *a lot* of money in those days. I remember feeling so humbled that my friends, who were building their own lives and families, could be so generous. Others stepped out of their comfort zones to canvass door-to-door. Betsy, as our self-described "herder of cats" who organized everyone's interest in volunteering, made sure there were friendly, familiar faces at as many of my own campaign stops as possible. "She needs us," Betsy told the gang. She knew that even before I did.

The faces that I knew and loved so well were there in the crowd in Little Rock on election night 1992 and then in Washington for Bill's first inauguration in January 1993. Patsy and Cheryl remember seeing me at the inaugural concert at the Lincoln Memorial, separated from my friends by a wall of bulletproof glass. "That's when I knew that your life had changed and things would never be the same," Patsy told me many years later. Those big events with their massive crowds were a blur for me, but there was one clear takeaway: I would have to be extra intentional (with Betsy's organizational and planning help) about staying connected to the people whose friendships I treasured.

I hosted a proper "Park Ridge Girls" celebration in July 1993, when I invited the whole group to the White House. I was still finding my legs as First Lady and as a mom trying to make that grand historic residence a home for Chelsea. What a treat it was to see the place through my old friends' wide eyes. Everything was new and exciting to them: the pastry kitchen, the family theater, the florist's studio. Patsy was even taking pictures of doorknobs! For me, the familiar and comfortable were what mattered most that girls' weekend. My friends weren't buzzing about any of the controversies already nipping at me (the West Wing office, my role putting together a universal health care bill, so-called Travelgate). We were all just excited to be together, like old times. Talking about our kids and how hard it was to get them to do chores. (Try enforcing chores when there's a whole household staff at your teenager's service! To Chelsea's credit, she stepped up even then.) Talking about our parents, the books we were reading, the vacations we dreamed of. I felt at home. At one point, Kathleen and I were riding the elevator from the state floor to the second-floor private residence. I looked at the usher manning the elevator and asked, "Do you know what all these women are here for?" He looked at me with a nod. "Slumber party, ma'am."

November 2016. "Next year in Val-Kill" was a running joke—part consolation prize, part rallying cry—between Betsy and Allida ever since I lost the Democratic presidential nomination to Barack Obama in 2008. For eight years, whenever something went blessedly right or horribly wrong for one of us girlfriends—an electoral defeat for me or, much more serious, a cancer diagnosis for Betsy and then for Hardye—Betsy and Allida would pledge to each other that they were going to sweep me off to Val-Kill, Eleanor Roosevelt's serene cottage in the woods of Hyde Park, New York. There, we would either celebrate or drown our sorrows in a contraband bottle of champagne, right in the former First Lady's living room.

Now, this story will make the most sense if I back up a bit and note that Allida is an Eleanor Roosevelt scholar. It's one of the reasons I, an ardent admirer of the former First Lady, was drawn to Allida when she sought my help when I was First Lady to finish cataloging Mrs. Roosevelt's papers. Allida is the founder of the Eleanor Roosevelt Papers Project, the editor of *The Eleanor Roosevelt Papers*, and a trustee of the Franklin D. Roosevelt Presidential Library. She always has a project she's tackling, a friend she's helping—like so many of us do. Meanwhile, I went from the 2008 presidential campaign to the State Department to grandmother to the 2016 presidential campaign. Life just kept putting off Allida and Betsy's fantasy getaway—hence their catchphrase: "Next year in Val-Kill!"

At last, 2016 was going to be *the* year we made it happen. Despite her failing health after a recent cancer diagnosis, Betsy had been with me throughout the ugly campaign against Donald Trump. In the roll call of state delegates at the Democratic National Convention in Philadelphia that July, it was Betsy who cast Illinois's ninety-eight votes for me, saying, "My sweet friend . . . this one's for you, Hill." Then, on

October 28, she was traveling with me when then FBI director Jim Comey upended our campaign eleven days before Election Day by announcing that the investigation into my emails that he had closed in July was being reopened. We were on a plane, headed to a women's rally in Cedar Rapids, Iowa. We landed and got into a car. Neither one of us spoke. Betsy understood that what had just happened was devastating and unfair. But there was no venting, no hysterics. She just sat there, holding my hand and holding on to faith that I could still win.

On election night, Betsy again herded cats—some thirty friends from the Park Ridge pack, plus one friend Betsy had made just two months earlier, the Canadian mystery writer Louise Penny—inside New York City's Javits Center, where my campaign threw a returns-watching party under a massive glass ceiling. It was important to me that they were there, the women who were with me in the very beginning and never left. The women who never cast a cynical side-eye at my commitment to serve or doubted my motivations. To commemorate all that we had shared leading up to that historic night, Betsy suggested I commission the Chicago glazeware artist Mary McLaughlin to create for each of my longtime girlfriends a porcelain dish inscribed with the words we'd learned all those years ago in Sunday school: "Do all the good you can, by all the means you can, in all the ways you can, in all the places you can . . . to all the people you can." Betsy and Mary presented the dishes over lunch that day, and then everyone scattered to get ready for victory-night festivities. That was before the Electoral College canceled the party.

I was ready to be president, had developed policies and plans that were ready to go once I was in the White House—to do all the good I could for every American, no matter whom they voted for.

Now what?

"Dammit! We are *going* to do this," Allida told Betsy sometime in January 2017. We had all been down in the dumps for weeks. There was Trump's inauguration. Betsy's cancer. My ruminating about the campaign. (I actually wrote a book about it, *What Happened.*) My friends' worry for Betsy and for me, for different, loving reasons. "Next year in Val-Kill" was now. "Let's just go," said Allida. "Let's go get sloshed in Eleanor's living room." (Did I mention Allida is a brassy one? And no, we didn't get sloshed.)

Betsy and Allida thoughtfully planned the whole day and included some of the other women closest to me, some of whom worked with me in the White House and at the State Department: Maggie, Huma, Cheryl M. (another Cheryl, not the one I grew up with), and Heather. Some special men who are also like family to me—Oscar, Brendan, Rocco, and Maggie's husband, Bill—came too, along with a new friend, Louise. It was the first Tuesday in March, and our first stop was the Franklin D. Roosevelt Presidential Library, where, in a private reading room, Allida had asked the archivist to lay out specially selected readings from Mrs. Roosevelt's papers for each of us to see. One was an accounting of Eleanor's days after Roosevelt died of a cerebral hemorrhage on April 12, 1945. She had to bury her husband and pack up their things in the White House, making way for Vice President Harry Truman to move in. Another was the last letter Eleanor wrote, to her friend and confidante Lorena Hickok, before leaving the White House for good on April 19, 1945. Eleanor, too, was pondering, *What now?* I bent low to read the type: "Franklin's death ended a period in history and now in its wake . . . we have to start again under our own momentum and wonder what we can achieve."

Almost seventy-two years after Eleanor wrote those words, that's exactly what I felt, mourning a different kind of loss and wondering what I could yet achieve. As I straightened up from the table, the reading room was quiet. Our group had been in a sort of morose suspended animation all afternoon, still shell-shocked from the events of the past several months. Heck, the whole previous year was traumatizing. We fought so hard to beat back Trump; Betsy was fighting for her life; and Louise had recently lost her husband, Michael, after a years-long goodbye during which dementia stole him away. I looked around, amazed. *Here we are,* I thought. *Together. Having each other's backs. Whatever I can yet achieve, we'll do it together.*

Then we visited the current exhibit at the Roosevelt Library and watched a film on the internment of Japanese Americans during World War II. In the dark of the theater, I found Allida's hand and gave it a squeeze to thank her for arranging our time there. The day was much-needed therapy for us all. And it concluded just as Allida and Betsy had dreamed it would. Down the road from the Roosevelt Library, in the living room of Eleanor's home at Val-Kill, Allida produced from her backpack a bottle of champagne and a dozen plastic flutes. She and Betsy made toasts whose exact words elude me now, but which boiled down to one essential truth: *We love you.*

Looking back on that emotionally intimate experience now, I marvel at how awkward it might have been for Louise. She and I had met for the first time the prior weekend, but I felt as though I already knew her from reading all her books. Louise and Betsy had become friends in August, at the apex of the 2016 White House race, when Louise's publisher arranged a get-together after reading a newspaper story that included the fact that Betsy and I were both in the middle of Louise's latest mystery novel. I didn't get to meet Louise until the first week of March, when she and Betsy came to Chappaqua to stay with Bill and me for a couple of days. It was like I had known Louise forever. The writerly Louise puts it more evocatively: "It's like you were saving a place at the table for me all along."

By that summer, she was hosting us in Quebec, in the area where she sets her stories. It was Betsy and Tom, Bill and me, Chelsea and Marc and their two children, Charlotte and Aidan (Jasper wouldn't arrive until 2019). We were also joined by a few other good friends—Susie Buell, Terry and Dorothy McAuliffe, Brian and Myra Greenspun—to celebrate Bill's birthday that week. Louise took us on a tour of the sites that feature in her popular Armand Gamache series. "I've never been on a vacation Murder

Tour before," Bill joked. We swam in the middle of Lake Massawippi and savored the mountain air. It was the perfect getaway. That
fall, Louise joined us again in Chappaqua for our annual family
Thanksgiving with those of Chelsea's and Marc's friends who aren't
Americans or can't travel to be with their own families. We pushed
four tables together to fit some thirty of us around a massive dinner
table. Before digging into the buffet set up in the kitchen, we each
took turns sharing one thing for which we were especially thank-
ful. With a nod to me and then Louise, Bill raised his glass and said
what I was feeling: *What an extraordinary gift it is, at this time in life,
to be making new friends.*

Amen.

October 2023. You know that reflexive *uh-oh* you feel in the pit of
your stomach when your phone rings in the dead of night? That's
what I felt when this appeared on my calendar for Friday, October 20
(and even before you ask, yes, my life is scheduled—down to the pre-
cise minute, thanks to Lona, my extraordinary scheduler):

> 10:01 a.m.–10:14 a.m.: Phone Call with Cheryl Mills, Capricia
> Penavic Marshall, and Minyon Moore

I feared that something was wrong in Hillaryland. Someone sick.
Or worse.

Hillaryland is the nickname for the tight-knit network of women
who have worked with me in the White House, Senate, and State Department and stuck with me through the years. It dates to Bill's 1992
presidential campaign, which was headquartered in Little Rock. Capricia, who started as an advance aide there—then worked with me
in the White House and, later, the State Department—is the unof-
ficial mayor of Hillaryland. If one of our own is having a wedding,
baby, midlife crisis, divorce, or major surgery, Capricia will know

about it and rally our troops—for showers, flowers, or happy hours; meals, prayers, and hugs.

Capricia, Cheryl M., and Minyon, along with Maggie, Melanne, Lona, Huma, Lissa, Karen, Tamera, Neera, Patti, Ann S., Evan Lisa, Kelly, Jen, Rachel, Ann O., Kiki, Tina, Aprill, and other stalwarts, are the still-beating heart of Hillaryland. Where once they called me Mrs. Clinton or Senator Clinton or Madam Secretary, today they refer to me as "Big Girl." As in, "Has anyone heard from Big Girl whether she's in town to meet us for dinner?" I like that it's not "Boss" or (God forbid) "Top Banana." Big Girl suits me—and the leveling of any hierarchy to these relationships—just fine. Most of the Hillaryland women are a good fifteen to twenty years younger than I. They have been my blanket, my sword, and my shield. They stepped up every day in their demanding jobs. And then they stepped up in 2008 and again in 2016, volunteering for the hard nuts and bolts of campaigning— block-walking in key precincts, knocking on doors, and winning voters one at a time. After a long day of that, they would show up at my nighttime rallies so that their familiar faces in the crowd and their hugs along the rope line would energize me for the next day.

For no more reward than my gratitude and friendship, the women of Hillaryland have remained at my side and had my back through ... well ... everything. The highest highs, the lowest lows, the mundane middle, and hilarious high jinks in between. (Here's one great example: In a vain attempt to protect me from fashion critics as First Lady, Capricia took it upon herself to secretly cart away the most "egregious" of the clothes I brought to the White House from Arkansas, something I discovered only when we moved out eight years later and Huma finally reunited me with all my giant shoulder pads and big, fuzzy sweaters that Capricia had stashed in a third-floor closet.)

These extraordinary women were there for the wounds and suffered the wounds themselves—from battles political, legal, and personal. They never judged me or questioned my heart. Nor I, theirs.

When the White House started to feel like one big hall of

fun-house mirrors, in which the image reflected back at me through the press and our political adversaries was so distorted and grotesque that I didn't recognize myself, it was in Hillaryland that I could count on support, constructive criticism, and love.

I loved them right back, these women of Hillaryland. I still do. Through bad dates, difficult pregnancies, divorces, deaths in the family—all the trials of a full life—I tried to be there for them, with advice or just a sympathetic ear. And because I loved them, I tried to protect them. I trusted them with my life, but I had to avoid confiding in them about many of the trials I faced. Because the warped thing about friendship in Washington, D.C., is that once you vent to a friend about your troubles, you increase the chances your friend will need to hire a lawyer.

And so, when I was tearing my hair out over the contrived twists and turns of the bogus Whitewater investigation and Bill's impeachment ordeal, or losing hold of my dream in the 2008 primaries and then burying it in 2016, my Hillaryland stalwarts knew that all they had to do was be there, keeping me busy, keeping me company, keeping me from feeling alone. Our bond is so unusual that Lissa, a former reporter and one of my longtime speechwriters, is finishing a book called *Hillaryland* explaining our time in the White House.

It was Betsy's shoulder I cried on. I will always be grateful that, at the end of the 1990s, when both my marriage and Bill's presidency were imperiled, Betsy just showed up at the White House. She knew that I needed her—her comfort, support, and guidance—without me having to say a word.

And then there was Diane.

Diane, a political scientist, was one of the two close friends I made in Arkansas when I followed Bill there in 1974 and started teaching law at the University of Arkansas, Fayetteville, where Diane was a political science professor and Ann H. taught at the business school. Ann H., a native Arkansan, became my guide to my new home, advised me on matters big and small, and hosted my wedding reception at her home in 1975. She still keeps me updated about the goings-on of her family and our friends. Diane and I bonded as transplants to Bill's home state (Diane had moved there from Washington, D.C., eleven years earlier), had a standing lunch date in the student union, strategized over the Equal Rights Amendment in our free time, played tennis, and traded favorite books. Bill and I loved Diane and her husband, Jim. They had a weekend home on Beaver Lake where we would relax and recharge. We trusted their counsel. Diane served as senior researcher to Bill's 1992 campaign and senior advisor in 1996. In between, she took a position at the Brookings Institution, a Washington think tank, so that she could be close by—with a life raft—as we learned to navigate D.C. waters.

Diane, like Betsy, was wickedly smart and irreverent, with a special knack for leavening the absurdities of public life and making me laugh. Also like Betsy, Diane treated me not like the First Lady and not like a porcelain doll. They treated me like plain old Hillary, the Hillary each had known before all the trappings, perks, and perils of my new position. Here's a fun example: During Bill's second term, I was speaking at a formal dinner. Diane came along, as did Huma, who had already worked her way up from East Wing intern to my personal aide. That job on that night included holding my evening bag while I greeted people and shook hands. At one point, I asked Huma for my lipstick. Next thing I knew, both Huma and Diane were wrestling with the tiny purse's fancy rhinestone-cheetah clasp. Huma pushed and pulled at that precious cheetah. "What in the holy heck are you doing carrying a ridiculous bag like this?" Diane finally chided in exasperation. "You don't deserve your lipstick!" The whole scene still makes me laugh.

Diane saw how the fun-house mirrors twisted everything I did and said. Ever the academic, she resolved to do all she could to make sure that history, at least, produced an accurate portrait of my tenure in the White House. She kept records of my work and notes on how I was experiencing the swirl of politics that sometimes felt like it would swallow me whole. Her attention to my truth was a comfort, giving me hope that someday, long after Diane and I were gone, historians would have access to Diane's papers and maybe see me in the unvarnished way that she did: flawed and human, but genuine in my thirst to improve people's lives, especially those of women and children.

Painfully, that someday came far too soon. Diane was diagnosed with lung cancer in May 2000 and dead weeks later. Losing her crushed me. In 2011, I lost my mother. Then, in April 2019, I lost Ellen, a dear friend and former California congresswoman who came to work with me at the State Department as undersecretary for arms control. After the 2016 election, Ellen was one of my trusted confidantes as I worked through the consequences and pain of that political loss. Little more than one month after Ellen's death, my younger brother Tony died at the beginning of June 2019, leaving us way too soon. My surviving brother, Hugh, and I talk about him all the time. And I delight in the time I get to spend with Tony's children, Zach, Fiona, and Simon, and my sister-in-law Megan. Then, at the end of that July, I had to say goodbye to Betsy. A cascade of grief followed.

Intellectually, I obviously accept that death is a part of life—a steadily bigger part as so many of my friends grow old alongside me. But it was so much loss in such a short time. You adjust your sails and carry on, but I don't think you ever get used to those goodbyes. Maya Angelou, who was eighty-three when she spoke to *Essence* magazine about friendship, described losing two of her closest sister friends this way: "I can see the perimeters are coming in closer and closer, but I'm still loving, living and giving it my best shot. I fill my days with gratitude, laughter and work and keep on stepping." She kept her heart open to new relationships. As she wrote in her 2008 *Letter to My Daughter*, "A friend may be waiting behind a stranger's face."

I have tried to follow Maya Angelou's lead. And I have found that there is real joy in full days, gratitude, laughter, and new friends. Especially women friends who instinctually just *know*. They know the juggling act of being a woman, a wife, a mother. They know menstrual periods, pregnancy brain, hormones, and menopause. They know what it is to be worried about an unhappy child, troubled by your marriage, or caring for a dying parent. They just *know*. They see you and they *know*. And we meet each other where we are now.

For example, Maria is someone I knew for years because of her longtime work providing microloans for poor women. I asked her to join my State Department team in 2009 as undersecretary for civilian security, democracy, and human rights. Maria and I are similarly situated on the staircase of life, and I relish her years of experience and earned wisdom. We traveled together to Spain twice, staying with our friend Julissa, the U.S. ambassador, who whipped up fabulous itineraries in Madrid, Barcelona, and Seville. At one point, Maria and I confessed to each other that we were now living in bodies we didn't recognize. Together we commiserated and shared strategies for confronting the postmenopausal disappearance of our waistlines. Maria's tip was to burn hundreds of calories just by jogging in place for five minutes at a time while watching TV or even on a flight, in the airplane bathroom. Of course I tried it! Until Capricia found out what I was doing, did some fact-checking, and told me I had misheard Maria: I need to jog in place for *forty-five* minutes at a time. There went that plan!

My idea, borrowed from Wanda Sykes, was to give our newly thick midsections names, owning them. When Chelsea and I were filming our 2022 *Gutsy* docuseries for Apple TV+, Wanda told us she calls her postmenopausal belly Esther Roll. I now call mine Beulah; Maria's is Bertha. They are stubborn old gals, so Maria and I decided that if the two of them won't go away, we might as well get on speaking terms with them.

For all the laughter and positive outlooks, I still felt a twinge of panic over the October 2023 calendar invite to that conference call with Capricia, Cheryl, and Minyon. The three of us, with Kiki, had been making fairly regular road trips to Rhode Island over the past few years to see Maggie. She hadn't been well, and we worried about her. When Capricia, Cheryl, Minyon, and I finally connected on the call that Friday in October, I heard only mischief in their tones before Cheryl took the lead and announced:

"Your birthday is coming up. And, wow, you're going to be really old!"

"Thanks," I said. "I really don't need to hear that."

"Yes, you do," Cheryl went on, "because to help you forget, we're taking you to Vegas this weekend to see Adele!"

Apparently I had offhandedly mentioned during our last Rhode Island trip that I would love to see Adele before her Las Vegas residency ended. And, voilà! I was turning seventy-six and getting a girls' weekend in Las Vegas. We ate, we laughed, we danced like no one was watching. Friendship, Adele, and an all-you-can-eat breakfast buffet? Life doesn't get any better.

Summer 2021. Louise and I had a special project about to debut. Back before the pandemic, a publisher who knew that we're friends convinced the two of us to co-author a novel combining her mastery of mystery with my inside knowledge of politics and national security. Louise and I thought it would be fun, and we had visions of writing together at some luxe spa or exotic resort. But COVID-19 had other plans, and we ended up collaborating over Zoom—still doing a fair share of work in robes and slippers, but without the massages and room service. We were pleased with the result, a political thriller titled *State of Terror* that was set to be released that fall. We had named the main characters Ellen and Betsy after my two friends who died in those terrible months of 2019.

Now, my co-author and I were back at Lake Massawippi, this time with a bigger group that included many of my Park Ridge friends. There was fun in the sun, but we were all feeling Betsy's absence. One evening, in the rose garden of the Manoir Hovey where we were staying, Louise and I had to take some casual author photos for publicity for our book. On a whim, I asked Bonnie, the girl from class council who once helped me decorate for high school dances, to braid my hair right there in the garden like we were fourteen years old again. I sat, and Bonnie braided, surrounded by the group of girlfriends that Betsy held together all those years like glue. I was reminded of one time when this Park Ridge gang happened to be visiting the White House while my mother was staying there. Mom just listened as we all chattered about the latest happenings in our lives, at one point telling Kathleen, "It's amazing, you girls—it's like you've never been apart." By our 2021 reunion in Quebec, my mother had been gone almost ten years. How precious it is to have so many women in my life who knew Mom and are still generous with memories of her that I never tire of hearing.

Just before Betsy died, Louise gave Betsy and me identical watercolor paintings of the two of us that Louise had commissioned some months earlier. The artist rendered Betsy and me arm in arm—not in our youth, but in the fullness of age, perfectly capturing our lifelong friendship. Bill hung the painting in our bedroom, where I can look at it every day.

At our next reunion in Quebec, in the summer of 2023, we were mourning Hardye, who had passed that February. *"I can see the perimeters are coming in closer and closer..."* Again I stood in the lakeside rose garden with my friends, including Hardye's husband, Don. He had made T-shirts featuring the name Agent Hardye Moel, the character in Louise's latest mystery that she had named for our friend. Misty-eyed, we all wore the T-shirts and shared memories of Betsy and Hardye as the sun set and we prepared to go inside for dinner.

Recently, a journalist shared with me a never-published interview with Betsy from late 2016 that was meant to be published if I won the White House. The interview was about our relationship and the thirty or so friends who were headed to New York City to be with me on election night. "It's wonderful at this age to realize that the choices you made when you were ten or eleven years old, as far as friends are concerned, can bear fruit as sweet as this," Betsy had told the reporter.

Betsy's last gift to me. And how sweet it is.

> *Make new friends, but keep the old.*
> *One is silver, and the other's gold.*
> *A circle's round; it has no end.*
> *That's how long I want to be your friend.*
>
> —"Make New Friends"

WHITE SCARVES

The two-page "kill list" was chilling to read. One hundred and twenty-five names—Afghan women I knew and admired—likely to be targeted by the Taliban after the last American troops left Afghanistan in September 2021. The departure would mark the end of the longest war in American history. It would also mark the start of a new hell for Afghans—especially women. The list had been put together by a coalition of women's rights organizations in the United States and Afghanistan who feared that these women faced a terrible fate at the hands of the Taliban, who were known to torture or execute women who did not follow their extremist edicts. They shared it with the White House, and a concerned White House official had covertly shared it with me.

By late spring 2021, the Taliban were making steady, alarming gains. With the United States preparing to depart after twenty years of war and reconstruction, Taliban fighters were marching through the countryside and pushing back the American-trained Afghan national army. U.S. intelligence predicted that the Afghan government, led by the ineffective president Ashraf Ghani, would hold for up to a year. But that window seemed to get smaller by the day.

This was all set in motion by Donald Trump in February 2020, when he made an agreement with the Taliban (without telling President Ghani) that pledged the full withdrawal of U.S. troops. President Biden inherited this commitment when he took office in January 2021 and faced a difficult choice. Honoring Trump's deal could doom Afghanistan to Taliban rule and prove that two decades of extraordinary effort and sacrifice had been a failure. Renouncing the agreement would mean renewed war and would require more U.S. troops put in harm's way. Biden made the call: It was time to go. The "forever war" had to end.

As spring turned into summer and the September deadline approached, the Biden administration quietly began focusing on evacuating American troops, diplomats, and Afghans who had worked for our military and embassy in Kabul. That was a big, important undertaking. But as conversations about potential evacuations took place, I worried about the many vulnerable women who did not fall into those categories and yet were at risk for retribution by the Taliban. Leaving them behind could be a death sentence.

As I read their names, I thought about their stories—many of which I'd shared and celebrated over the years. A professor at Kabul University whose lectures on human rights and gender equality inspired countless students to continue pursuing an education. A prominent human rights lawyer who'd dedicated her life to prosecuting sexual violence and child exploitation in Afghanistan. A deputy minister in Ghani's government who was a Fulbright Scholar to the United States and fought for women's rights. Founders of women's rights organizations. Judges who prosecuted the Taliban. Women who worked with the United States Agency for International Development (USAID) to rebuild their country over the last two decades with American support and encouragement. We couldn't abandon them now.

When the Taliban first seized control of Afghanistan in the mid-1990s after a bloody civil war, women were forced to stay out of public view. They were required to wear full burqas, covering their bodies completely from head to toe with only a mesh-covered opening for their eyes, and barred from leaving their homes unless accompanied by a male family member. Girls and women were banned from schools and denied social and economic rights. The stories that filtered out of the country were horrifying. I remember hearing about an elderly woman who was flogged with a metal cable until her leg was broken because a bit of her ankle was showing under her burqa. I saw photos of public executions in sports stadiums.

When Biden made the final decision in late spring to withdraw American troops, I quietly but forcefully reminded former colleagues in the White House and State Department not to forget the women. As the days slipped by and the Taliban marched closer to Kabul, I decided it was time to stop asking and start doing. If the U.S. government had its hands full, we would find more hands.

Melanne Verveer was my first call. We go way, way back. Melanne and her husband, Phil, had studied at Georgetown with Bill, and she had gone on to do great work on Capitol Hill and at People for the American Way before joining my team at the White House during the Clinton administration. For the decades I've known and worked with her, Melanne's energy has been simply unstoppable—never tiring, always ready to board another plane, visit another country, meet another aspiring and inspiring leader, forge a new partnership, break another barrier.

Melanne was my chief of staff in the 1990s when the Taliban first seized power in Afghanistan. Humanitarian groups asked us to help ensure the Clinton administration did not recognize the Taliban's new theocratic regime as a legitimate government. The more I learned about them, the more horrified I became. I began rallying international condemnation. "There probably is no more egregious and systematic trampling of fundamental rights of women today than what is happening in Afghanistan under the iron rule of the Taliban," I said at the UN's International Women's Day celebration in 1999.

When I became a senator, I convened a hearing on Afghan women's lives under the Taliban with the help of Melanne and Vital Voices, an organization we created with Madeleine Albright and the activist, philanthropist, and former U.S. ambassador to Austria Swanee Hunt, to support women leaders and promote human rights around the world. Afghan women in exile shared terrifying stories of Taliban fighters showing up at their homes and offices and asking, "Do you realize how easy it is for us to kill you?"

After 9/11, the United States overthrew the Taliban. As a member of the Senate Armed Services Committee, I traveled to Afghanistan three times to visit our troops and talk with Afghan leaders. Each time, I also made a point of meeting with Afghan women and was impressed by the contributions they were making to build a fledgling new democracy. In 2003, I helped one of the women, Farida Azizi, who needed medical treatment after a long bout of illness, get a visa to America. We appeared on national television together to talk about the importance of centering women's rights in U.S. policy in Afghanistan. Years later, as the Taliban resumed control, I would be trying to evacuate more of those very women I'd first met with years before.

When I became secretary of state in 2009, I insisted that the Obama administration prioritize the needs and concerns of Afghan women as we surged military and economic assistance into the country and worked to build up Afghan political institutions. It wasn't always an easy sell. "Gender issues are going to have to take a back seat to other priorities," one senior administration official told the *Washington Post*, anonymously of course. "There's no way we can be successful if we maintain every special interest and pet project. All those pet rocks in our rucksack were taking us down." It's typical of a certain myopic D.C. male point of view to consider the needs of half the population a "pet project." Melanne, whom I had asked to serve as the first U.S. ambassador for global women's issues when I became secretary, started calling her team the "Pet Rock Office" and redoubled her efforts. I'll never forget when she came home from a trip to Afghanistan and reported that the women she'd met told her, "Please do not look at us as victims, but look at us as the leaders that we are." Those words stayed with both of us.

America's efforts in Afghanistan, along with those of our allies and the Afghans themselves, produced results: From 2001 to 2012, the average life expectancy of an Afghan woman jumped from forty-four years to sixty-two. By the time I left the State Department, infant mortality had declined by 22 percent. Under the Taliban, only nine hundred thousand boys and no girls had been enrolled in schools. By 2010, more than seven million students were enrolled, and nearly 40 percent of them were girls. Afghan women received more than one hundred thousand small personal loans that allowed them to start businesses and enter the formal economy. But corruption was rampant, the government was weak, and the Taliban proved a resilient enemy. Sometimes it felt like we were trying to help build a democracy on a foundation of quicksand. I kept reminding myself that an entire generation of Afghan women were enjoying unprecedented freedom and opportunity in large part because of American investments and sacrifices. If I forgot, Melanne was always there to remind me: The women of Afghanistan were counting on us, and Afghanistan's future was counting on them.

This was never more true than in the final days before the country fell once more under Taliban tyranny. Melanne shared my urgency to organize an operation to help evacuate Afghan women activists, academics, government officials, and others on our list of women likely to be targeted by the Taliban. She mobilized colleagues at the Georgetown Institute for Women, Peace, and Security, which she'd founded after leaving government. What we didn't know yet was just how quickly we'd need to mobilize and how many names would ultimately be added to the list—but we wanted to be ready.

We made dozens of phone calls to friends and former colleagues who worked in the Biden administration and at NGOs who we knew would want to help. Almost overnight, a small team of women came together: Allie Smith and Jess Keller at the Georgetown Institute, Alyse Nelson at Vital Voices, Tanya Henderson and Teresa Casale at Mina's List, Olivia Holt-Ivry in the State Department, Jen Klein on the White House Gender Policy Council, Julissa Reynoso in Dr. Jill Biden's office, my longtime aide Huma Abedin, and, crucially, the Afghan women leaders Belquis Ahmadi and Horia Mosadiq.

I first met Belquis at the White House in 1999, when Bill and I presented her with the Eleanor Roosevelt Award for Human Rights. She was a twenty-seven-year-old women's rights activist who fled Afghanistan when the Taliban seized control the first time and prevented her from attending school. At the time, she was working full-time, taking university courses, and caring for her three younger siblings while living in Virginia.

"Afghan women have lost lives, family members, basic human rights, human dignity and the right to be respected," she told the White House audience. "Soon they might lose something that destroys humanity. They might lose hope."

Belquis and I remained in touch over the years while she pursued a career in law, led USAID programs in Afghanistan, and became a senior program officer at the U.S. Institute of Peace. Her more than twenty years in exile and her ongoing work in Afghanistan meant that she had an intimate knowledge of the extraordinary women's network across the country—and knew many of the women on our list.

Like Belquis, Horia Mosadiq fled Afghanistan after the Taliban took control in the 1990s. She had been studying journalism at Kabul University and worked as a journalist in Pakistan before she completed her studies in America. She returned to Afghanistan with Amnesty International in 2001. She was frequently targeted by extremists who opposed her work on behalf of women and girls, but it wasn't until her husband and daughter were attacked that she decided to flee Afghanistan again. She settled in London, where she works to support at-risk human rights activists and advocates for women in Afghanistan. Her connections would be a lifeline for our operation.

With Belquis and Horia advising our team every step of the way, we began putting together a plan. Belquis and Horia, both fluent in

Pashto and Dari, began contacting women on the list via WhatsApp and collecting addresses, passport numbers, and information about family members. At first, many of the women were reluctant to evacuate. They didn't want to leave Afghanistan or their loved ones behind. But by July, Taliban fighters had taken control of nearly half the country as the Afghan military melted away before them. On August 6, the Taliban toppled the provincial capital of Zaranj, on the border with Iran. The next day, they had taken a second provincial capital. The next day, they took three cities. By August 12, the Taliban had defeated the Afghan national forces in Kandahar and Herat—the two largest cities after Kabul. Taliban fighters were pictured holding rifles and riding through the streets in the back of armored Ford pickup trucks. It felt like a sickening time warp. No one could quite believe the speed with which they were advancing and how easily the Afghan military was giving up. The streets of Kabul were quickly becoming crowded with terrified families who had fled provinces now under Taliban control. Belquis received a phone call from one of the women telling her that the Taliban was near and she needed to say her goodbyes.

We knew we had to move fast. We grouped the women based on where they lived, connected them via WhatsApp, and organized shelter and transportation to the airport neighborhood by neighborhood. We secured safe houses from local domestic violence shelters and hotel rooms near Kabul's airport so that women on our list could be in position when the time was right. One woman housed thirty-five fellow evacuees in her two-bedroom apartment for a night. Women were asked not to tell their family members where they were going. *Don't wear jewelry under your clothes or pack luggage. When you leave home, it should look like you're going to the market. Bring an extra phone battery if you have one and extra diapers if you're bringing an infant. Wait for our signal that it's time to head to the airport.*

Alyse and her team at Vital Voices created a fundraising

campaign to rent buses, pay drivers, and charter flights, led by board member and my good friend Diane von Furstenberg. They raised $10 million in just two weeks.

Our team also set up a 24/7 Zoom room where we could immediately share information with one another across continents and time zones, particularly in emergencies. Huma and other team members would fall asleep with their laptops open beside them and wake in the middle of the night to a voice asking, "Are you there? Is anybody there?" The Zoom room stayed open for the next three months. Someone was always there.

Word spread to other Afghan women and their families. The team was quickly overwhelmed by a flood of messages from women all over the country. They'd send photos of their family members who had been beaten by the Taliban or of their children, begging us for help. *Look at these faces,* they'd write. *Is Hillary going to leave our children to die?* It was overwhelming. Our list grew from 125 names to 500 to more than 1,500. By the end of summer we were working with thousands of names of women and their family members. Belquis and Horia had heartbreaking phone calls with the women about which family members they could bring with them. Some family members didn't have passports or even the Afghan national IDs needed to board a plane. Other women were weighing impossible choices, like whether to leave behind a son in order to evacuate a niece likely to suffer more under the Taliban's gender apartheid regime.

On August 13, U.S. marines arrived in Kabul to provide extra help evacuating embassy personnel. That same day, Taliban forces captured Pul-i-Alam, another provincial capital, only forty miles from Kabul. Two days later, the Taliban arrived at Kabul's gates. The city fell into their hands without resistance from Afghan forces. President Ghani fled the country by helicopter. Photos and videos emerged of Taliban fighters posing with rifles behind Ghani's carved wooden desk in the presidential palace. Afghan flags were lowered across the city. Long queues formed outside banks as Afghans desperately tried to withdraw cash. I was heartbroken by what I was seeing on the news.

Amid this chaos, the first group of women on our list and their families were dropped off at the airport. But U.S. marines at the gate refused to recognize their e-visas, which we'd worked with the State Department to secure. There was clearly a miscommunication, and it left the women confused and exposed. They sent us frantic WhatsApp messages. What were they supposed to do now? They couldn't get past the airport gates, and they couldn't go home because the Taliban would be looking for them.

Thousands of miles away, our team scrambled to make sense of what to do next. Our most immediate concern was getting the women and their families to a safe location. Horia quickly managed to place most of our women in safe houses around Kabul. One woman retreated to a nearby gas station and spent the night hiding in a bathroom stall after she saw Taliban fighters gathering outside. Through the sleepless night, we devised a new evacuation plan.

By morning, Taliban troops were patrolling Kabul. They struck a tenuous agreement with U.S. officials to keep the airport open and allow evacuations to continue. The Taliban wanted to be sure U.S. troops really did leave as promised and seemed to understand that the alternative to cooperation was renewed fighting. But how long would their patience last? And did they have command and control over poorly trained fighters suddenly charged with working alongside "infidels" they'd spent their lives battling?

Time was clearly of the essence. Again, we found a plane that could fly the first group from our list to safety. Now we needed to get the women from the safe houses back to the airport, but it wouldn't be easy. An estimated twenty thousand Afghans had already surged into the airport, with thousands more trying to shove their way in. The airport gates became an unpredictable bottleneck, with U.S. soldiers, troops from partner nations, Taliban fighters, international diplomats, and huge crowds all jostling together.

On my flights into Afghanistan over the years I had landed either in Kabul or at the military airport, Bagram Airfield, just thirty-five miles away. But now Bagram was deserted. One thing I learned as a former member of the Senate Armed Services Committee and as secretary of state is that the U.S. military wastes no time in carrying out an order. Once the remaining troops in Afghanistan received word in mid-April that they needed to withdraw, they packed their bags. The military base that once housed forty thousand American troops was a ghost town by July 2021. This left Kabul's commercial airport as the main evacuation route.

From a security standpoint, the airport is terribly located. It can be approached by several roads that are narrow and lined with street vendors. One of the entrances, Abbey Gate, is bound by a sewage canal on one side. Large vehicles or crowds of people can quickly cause a bottleneck.

The rest of the city, including the roads leading to the airport, was now firmly in Taliban control. Reports emerged that militants were going door-to-door examining documents and electronic devices. Roadblocks and checkpoints went up. They were stopping cars and searching people's phones. Panicked Afghans began deleting foreign contacts and burning documents that might connect them to the Americans, ultimately making their evacuations harder. One woman on our list reported that the Taliban had shown up at her mother's door demanding to know where she was and threatening to kill her. Others reported that the offices of their NGOs had been ransacked, and they were terrified about what information the Taliban might have gleaned from their files.

With Belquis's and Horia's contacts in Kabul, we hired inconspicuous, run-down grocery trucks to pick up and transport the women to the airport. We'd told them to keep their phone locations turned on but to delete our WhatsApp chat history and foreign phone numbers in case the Taliban searched their devices.

Bill and I were vacationing with Louise Penny and friends in

Quebec, although it was impossible for me to focus on anything but what was happening in Kabul. While Bill and everybody else slept, I worked the phones and continued making calls over the following days. I called UN secretary-general António Guterres, asking for the UN's assistance providing water to the crowds outside the airport gates in the blazing August sun. I called Secretary of Defense Lloyd Austin, his chief of staff, and Secretary of the Navy Carlos Del Toro and told them about our small operation. They said they would put the names of our women on a list so that the U.S. marines guarding the airport would let them through.

We needed a way to make our group more easily identifiable in the crowds around the airport if the women had any hope of reaching the marines at the gate. Belquis quickly thought of a solution: white scarves. Every Afghan woman had one. Our team told the women to tie white scarves to their handbags. By the end of August, the U.S. military's CENTCOM was referring to us as Operation White Scarves.

I heard that Amed Khan, a philanthropist friend, was trying to secure planes from various countries that could help evacuate at-risk Afghans, so we joined forces. I called the Ukrainian government and asked if it would send planes to support our evacuation. It said yes. I called the Qatari government and asked for its help arranging flights, visas, and transport through Kabul. It said yes.

I called the prime minister of Albania, Edi Rama, to ask if he could accept some of our women en route to their final resettlement countries. He readily agreed to temporarily house a thousand of the women and their family members for one year in an offseason summer resort. I called the Canadian prime minister, Justin Trudeau, to ask if he would also accept some of our women and families. It was not clear that they would have a path to permanent residency in the United States—assuming they could make it there in the first place—and that meant they might be at risk of being deported back to Afghanistan. Trudeau was supportive and agreed to accept as many as a thousand women and family members on refugee visas.

I called Huma constantly for updates. She had little good news. Desperate Afghans were scaling the airport walls with ropes, climbing over airport fences, running onto the tarmac, rushing onto unguarded planes, and huddling beside the runway hoping to get on a plane to anywhere. The U.S. forces did an amazing job under impossible circumstances, but there were too few of them, and the situation spiraled out of control—all of it captured on live television. When the first military planes took off, Afghans clung to the wings and wheels. Panic superseded logic. A young Afghan dentist fell to his death from the wing of a plane, and his body was found on a rooftop four miles away. I watched in horror alongside millions of people around the world as news footage of the chaos showed another young man, a teenage soccer player, plummeting to his death on the tarmac. In an effort to prevent any more of these appalling tragedies, the airport grounded all flights until the runway could be cleared. U.S. troops worked with soldiers from Turkey and other partner nations to secure the airfield.

Our group of Afghan women, who we called "The White Scarves," were still stuck outside the gates. With crowds clogging the streets, they abandoned the grocery trucks and tried pushing their way to the airport on foot. In the 24/7 Zoom room, our team listened on speakerphone as one of the women reported there was no way to access the airport. The crowds were too massive. Then gunshots rang out and the call went quiet. Everyone in the Zoom room held their breath. Had we lost her? What was happening on the other end of the line? Finally, the woman's voice returned. Someone had shot into the air to try to control the crowd. It hadn't worked.

A group of White Scarves made it to the airport's Abbey Gate and showed their white scarves to the marines stationed at the entrance. The women said they were on "Hillary's list" and that a plane was waiting for them. The marines said they hadn't heard of the list. They wouldn't let the women pass.

Frantic, a member of our team called a contact at the Department of Defense to plead for help. The contact said the women should go to the east gate. Our team member relayed the message to the White Scarves, hoping they could make it there before sundown. The Taliban had imposed a curfew, and nobody knew what they would do with the hundreds of people still trying to get into the airport. Would they round people up? Start shooting? As light began to fade, the shared sense of panic deepened. By this point, the White Scarves and their families had been on their feet for fifteen hours without food, water, or access to a bathroom. One member of the group had broken an ankle. A pregnant woman fell ill. Kids were trampled. It was getting dark. Nobody knew what abuse awaited these women, and they had nowhere else to go.

Melanne called the White House Situation Room. Jess and Allie called the Department of Defense and congressional offices to ask for immediate help getting our list of names to General Frank McKenzie, commander of all U.S. forces in the region. I called former U.S. ambassador to Afghanistan John Bass, who had worked closely with me at the State Department and now was President Biden's point person on the ground overseeing the evacuation. Among prominent Afghan women leaders, our list had become the only hope for evacuation. Yet despite the mounting stakes, lines of communication within the airport were breaking down. It was difficult to get word all the way to the troops guarding the airport gates. I called Robby Mook, the manager of my 2016 presidential campaign, who was now a lieutenant in the Navy Reserve and assisting with the evacuation at Kabul Airport. He also directed our group to the east gate. We urged the women to stay together as they made their way—and to make their white scarves visible to U.S. soldiers.

By 10:30 p.m. local time in Kabul, most of our women and their families had made it inside the airport, but sixteen women and their families remained stuck behind a Taliban checkpoint. One of the women had been at the airport gate with her children for over twenty-four hours. She texted the group to say her kids had fainted several times. The crowds were too much. "My legs cannot hold me anymore," she wrote. Women were beginning to lose hope. Some retreated to safe houses that our team had found; others stood through the long night hoping to press forward through the crowds.

As the sun rose the following day, large crowds gathered around the airport to protest the Taliban's takeover. The roads were impassable. Inside the airport, we finally had a breakthrough. Our team secured fifty-eight seats on a military plane. There was still a thirty-six-hour wait before the plane would take off and conflicting information about where its final destination would be. The women and families huddled inside the terminal anxious to leave and desperate for food, water, and freedom. Finally, they boarded a U.S. military plane. We thought it was bound for Doha, but the women ultimately touched down in Bahrain, en route to Kuwait. But that hardly seemed to matter now. The team received a text from one of the women on board: "Give our love to all those who worked day and night to save our lives and get us out." It was the first successful evacuation of the White Scarves.

Huma called to tell me the good news. I was so proud of our small team for pulling off what just days ago had seemed impossible. For a moment we both breathed a sigh of relief. But with the list now at more than 1,500 names, we still had many, many more to go. And the stakes were only getting higher as the date of the final U.S. withdrawal approached. After a few moments of relief and celebration over Zoom, the team quickly got back to work organizing the next evacuation plan.

Back home in Chappaqua, I was on the phone with Qatar's defense minister, asking him to help us execute our next plan: transporting three buses of high-profile Afghan women and their families from the Kabul Serena Hotel to the airport. This would require passing through several Taliban checkpoints, an impossibility without protection from someone the Taliban trusted. Someone like the Qataris. The minister agreed. Huma was also working with her contacts in the Qatari and Emirati governments to arrange humanitarian aid and resources when the women eventually reached Doha. Meanwhile, Belquis and Horia were securing hotel rooms and safe houses for the women. That's when we ran into a new problem: ATMs were down, banks across Kabul had closed, and the hotel would accept only U.S. dollars. Without cash, the women couldn't check into their rooms, and it was too dangerous for them to turn back. So Belquis started calling friends around Kabul who might be able to help. Soon enough, someone arrived at the Kabul Serena Hotel with enough cash to pay for the rooms. It was an incredibly brave act of kindness.

The next morning, on August 26, a large group of women and their families, including two pregnant women, emerged from their hotel rooms and safe houses around Kabul and quietly made their way to the Kabul Serena Hotel parking lot. They boarded three buses that the Qataris promised to safely escort to the airport.

Then disaster struck. A suicide bomber from the Islamic State–Khorasan, or ISIS–K, detonated near the airport's Abbey Gate. Thirteen marines and 170 Afghans were killed. As I watched the breaking news on TV, I was horrified by the senseless loss of lives and the deaths of the young marines. Fearing the airport would be closed, Melanne began exploring land routes through Pakistan, Uzbekistan, Tajikistan, and Turkmenistan. But with the Taliban's tight grip on most of the border crossings, it seemed too treacherous.

The buses sat for fifteen long hours in the Kabul Serena Hotel parking lot while the Qataris negotiated with the Taliban. A designated point of contact remained on the phone with Belquis and Horia, who were dialed into the 24/7 Zoom room so that our team could hear what was going on. Finally, an agreement was reached, and the buses began to move. We tracked the buses using GPS from the women's phones.

Huma frequently sent me reports, screenshots, and videos of what the women on board were experiencing. Traffic wasn't moving. Taliban checkpoints were everywhere. Panic again set in. Then a Taliban fighter boarded one of the buses. He demanded to see passports and told the women to remove their face coverings so he could check their faces. The women were horrified; this was against the religious beliefs the Taliban purported to uphold. Then the rules changed again. The bus couldn't continue until every passenger on board showed proof of a visa. There were no visas. A quick-thinking friend of Vital Voices in Albania got word of what was happening and looked around for a solution. He snapped a photo of the QR code on a bag of potatoes in a grocery store and doctored an "official e-visa" to enter Albania. Mercifully, it worked.

Meanwhile, one of the pregnant women started bleeding. Her husband, who had been on President Ghani's foreign policy team, demanded that they be let off the bus to find a hospital. Our team begged them to stay, promising that U.S. medics would assist them inside the airport. It was an impossible situation. They left the bus. I'd later learn that the woman miscarried and paid an enormous amount of money to be smuggled out of the country with her husband.

Before letting the buses leave, a Taliban fighter came on board each bus and called every passenger's name as he checked the e-visas against the passenger manifest. This was new. Even as he spoke in Pashto, it was clear to everyone half a world away listening in the Zoom room via an open line, muted on our end, what his message was: *The Taliban knows your name and that you're attempting to flee with American support. If you fail to make it out of Afghanistan, you and your family will be punished.*

Finally, the Taliban finished, and the three buses lurched forward. We watched breathlessly as, inch by inch, the red GPS dots indicated that the buses had rolled through the airport gate. The journey from the hotel to the airport was less than five miles but took over seventy-two agonizing hours.

And then the plane wasn't there. It had taken off without them. I was devastated but not ready to give up. After more phone calls and strings pulled with well-placed officials in the U.S. government, the women were able to board a C-17 plane bound for Fort McCoy, Wisconsin.

Everything about our rescue operation was a scramble that changed day by day, hour by hour. One day the cost of chartering a plane was $150,000, the next it was $750,000. One hour the east gate was open for passengers to enter, the next it was closed indefinitely. One minute three buses full of high-profile women and their families made it to the airport, the next minute there was no plane. Here is what I know from a long career in politics and diplomacy: The best-laid plans fall apart. It takes a lot of careful planning, courage, and creativity to make things happen.

Zarifa Ghafari was one of the few female mayors in Afghan history and one of the youngest. On her first day in the role, at just twenty-six years old, her office was mobbed by men refusing to be governed by a woman. Undeterred, she showed up day after day—even after the Taliban murdered her father, a former military officer, and tried to assassinate her three times. But the immense loss and feeling of guilt only spurred her on in her work on behalf of Afghan women and the poor. In 2021, she had a budding political career, a fiancé, and plans to start a family in her new Kabul apartment. All that changed when Kabul fell to the Taliban.

Like so many other Afghans, Zarifa was reluctant to leave her country. She loved her homeland and wanted to do whatever she could to help keep it safe. But as she considered the future of her young sisters under Taliban rule, she decided it was time to leave. One night in late August, as she considered her escape, she called Huma and said she was worried that the Taliban was outside her apartment. Her siblings were hiding in a closet, terrified. She had to leave immediately.

Zarifa got into a taxi with her family and headed for the airport. She called Huma again and said that the crowds were impassable, but she recognized the Turkish deputy ambassador's car. Zarifa flagged him down and explained the situation: *Hillary Clinton will vouch for us, please help us get into the airport.* Zarifa handed her phone to the official, and Huma explained that Zarifa was on our list and it was important to get her out of Kabul. The deputy ambassador pulled Zarifa and her entire family—mother, siblings, and her fiancé—into his car and ushered them safely into the airport. There was a C-130 leaving in thirty minutes, and the ambassador saw to it that the Turkish military would take Zarifa and her family with them.

Zarifa was in tears. She and her family had just escaped the Taliban and were buckled into a military plane taxiing down the runway to safety (where exactly that was, they weren't sure). But suddenly Zarifa didn't want to go. She didn't want to let the Taliban win or leave her countrywomen behind to a dangerous, uncertain future. She called Huma, her voice quivering, and said we had to stop the plane. But the plane was moving. The line went dead as Zarifa and her family were carried over the Hindu Kush mountains.

Other women took similar risks to get out on their own. Shabana Basij-Rasikh was one of the first women to reach out to me for help when the United States announced its withdrawal. Since 2016, Shabana had been running the first and only all-girls boarding school in Afghanistan. By 2021, her school, which particularly focused on enrolling girls around the age of puberty when they would typically drop out, had nearly one hundred girls enrolled from twenty-eight of Afghanistan's thirty-four provinces. It was all but guaranteed that the Taliban would not only outlaw the school but target its students and staff.

Shabana was one of the names on our team's list, but she understandably grew impatient with how long it was taking for plans to come together. She took matters into her own hands. She had already been preparing to take her students abroad for a semester to wait out the insecurity in Afghanistan. When Kabul fell, her plans moved up. They had to pack, evacuate, and get on a flight quickly. She knew the girls would be recognized as a school group and turned away if they arrived at the airport together, so she divided her students into pairs and trios, with some of them pretending to be children of staff members.

Most made it through the chaos into the airport, including Shabana. Because she was on the list of likely Taliban targets, she was approved to fly out, but she refused to leave any of her students behind. She spent that night and the next in the airport. On the third day, with fifty or so students still left outside the airport gates, she refused to wait any longer. She found a U.S. Marine captain, explained what was going on, and asked him to take her back outside the gate to find her students. Along with two other marines, they left the relative safety of the airport and managed to find the remaining students and extract them from the crowds. Finally Shabana and her students, staff, and graduates—all 256 of them—made it onto a plane bound for Rwanda. Four days later, they resumed classes. Before she left Afghanistan, Shabana burned the school's records to protect her alumni, students, and their families. As feared, the Taliban has not allowed girls older than ten to return to school since 2021.

Shabana's school continues to teach its students in Rwanda. She launched an online curriculum for girls still in Afghanistan to continue their education if they're able to access the internet. Unfortunately, very few do, but Shabana refuses to give up on the generation left behind.

These stories were bursts of hope in otherwise heartbreaking, difficult days. Our team was working around the clock. No one was sleeping. Nerves were frayed. It was impossible to think of anything but what was happening in Kabul. Every time I talked with my grandkids over FaceTime I felt a deep ache for the terror that other moms and grandmas were experiencing half a world away. We were all doing our best to help them, but time was running out and our list kept growing bigger. Once word spread that we were successfully evacuating people, requests came flooding in. We were asked to help evacuate American and Afghan journalists from the *Wall Street Journal* and Bloomberg, which somehow we were able to do. A. G. Sulzberger, publisher of the *New York Times*, called because he had learned I was helping evacuate Afghans. He said he needed eight seats on a plane for his reporters and their family members. I told him I had five seats left on the plane we were using, but he didn't want to leave anyone behind. I offered to connect him to the White House, and they were able to put all eight people on a U.S. military plane. Malala Yousafzai, who survived being shot in the head by the Taliban on her way home from school in Pakistan as a young girl, called and said her team of education advocates in Afghanistan were receiving threats. We were able to put them in touch with our Qatari contacts, who got Malala's team on planes bound for Canada. We were also asked to keep adding women from across Afghanistan to our list. We knew we couldn't rescue them all, which devastated everyone involved, but we would help as many as possible.

In the end, we managed to evacuate roughly one thousand Afghan women and their family members. From Kabul they flew to Albania, Bahrain, Canada, Germany, Greece, Kuwait, Qatar, Pakistan, Rwanda, Turkey, Ukraine, the United Arab Emirates, and the United States. Some were stopovers; others were for the long haul.

The Biden administration, for its part, managed to evacuate an astounding 122,000 people. It was the largest civilian airlift in U.S. history (more than double the forty-five-thousand-person airlift from Saigon in the Vietnam War). More than eight hundred planes were cobbled together from thirty countries to transport the thousands of people from all over the world who needed to leave. Three babies were even delivered midflight during evacuation, one on a U.S. military C-17 plane. However, many people were never able to make it through the airport crowds and onto a promised evacuation flight. An estimated one to two hundred Americans and thousands more Afghans who worked on U.S. or NATO-funded initiatives remain in Afghanistan.

Evacuation was only the first step. When the planes touched down in faraway places like Albania, the White Scarves faced new challenges. The network of individuals and organizations we'd pulled together to help get women out of Afghanistan pivoted to supporting resettlement. Vital Voices played a crucial role in the months that followed, and I was once again enormously proud of the organization that Madeleine, Melanne, Swanee, and I started all those years ago.

As our evacuees started building new lives in Albania, they welcomed twenty-three babies into the world. Mothers and newborns received top-quality obstetrics and neonatal care. More than three hundred children and adolescents participated in educational courses and English classes. There was also mental health and trauma support, as well as case management, educational support, and legal aid to help families plan for resettlement. Alyse and her team at Vital Voices raised funds to provide cash stipends for the families, so they could buy new clothes and gifts for the kids, as well as have funds to observe Ramadan and celebrate Eid according to their traditions at home in Afghanistan. Vital Voices continues to support resettled Afghan women in the United States and around the world, and it recently launched a fellowship program called Aghaaz, meaning "rebirth" in Dari, to connect evacuees with universities, civil society organizations, and think tanks in Washington, D.C.

Several key members of our team, including Alyse, Belquis, Horia, and Jess and Allie from the Georgetown Institute, traveled to Albania to personally thank Prime Minister Rama for his government's support and to meet with evacuees. What they found was a community glad to be alive but also in deep grief for what they'd lost.

The White Scarves had been at the tops of their fields and careers. They'd made impossible choices to get themselves to safety. One woman, a former member of Afghanistan's parliament, was inconsolable over having to leave her children behind in Afghanistan. She was sick with worry that the Taliban would harm them before they could be reunited. Other women shared stories of family members being harassed by the Taliban and forced to move homes and feeling trapped inside their homes for fear of retribution. Nearly all wanted to return and help lead a free, democratic Afghanistan someday. In the meantime, they were organizing and leading in other ways.

Some of the women already had experience running refugee camps or humanitarian operations. The Taliban had internally displaced thousands of people during their previous rule, and millions more Afghans struggled with poverty, hunger, and homelessness for years afterward. The women in Albania put their experience managing those crises to work, no guidance needed. They divided the families into twelve clusters and democratically elected a leader to represent each cluster. They set up time-bound leadership terms and processes for holding cluster elections. Leaders were responsible for coordinating with Vital Voices and the Albanian government on behalf of their groups' needs—including managing visa applications, flagging medical needs, landing local jobs (at nearby restaurants and hotels) for people who could work, and visiting pregnant women in the hospital as they gave birth. One elected cohort leader was a fourteen-year-old girl who had been evacuated because of her role as a youth representative for the World Food Programme. Allie and Jess smiled every time they saw her running around the compound, answering phone calls, and going door-to-door to check on her cohort members.

With the support of Vital Voices and Melanne's Georgetown Institute, the women wrote a policy paper advocating for the U.S. Afghan Adjustment Act, which would allow those waiting for visas to begin working, earning, and establishing a permanent home in the United States. Without it, many Afghan refugees in America and in other countries like Albania risked deportation back to Afghanistan when their temporary visas expired after two years. The proposed legislation was introduced as a bipartisan bill in August 2022 and reintroduced in 2023 (and the White Scarves again came together to advocate for the legislation), but it has yet to pass in our divided Congress. To fill the gap, President Biden negotiated an increase of twelve thousand more Special Immigration Visas and an extension of current Afghan humanitarian visas to 2026. However, with eighty thousand Afghans like the White Scarves currently waiting for U.S. visas, there is still much to be done.

The women also continued their advocacy for human rights back in Afghanistan. The Georgetown Institute launched the Onward for Afghan Women initiative, and other women created the Women's Forum on Afghanistan, the Afghan Women's Policy Collective, and other groups to leverage their expertise advancing inclusive peace to ensure their voices are at the center of global policy debates. They have offered guidance to the U.S. government and the United Nations on responding to Afghanistan's ongoing hunger crisis, engaging Afghan women in development efforts, and classifying gender apartheid as a crime against humanity to apply pressure to the Taliban.

One very brave woman has even made a dangerous trip back to Afghanistan to continue advocating for the women left behind. Soon after Zarifa Ghafari, the young mayor who fled with her family by flagging down the Turkish delegation, resettled in Germany, she began making plans to return. In 2022, she worked through the German foreign ministry to coordinate with the Taliban for safe passage for herself and a small documentary crew from HiddenLight (the production company that Chelsea and I started together with Sam Branson). The Taliban saw Zarifa's trip as a tactical move. They desperately needed international aid to resume and hoped that publicly allowing an advocate for democracy and women's rights to travel through the country safely would make for good PR. She took a lot of heat online for her willingness to negotiate her trip with the Taliban. But she was undeterred: "I am prepared to speak with those I dislike and distrust, or whose ideas differ from mine, if it means that I carry on with my work. Better that than to shout from afar."

In Kabul, Zarifa took the camera crew to document displaced families living on the streets and struggling to survive. With the Taliban in control and the country's central bank reserves frozen, there is no longer any public aid available to help them. Zarifa distributed supplies of rice, flour, and oil. She asked women about their hardships and argued with men who harassed her for being an educated working woman. Zarifa also gave an interview to Afghanistan's largest private TV network. She called on the Taliban to release its female prisoners: "Those who have fought for women's rights, in the service of a better Afghanistan for everyone, should not be in a prison cell." The interview aired once Zarifa's plane had safely departed. Like so many of the evacuated women, she hopes to someday return for good to a democratic Afghanistan. You can see Zarifa's story on Netflix in the Emmy Award–winning documentary HiddenLight produced about her called *In Her Hands*.

As of May 2024, all but nine of the women we helped evacuate have been permanently resettled. This is an incredible success rate. Many are now living in the United States and Canada, and some are spread across Germany, Pakistan, Qatar, Rwanda, Turkey, the UAE, and Ukraine. The team continues to support those nine women still waiting for permanent resettlement. Vital Voices continues to support hundreds of women still inside Afghanistan and those who have fled to Pakistan through grants to women's NGOs and safe houses in both countries.

In the fall of 2021, when Chelsea and I were filming our TV show *Gutsy*, we traveled to Fayetteville, Arkansas (where Bill and I were married and taught at the nearby university), to meet with another women-led group resettling Afghan families. Canopy Northwest Arkansas assists newly arrived evacuees during their initial resettlement, including setting up their homes, providing food, and helping them enroll in school, find jobs, apply for benefits, learn English, and access health care. Chelsea and I jumped right in assembling furniture for a soon-to-arrive family of five that had fled Kabul.

Afterward, we had tea with Aqela Faizy and her sister-in-law, Basira, in their new home in another town, and they told us of their dangerous escape months before. Basira was in her last year studying for a medical degree at Kabul University and was learning how to drive when U.S. forces left Afghanistan. Aqela's husband, a Fulbright Scholar who earned his master's degree from the University of Arkansas, Fayetteville, and worked for President Ghani's government, called one morning and said everyone needed to immediately come home. "We thought it would take months for the Taliban to reach the capital, but it happened so quickly," she told us. Just after midnight on August 24, all fifteen members of the Faizy family made their way through the chaos to the airport. They boarded a transport plane bound for Virginia, where they spent weeks in a refugee camp before moving to Fayetteville with Canopy's help. Now, Basira is studying to become a dental hygienist and works for Catholic Charities, where she helps other refugee women and families from around the world resettle in America. She worries for her friends still in Afghanistan who have been abused by and forced to marry members of the Taliban.

When I think back on the evacuation and resettlement, I'm struck by what a collaborative effort it was among multiple organizations supporting and led by women. The ingenuity of our team to overcome immense obstacles. The bravery of so many Afghan women and their families to leave their homeland and start anew. A mantra emerged every time one plan failed: *There's always another way.* Together, we'd always find it.

I deeply regret that American leadership in Afghanistan across four administrations was not more successful in helping the Afghan people achieve the peace and security they deserve. I tried to make sure gender equality and human rights were at the forefront of our policies and not an afterthought of our military operation. And I'm proud that American leaders, starting with Laura Bush, worked to help Afghan women and girls reclaim their rights. As secretary of state, whenever I met with Afghan women I made a promise on behalf of our country: "We will not abandon you. We will stand with you always." In the end, we couldn't keep that promise. I lose a lot of sleep over that. That's why this evacuation was immensely personal to me. It's why I'm so grateful to Belquis, Horia, and all the others who shared my determination to get as many women and their family members out of Afghanistan as we possibly could.

I take some comfort from knowing that while the Taliban can close the schools, they can't take away two decades of girls' education. They can't erase the memory from millions of women's minds of what it was like to pursue careers outside the home, vote, and work together to effect change. No matter how brutal they are, they can't control women's minds or extinguish their dreams.

Here's one more story that will always stay with me: In the fall of 2021, after U.S. troops left Afghanistan, we continued to quietly evacuate women on our list from an airport in Mazar-i-Sharif, a city about 250 miles north of Kabul. One day we secured a flight but couldn't find safe shelter near the airport for the women to wait at until it was time to go. The hotels and safe houses weren't an option. Some were full, and some had been raided by the Taliban. We weren't sure what to do. Belquis said she knew of a wedding venue close to the Mazar airport. It was large enough to accommodate the women and families on our flight and was unlikely to raise suspicion. Belquis and Horia rented it out, paid for a catered meal, and hoped the Taliban would think a wedding was taking place. It worked. Women always find another way.

THIS REMARKABLE
SISTERHOOD

I never cared much for the question that so many reporters like to ask: *Do you have any regrets?* Maybe because it often feels like a can't-win trap, a gotcha question whose answer, whatever that answer might be, will be breathlessly framed as an admission of weakness, wrongness, or guilt. But mostly, I am not someone who spends a lot of time looking back with second thoughts—unless a publisher commands it (see: *Living History, Hard Choices,* and *What Happened*). I am more naturally present-day oriented, not inclined to dredge my memory for certain snapshots in time or ruminate on shoulda-coulda-woulda scenarios.

But when the news of former First Lady Rosalynn Carter's death broke on November 19, 2023, one memory from three decades earlier came back to me clearly. It involves a regret I feel to this day. It was the summer of 1993, and I had been First Lady for five months. One morning late that June, I read in the daily White House newspaper clippings that Pat Nixon had been laid to rest on the grounds of the Richard Nixon Library and Birthplace in California. This was in the pre-digital age before twenty-four-hour news, the internet, and social media would be bombarding us from all sides with this kind of news as it was happening. I saw from news photos that the funeral ceremony had been attended by two couples who had succeeded the Nixons in the White House: Betty and Gerald Ford and Nancy and Ronald Reagan. Seated in the first row, across the aisle from Richard Nixon and his children and grandchildren, the Fords and Reagans literally were at their fellow former president's side as he wept over the woman who was his wife of fifty-three years. It was a quietly powerful portrait of a man who had held his emotions in check when he resigned the presidency while Pat Nixon stood beside him holding back tears.

I don't remember what Bill and I were busy with that weekend. I have no idea whether the funeral was ever on my scheduler's radar or brought up to me by my staff or Bill's. All I knew was that I should have been there, showing respect for a woman who had once been our nation's First Lady during a tumultuous time. Especially because I believed in showing up for funerals, calling hours, and memorial services for people I knew and cared about long before Deirdre Sullivan's 2005 essay for National Public Radio, titled "Always Go to the Funeral," went viral. I try to never miss one of those opportunities to be present for family, friends, and neighbors. But I had never met Pat Nixon. And I didn't know Richard Nixon but for a brief handshake in March 1993, when Chelsea and I waited at the elevator in the White House residence to greet the former president upon his arrival for a visit with Bill. Nixon had done his homework. As he said hello to Chelsea, he added with a note of nostalgia that she was attending the same school in Washington that his daughters had. He didn't have much to say to me, knowing I had served on the impeachment inquiry staff that had investigated him in 1974 and recommended that he be impeached. The Judiciary Committee voted on a bipartisan basis to do so, which led to his resignation.

I didn't know Pat Nixon. I had no relationship at all with her. And yet I did. I just hadn't really understood that at the time.

Now I do. And I haven't missed the funeral of a former First Lady since.

November 28, 2023. The flight aboard Air Force One to Atlanta for Mrs. Carter's memorial service was a mini-reunion, as the ceremonies attending death are for so many families. President Biden had invited Michelle Obama, Bill and me, and former senator Chuck Robb and Lynda Bird Johnson Robb, President Lyndon Johnson's daughter, to catch a ride with him and Jill. In the president's conference room, Jill used the flight to catch Michelle up on what was new at the White House, while the president, the Robbs, Bill, and I talked about the wars in Ukraine and the Middle East. Despite the fraught topic, it was a comfortable chat. Familiar. Bill and I knew intuitively the sky-high stakes Joe was managing. Only eleven people alive that day could truly know, having lived it from inside the White House, exactly what that high-wire act really is, bearing on your shoulders the weight of war, markets, natural disasters, and whatever else the day could bring, all while dodging fire from critics, adversaries, and even friends. There on Air Force One were five of those eleven people, heading south to honor she who had, until days earlier, made us an even dozen.

Rosalynn's grandson Jason said it had been her wish that all the First Ladies would come together for her memorial in a show of unity in these divisive times. "My grandmother campaigned against and voted against some of their husbands," he said. "But she believed that there are some things that are more important than politics." So, when all of us flying together from Washington finally arrived at Atlanta's Glenn Memorial United Methodist Church and were shown to a large holding room in the basement, we expected to see Laura Bush. She had flown in from Texas and was, as always, a picture of polish and warmth. She said hello, leaning in to touch her cheek to mine.

That Melania Trump was also in the room seemed a huge surprise to everyone. If anybody at the White House or on Bill's or my Secret Service detail had been briefed on Mrs. Trump's plan to attend, they didn't tell me. I had not spoken to her since our briefest of hellos on the dais at the 2016 Alfred E. Smith Memorial Foundation Dinner in New York City less than three weeks before that fateful Election Day. I never quite knew what to make of the third Mrs. Trump. Back in 2005, when I was Donald's senator, I accepted his invitation to their wedding at his Mar-a-Lago resort in Palm Beach. I went out of curiosity. I was going to be in Florida anyway and thought it would be entertaining to see what a Donald Trump wedding was like. It was the first time I met Melania, and I just remember that she was young, very beautiful, and very tall. And that she didn't talk much, at least to me.

Now, here she was, standing alone as Laura, who'd looked to be chatting with Melania when the rest of us walked in, stepped away to say her hellos. Melania had a look on her face—very smiley but uncertain—that reminded me of the little kid at the birthday party who doesn't know anyone and is waiting at the edge of the circle, hoping people are going to be nice. We were. We all went up to her. President Biden walked over to greet her. Jill air-kissed her cheek, and Michelle Obama gave her one of her signature big hugs. As at her wedding, Melania didn't engage much. Bill tried to make conversation, asking her how she was, but he was met with a smile and few words. I reached out, shook her hand, and said, "Hello, Melania, it's nice to see you."

In the sanctuary, Melania, Michelle, Laura, Jill, and I sat in the front row as the Carter children and grandchildren took turns reading Scripture and sharing heartfelt reflections of Rosalynn. Amy Carter read a beautiful seven-sentence love letter that her father had sent home to her mother seventy-five years before from his deployment with the Navy. Amy is now a fifty-six-year-old mother of two, but with her familiar blond bangs and glasses, she reminded me of the young girl who moved into the White House in 1977. I had often wished from afar to give her a hug then. By 1979, I was the First Lady of Arkansas and expecting my own baby girl, Chelsea. I would see intrusive news photos and footage of Amy and worry over her privacy and innocence in the Washington, D.C., spotlight. Cameramen boorishly stalked her at school. Comics cruelly mocked her for having her nose in a book during a state dinner. What Amy endured warned me to fiercely protect Chelsea when she moved into the White House. Now, as the former First Daughter stepped off the altar shaking with grief over losing her mother, I felt again the urge to give her a hug.

Then Jason Carter stepped to the lectern and opened his eulogy this way:

"Secretary Clinton, Mrs. Bush, Mrs. Obama, Mrs. Trump, and Dr. Biden, thank you all for coming and acknowledging this remarkable sisterhood that you share with my grandmother. And thank you all for your leadership that you provided for our country and the world.

"Secretary Clinton and Dr. Biden, we also welcome your lovely husbands."

That last line got a good laugh from an audience well acquainted with how often First Ladies—or, really, any wives at events where they are plus-ones to the men who are the real stars of whatever show we're sitting through—are reduced to "your lovely wife" in an emcee's opening remarks. I have come to appreciate over the years how I present an even more nettlesome conundrum in these kinds of circumstances. In my husband's White House, I was Mrs. Clinton. (Mrs. Rodham Clinton was a bridge too far in 1993.) Then, for eight years, I was Senator Clinton. In Barack Obama's White House, I was Madam Secretary. Had 2016 turned out differently, I wonder now if I could have gotten away with President Rodham Clinton; I would have liked that as an enduring tribute to my parents. I hope the women presidents in our nation's future get to choose how they will be addressed, no matter how much of a mouthful it is. I've loved every chapter of my story and the titles that attended them. I know that, for all the paths I've walked since being First Lady, there will still be spaces where I am Mrs. Bill Clinton. That's okay. (If you ask Bill, he'll tell you there are times when he feels like Mr. Hillary Clinton.)

You can also just call me Hillary.

So while we all enjoyed Jason's knowing nod to "your lovely husbands," what made an even deeper impression on this former First Lady were three other words: "this remarkable sisterhood."

I never had a sister. Never really thought about what it would be like to have one. Two younger brothers were enough for me when it came to siblings. And I can't say that I ever thought of the women who have borne the title First Lady as sisters. We didn't sign up for a sorority, and the title is no personal achievement, excepting the work we did to help get our husbands elected. The title itself was never conceived by our founders; it unsteadily evolved from alternatives tried in the 1800s, like "Lady Presidentress" and "Mrs. President." I can't help but think how the Right would have delighted in using both as slurs when they burned me in effigy for trying to improve Americans' health care when I was First Lady. For all the heartburn that came with the failure of "Hillary Care" (the Right's actual slur, but one I'm proud to own simply for trying), Whitewater, and the rest, I loved my years as First Lady. The state dinners, international travel, grand Christmas decorations—I was proud to be the nation's hostess, and, let's face it, those things were a lot of fun.

But even more important to me was the opportunity to work, with real influence, on the things I had always cared about, like women's rights and early childhood development. Still today, I'll meet mothers, some of them now grandmothers, who say they learned from me the developmental value of reading, talking, and singing to their newborns. Credit really goes to then new brain research we highlighted at the 1997 White House Conference on Early Childhood Development, but I prize the compliment as proof that I accomplished some lasting good as First Lady. The fact remains that the job of First Lady is not a real job. There is no job description, no salary, only a generally agreed-upon unfunded mandate: helpmate to the president, hostess to the nation, and avatar for ideal womanhood, whatever that happens to be when history finds us in the White House.

As for the club of former First Ladies, if anything, we are like the neighborhood book club of moms that never got off the ground because it was impossible to find a night that worked for everyone, let alone agree on a book and then make the time to read it. Before the service for Rosalynn, five whole years had passed since the last time the small group of us got together—at the 2018 funerals of first Barbara Bush and then her husband, former president George H. W. Bush. Funerals, presidential library dedications, and a gala for the U.S. Botanic Garden. Those are the few occasions that lured us away from our separate lives, busy with family, advocacy, and our personal commitments. I felt a much more genuine sorority with my fellow gubernatorial wives in the 1980s and then with the women with whom I served during my eight years in the U.S. Senate. The group of us women senators worked really, really hard at getting along as people and working together as lawmakers. We regularly got together for dinner as a group, and when Republican senator Susan Collins of Maine got engaged just before Valentine's Day in 2012, I threw her a girls' night dinner party at my house. Before the tribalism of today took over political life, I found the company of the women senators—and, before them, the state First Ladies—to be a supportive safe space, where we could ask questions and talk through concerns as women, not as political rivals. When the governors' wives got together, which was at least twice a year around the governors conferences, we could talk through serious policy challenges back home, like improving schools, or more mundane ones. I remember my friend Lynda Bird Johnson Robb, then the First Lady of Virginia, saying in one especially freewheeling discussion group, "What can you ask these First Ladies that none of your other friends could ever answer? It's 'What do you do with all your plaques?' Everywhere I go, I'm given a plaque."

When it came to us few presidential wives, "sisterhood" was a bit of a stretch. We were certainly connected, as Jason recognized, but I wasn't sure it was a fair description.

I thought about sisterhood some more when I was asked weeks later what it was like seeing Mrs. Trump in Atlanta. Social media had been abuzz with catty (read: sexist) takes on Melania's gray tweed coat and the body language among us "sisters." The *Washington Post* reported that we "barely looked at each other or smiled, and appeared to take pains to stare straight ahead after entering the church." The *Post* also observed that Michelle, in the seat beside Melania, appeared at times to be "leaning away" from her. Typical. Also, ridiculous. Of course, reporters couldn't *see* into the First Families' holding room before the service to know that Michelle hugged Melania. So they saw what they wanted to see in the sanctuary (female rivalry at any level, real or imagined, makes good copy), never stopping to consider that perhaps the five of us First Ladies didn't enter the sanctuary all smiley and sociable, like we were walking into a chick-flick matinee, because, you know, *we were at a funeral.*

As for what we wore that day, the *New York Times* fashion critic Vanessa Friedman noted that four of us were "united" in black, while Melania's choice of gray made her stand out, not a team player—as if the rest of us had a group chat and worked out beforehand what we would all wear—calling it "a sign, perhaps, of Mrs. Trump's historic ambivalence toward the role of first lady and her reluctance to play to the expectations that surround it." On the social media site X, commentary was not so delicate, with one user writing that Melania's decision to eschew black was "distasteful and gross."

Let's get real. The Victorian-era tradition of donning black for funerals has gone the way of the edict against wearing white after Labor Day. Jason Carter wore a gray suit to deliver a tribute to his "cool grandma." President Biden was in blue. As far as I can tell, neither of them got any flak for it. Was I really feeling some sympathy for Melania Trump after all the ugliness and turmoil the Trump family had heaped on the nation, the world, and my own family the past several years? I won't go that far. But in my view, what Melania wore to pay tribute to Rosalynn (who herself was pointedly critical right back at the Trumps) was perfectly appropriate, and I was sorry that Melania got slammed for something so petty. She came. That's what mattered. After the shattering of so many norms by the Trump White House, the former First Lady came to Atlanta to embrace one still-sacred American tradition: unity in mourning. I give her points for that. I can appreciate how awkward it must have been, not knowing what kind of reception she would get after all her husband's insults directed at us Bushes, Bidens, Obamas, and Clintons alike. When I thought of Melania at all, I found myself conflicted. On a gut level, I have never believed that a wife bears responsibility for the actions of her husband. But did she aid and abet her husband's worst instincts? Was she quietly complicit in his bigotry and hate-mongering? I can only think of what she wore to a Texas shelter for migrant children separated from their parents: an army-green jacket with I REALLY DON'T CARE, DO YOU? boldly scrawled on its back. It sure seemed on brand for *Donald* Trump. As for *Melania* Trump, I'll stick to my own edict of not passing judgment on another woman's appearance. We get too much of that already.

January 20, 1993. I thought we were *supposed* to wear hats.

Leaning into the "lady" of First Lady and Second Lady, Tipper Gore and I both showed up to the White House in hats—hers purple, mine a royal blue—on the sunny winter morning our husbands were being sworn in as vice president and president. Before the ceremony and celebration began the long day ahead, it was tradition to meet up at the White House for tea (coffee, in our case) with the outgoing president and First Lady (in our case, George H. W. Bush and Barbara Bush). It was all part of the peaceful, *civilized* transfer of power.

It had been a bruising election, turning the Bushes out after a single term. But Barbara met the day with an élan that I admired. In her diary-style memoir the following year, she would remember this: "The ladies looked great and both wore hats. It reminded me of how critical everyone had been about Marilyn Quayle's hat four years before, and I wondered if Hillary and Tipper would get away with theirs." These are the things you think about after being put on a pedestal under a spotlight and picked apart—how you look, the way you sound, and what you care about—for four or eight years.

This wasn't my first time as Barbara's guest in the executive mansion that would next be mine to make into a home. In mid-November, after the election, she had given me a tour of the White House family quarters. She greeted me on the south driveway with a hug and held my hand as she led me inside. It was crystal clear that she was still smarting, badly, from her husband's defeat. As she showed me the rooms where her grandchildren had sleepovers and filled me in on things like how we would get our mail, she also vented about the election and how James Baker should have left the State Department sooner to help George's campaign. At one point, she asked me, "Do you think Ross Perot knew his third-party candidacy would help you?" It was a little uncomfortable at the time. Today, I remember it as vintage Barbara.

Eight years later, I held Laura Bush's hand in the same spot on the driveway where Barbara and I had stood. Laura had visited the White House numerous times when her in-laws lived there; surely she didn't need a tour from me. But she came anyway, because before she could put her own stamp on the house and our history (most notably as a champion for education, literacy, and the Taliban-oppressed women of Afghanistan), she had a role to play in this other decades-long tradition of the peaceful transfer of power, unbroken until 2020, when Mrs. Trump neglected to extend an invitation to Jill Biden after Joe Biden's election. Years later, when Laura's memoir, *Spoken from the Heart*, came out, I was charmed to read what she wrote about our visit. How she and George ended up growing tomatoes in pots right where Chelsea had told her our tomato plants had thrived. And the "kinship" she felt in the easy warmth of our time together, just as she'd felt with other wives of political leaders. As Laura described it, "There was a similarity and at times a strangeness to our shared circumstances that created an instant bond."

Also instant was Laura's baptism in the gratuitous and cruel snark aimed at women who step onto the public stage. Coverage of her White House visit panned the outfit she wore, an immaculately tailored skirt suit. A "purple plaid upholstery suit," jeered a fashion critic in the *Washington Post*. Laura's home-state *Texas Monthly* was no more charitable, regurgitating a review that said her "terrible purple plaid number" made our incoming First Lady look "like nothing so much as a country mouse." It was unfair to her, and I felt awful.

From far outside the gates surrounding 1600 Pennsylvania Avenue, a walk-through of a handful of rooms might seem incidental. But it was a gesture of continuity so historically powerful and personally meaningful—woman to woman, as one is moving out and another is moving in—that Jacqueline Kennedy, busy with trauma, grief, and two young children, made time to host Lady Bird Johnson for tea and a tour just one day after President Kennedy's burial. In her memoir, *A White House Diary*, Lady Bird recalled walking with Jackie through the Yellow Oval Room, the same sunny refuge where Chelsea, Bill, and I would put up our personal Christmas tree and spend time outside on the Truman Balcony. "There on the table," Lady Bird wrote, "were the black boots—the boots that were on the riderless horse in [President Kennedy's] funeral procession. There was also a folded flag."

Life happened in those grand spaces that were handed down family to family along with the furniture, the artwork, and the household staff who kept the place running. On our first morning in the White House, Bill and I learned pretty abruptly just how much we had inherited from our new home's previous occupants. After the long day and late night of inauguration festivities, we had been asleep just a few hours—in the bedroom vacated by the Bushes only twenty-four hours earlier—when we were awakened at 5:30 a.m. by a tuxedoed butler carrying coffee on a silver breakfast tray, just as George and Barbara had liked it.

In 1976, about six months after Bill and I got married and before I joined the Rose Law Firm in Little Rock, Arkansas, I worked as the Indiana field coordinator for the Carter presidential campaign. Carter didn't carry Indiana (to be fair, it was always a long shot), but I came away deeply admiring our new president-elect and incoming First Lady. They were an unusual couple, for sure. They could drive you crazy with how single-minded they could seem, so possessed of their own righteousness and urgency to act. Jimmy was governor of Georgia when I first met him in early 1975. He stuck his hand out to shake mine, saying, "I'm Jimmy Carter. I'm going to be your next president." He hadn't even announced his campaign yet, but that's who he was. He had a sense of destiny about him.

Rosalynn was the same way. She was a hard worker and a serious, somewhat reserved person who really wanted to get things done. When you saw her, there were few pleasantries. She would dive right into whatever passion project she was working on at the time, whether it was mental health, childhood immunization, or the Equal Rights Amendment. She had a deep confidence in the contributions she could make, and she was unabashed about being Jimmy's full partner—in everything. She went to cabinet meetings and attended whatever interested her on her husband's Oval Office schedule. Feminist chutzpah to some, maybe. But I saw it as reflective of her relationship with Jimmy and the religious faith they shared. They had this clear sense that they were meant to do great things, and they were going to take up every minute that they could trying to get those good things done. Their approach spoke straight to the heart of this Methodist girl who, well before I was confirmed in the sixth grade, could recite church founder John Wesley's golden rule: "Do all the good you can." It was with Rosalynn that I first felt that kinship Laura Bush would later enunciate. I had been First Lady of Arkansas for just a little over six months when Rosalynn came to Little Rock in July 1979 for a childhood immunization event on the back lawn of the governor's mansion. It was a big deal for the nation's First Lady to come to Arkansas. It was a big deal to me. And it was a big deal to celebrate vaccinating children against dangerous childhood illnesses.

In the years ahead, it was probably Rosalynn's pragmatic, activist example—she with her notebook at cabinet and Oval Office meetings—that made me think it would be no problem to take a West Wing office after Bill asked me to lead his health care reform initiative. And, even later, it was partly Rosalynn's indefatigable good works in her First Lady afterlife that emboldened me in my own political afterlife, even though some loudmouths on the Right wanted this "former" (former First Lady, former senator, former secretary of state, former presidential nominee) to go home, stay home, and keep quiet.

Don't get me wrong. I'm not suggesting we were a cozy, "Kumbaya"-singing foursome of like-minded Democrats. Google "Bill Clinton Jimmy Carter North Korea" and you'll get just a taste of how complicated the relationship was between the Carters and us Clintons. For more, try "Did Jimmy Carter vote for Hillary Clinton in 2016" and you'll see what I mean. (He apparently didn't in the primary and then did against Trump. Carter also famously said that, in his opinion, Trump "didn't actually win the election in 2016" but was "put into office because the Russians interfered on his behalf.") But the important thing is that, throughout, we respected that each of us was trying to do what we individually believed was best for the American people. As "formers," I think we all came to see that perhaps our most critical role was in preserving the norms of the presidency, as is enshrined in the peaceful transfer of power, and protecting democracy.

Bill and I last saw the Carters in July 2021, when we traveled to Plains, Georgia, for their seventy-fifth wedding anniversary. Frail and well into their nineties, they gathered hundreds of family, friends, and supporters at the local school that also houses the National Park Service site commemorating their life stories. They had finally given up building houses with Habitat for Humanity but were still engaged in the global humanitarian work of the Carter Center. Inside a classroom, Bill and I greeted Rosalynn, who was using a walker, and Jimmy, who was in a wheelchair and wore a gardenia in his jacket's buttonhole. They both expressed their appreciation for us coming and told us to be sure to look around at the exhibits while we were there.

Once I sat and thought about the web of connections that I had enjoyed with my fellow First Ladies over the years, I started to see that sliver of my life as an almost Forrest Gump–like walk through modern American women's history. Jackie and Lady Bird were perhaps the last of the traditional First Ladies who disavowed—in public, at least—any hand in their husbands' work. (It's worth noting, however, that a 2021 biography of Lady Bird and her behind-the-scenes politicking was subtitled *Hiding in Plain Sight*. And historians credit Jackie with quietly cultivating improved diplomatic relations between her husband and the leaders of France, the Soviet Union, Pakistan, and India.) From these two women, I savored small kindnesses that were huge to me in difficult times. Jackie endorsed Bill in 1992, and over the course of that campaign, I got to know the transcendent woman I had admired for so long. I wasn't First Lady for more than a couple of days when I placed an SOS call to Jackie in New York City. Already, the White House was overwhelming and isolating with its bustle of staff, security, and press. I had no idea how to make life normal for Chelsea—and for me. Jackie didn't hesitate: *Come to lunch, we'll talk.* Six days after the inauguration, I was at her doorstep. Her Fifth Avenue apartment in Manhattan was literally decorated with books, a design trick I subsequently tried to copy with the mountains of books that Bill and I own, but they never look as elegant as Jackie's. We ate lunch at a table beside her living room window overlooking Central Park. Jackie was generous with moral support, practical advice, and her wicked sense of humor, especially her droll impersonations of certain political figures. (Who? I'll never tell.) *Don't let the Secret Service agents overprotect Chelsea,* she advised, recalling how agents would try to keep her young son John Jr. from falling off his bike. "But that's a part of growing up," she wisely insisted. Another tip was to use Camp David as much as possible, because there's much more freedom and privacy there.

It was a darker time of uncertainty for me when Lady Bird reached out with her own style of moral support. She had been watching TV on December 19, 1998, and caught coverage of me in the Rose Garden, joining Al Gore and a crowd of congressional Democrats in a show of solidarity with Bill after the Republican-led House voted that day to impeach him. I was holding my marriage together with wisps of faith, but I knew Bill was a good man and a great president, so I joined the fight to keep him in office. Not long after that, I got a letter from Lady Bird: "You made my day! When I saw you with the President on television with you by his side (was it the South Lawn?), reminding us of the country's progress . . . and how far we have yet to go, I sent a prayer your way." Like Jackie, Lady Bird had lived with the background noise of whispers about her marriage. She understood the pressure I was under, and her words were a uniquely powerful sort of kindness, just when I needed it.

After Jackie died in May 1994, her son John F. Kennedy Jr. sent Bill and me a handwritten letter—and the great gift of knowing that we had given something back to Jackie when *she* needed it. The letter, on stationery monogrammed "JFK," was dated June 5, 1994, two weeks after Bill and I stood with John and his sister, Caroline, as their mother was laid to rest in Arlington National Cemetery beside their father. The former First Son wrote, in part:

It seems like ages ago since we last met at Arlington—the day, though, remains vivid in memory. I've been rolling these words around in my head, not quite ready to part with them. But time rolls on and I'm not getting any more eloquent, so it's time I share them.

I wanted you both to understand how much your burgeoning friendship with my mother meant to her.

Since she left Washington, I believe she resisted ever connecting with it emotionally—or the institutional demands of being a former First Lady. It had much to do with the memories stirred and her desire to resist being cast in a lifelong role that didn't quite fit. However, she seemed profoundly happy and relieved to allow herself to reconnect with it through you.

With his signature boyish charm, John added a postscript:

P.S. Sorry for the smudges. Being left-handed in the sweltering New York summer has its drawbacks.

Bill and I have hung on to that letter all these years. And still, today, I mourn not having more time with Jackie.

When I think of my friendships with the vastly different women who had walked their own paths into the same house, the same crucible, political party is nowhere in the frame. Up close, I got to see Betty Ford's personal dedication to the treatment of addiction. She once led me on a private tour of the Betty Ford Clinic in California, and it was dazzling how she knew everyone by name. "Treatment saved my life," she told me. "I want to save other people's lives." And so, she did. In August 1993, Betty even generously offered us her family's house in Beaver Creek, Colorado, where Chelsea and I hiked and went to the Bolshoi Ballet performance during the Vail Dance Festival and Bill played golf with Jerry Ford, Jack Nicklaus, and others. Betty knew how important it was to get out of Washington to breathe now and then.

After the September 11 attacks brought war with the Taliban in Afghanistan, Laura Bush invited me to join her as co-chair of the U.S.-Afghan Women's Council, bringing aid, education, and opportunity to Afghan women and girls. It's a commitment she and I still pursue. I had many disagreements with her husband while serving as a senator, but she and I found common ground around the Afghan women.

My relationship with Michelle Obama was never a sure thing. It had to grow, little by little, from the wounds of the tough 2008 Democratic primary fight between her husband and me. I came to appreciate that Michelle doesn't brush things off as easily as Barack does, and so the relationship that she and I forged during the time I served President Obama as secretary of state was all the more meaningful to me. Michelle and I never addressed any personal tension. Our relationship just naturally warmed as we came to know each other. I like to think that she saw my loyalty and effectiveness as secretary and grew to trust that I wanted not only for Barack and his administration to succeed but for her and her girls to succeed as well. In a phone conversation before the family moved to Washington, Michelle and I talked through how Bill and I had picked a school for Chelsea sixteen years earlier and what she was thinking about for Sasha and Malia. Once they were settled in the White House, Michelle asked me to lunch in the Yellow Oval Room on the second floor of the White House. At a small table looking out over the Truman Balcony, we bonded over the challenges of raising a family in a fishbowl and over her plans to use her platform as First Lady to promote child health through nutrition and exercise. (She was practicing what both she and her husband preached about healthy eating and exercise. I agreed with them in principle but fell short in practice. Lunch was delicious but portion-controlled, and I remember getting back to my office at the State Department in urgent need of a snack.) I was touched when Michelle later asked Chelsea to come talk with her daughters about living in the White House, sharing her experiences being a teenager in the spotlight followed by Secret Service agents to parties.

Michelle was one of the most passionate and most impactful cheerleaders for my bid to succeed her husband. She campaigned her heart out for me in 2016. The last time I saw her that year was at an election eve rally of tens of thousands of people at Philadelphia's Independence Hall. After all the speeches and ovations and even an appearance by Bruce Springsteen, I hugged Michelle and Barack and thanked them both. He whispered, "You got this." It was tough seeing Michelle for the first time after that, which was at Donald Trump's inauguration. In the joyless blur of moving through that January day, Michelle and I never got to speak on the Capitol's west front during the ceremony. But when our eyes met in the middle of the proceedings, we shared a look that hovered somewhere between disbelief and dread. We had already seen the ugly racism he was unleashing, and my heart broke for Michelle and her girls, for all the little girls. By failing to defeat Trump, I had let them all down.

It made news when I all but stopped wearing skirts as First Lady when I started running for the Senate in 1999. Michelle Obama's summer vacation shorts (shorts!) aboard Air Force One also made news. Or, as she called it, "a huge stink." When Jill Biden took the mantle, she got flak not for her clothes but for her preference to be called *Dr.* and not *Mrs.* Biden, as if her hard-earned advanced degree in education, which she puts to use every day in her day job— unprecedented for a presidential spouse—as a community college professor, were nothing but an uppity ornament. The *Wall Street Journal* had the nerve to call Jill's preferred title "fraudulent, even comic." Two steps forward, one step back. I was a partner in my law firm and building a college fund for Chelsea when Bill was elected president. I thought I could continue to practice law alongside my hostessing, traveling, and advocacy duties as First Lady, just as I had done as First Lady of Arkansas. I broached the idea with Bill's advisors. You would think I had proposed painting the White House in pink stripes. The notion was so far-fetched to them that it was shot down immediately. When I look now at Jill and how she has held on to this separate piece of her identity and found such fulfillment in it, I wonder: If I *were* the shoulda-coulda-woulda type, would I wish I had pushed Bill's team harder to let me keep being a lawyer? (Given that Second Gentleman Doug Emhoff had to give up being a lawyer when his wife, Kamala Harris, became vice president, I think the answer would have been the same: no, because of the potential for conflicts of interest.)

I recently had a look at notes from the First Ladies' Symposium on Children of the Americas that I convened in Miami in 1994 as a companion to Bill's first Summit of the Americas. We both saw rich opportunities for working with our neighbor countries of North, South, and Central America and the Caribbean on region-wide health and prosperity policies. On one handwritten page, someone on my staff (I don't recognize the handwriting all these years later) noted that some of my counterparts from "Belize et al. object to 1st lady label and role—[because we] are professionals." And so our annual conferences came to be called the clunky "Wives of Heads of State and of Government of the Americas." Today, I think California governor Gavin Newsom's wife, the award-winning filmmaker Jennifer Siebel Newsom, hit the nail on the head when she coined for herself the title "First Partner."

Good for Jill—for *Dr. Biden*—and Jennifer for pushing open that door to presidential and gubernatorial wives maintaining their individual and professional identities. I expect we will see more of that ahead. We need to model and normalize women—*all women*—as autonomous individuals. That shouldn't have to be said. But, well, there's *Dobbs*, the decision where the Supreme Court overturned

Roe v. Wade after fifty years. We're fighting for women's basic rights to privacy and autonomy all over again.

Here in the world of the "formers," I wonder if there isn't more that the few of us can do together in our afterlife. First Ladies typically leave the White House with much higher public approval than their husbands. Harness that popularity with the kinship that Laura Bush identified and that I experienced, and just think of the multiplier effect. (With apologies to Jason Carter, I'll use "kinship" over "sisterhood" if only to make a path for a future First Gentleman.) The ex-presidents get a lot of ink for joining forces to raise money for disaster relief or promote COVID vaccines. Imagine the power of former First Ladies—Democrat and Republican, Melania included—linking arms as mothers, grandmothers, and women. Working together as allies for America's children. Standing together to stare down hate, protect democracy, and secure those children's futures.

Imagine.

Will it happen? Probably not. I am not Pollyannaish when it comes to the people in this blood sport of politics. I know that pulling off this kind of united front by even just five women would be a feat of scheduling, logistics, ego, and marital dynamics. But when, today, so much in that realm feels turned upside down and torn inside out, I will take any sign of decency and normalcy as cause for hope—like reporting in the *New York Times* last February that, even after all the ugliness of the 2020 election and January 6, 2021, Jill sent Melania a birthday card that April. And Melania reciprocated two months later when Jill turned seventy. It's not nothing. Not when all of us, as families and communities and as a nation, have been so battered in recent years. Any reminder that we're all human and we're all in this together—I'll take it.

PUTTING PEOPLE FIRST

It was hot. At least 90 degrees Fahrenheit at 11:30 a.m. In the dead of winter. I stood sweating in my straw hat and light cotton shalwar kameez as the sun climbed above the baking desert in the Little Rann of Kutch, nearly four hours by car northwest of the city of Ahmedabad in India. It was February 2023, and I was looking at a salt pan—a shallow pool for evaporating water—and talking with women harvesting the crystals left behind when the water disappeared. I'm not an especially tall woman, but next to me these salt farmers were tiny. Each was wearing a unique and colorfully layered sari that stood out like a flag flapping in the wind. I watched as they tossed the edges of their saris over their shoulders and dragged enormous rakes—bigger than they were tall—back and forth across the pans. It looked cumbersome, but they managed it with finesse.

India is the third-largest producer of salt after the United States and China, and these women and their families are a big reason for that. They take pride in their work, but the conditions are grueling—and dangerous. The heat is tremendous and getting worse every year. It can now reach over 120 degrees in the summer. The risk of heat exhaustion and stroke is ever present. The women I met told me that it's also causing nausea, nosebleeds, and miscarriages. Higher temperatures are forcing these farmers to change their hours, starting before dawn to beat the sun, taking longer breaks in the middle of the day, and losing pay as a result.

Then there is the constant exposure to salt and salt water. Just imagine having a cut or scrape on your foot, then having to submerge that foot in salt water while you work all day, and the next, and the next. A quick rinse with salt water might debride a wound and help it heal. But extended contact with salt water prevents small infections from healing, turning them into large ones. It causes boils on the farmers' skin. Many go blind from the searing sun reflecting off the vast white expanse of salt and sand. The average salt farmer lives to just sixty years old.

Rann means "desert" in Gujarati. Little Rann is a stretch of salt marshes that was underwater until about two centuries ago, when a series of earthquakes raised it above sea level. Now, the area is submerged only during the monsoon season between June and October, when the rains replenish the saline groundwater. This ecological idiosyncrasy means that the Rann is rich in salt—a commodity so prized that in centuries past it was equal in value to gold.

Before making this trip, I'd been briefed on the basic operations of the salt flats. But the briefings couldn't capture what daily work looks like for the women who have farmed these salt marshes for generations. Each autumn, as the monsoon rains ebb and the waters recede, they travel on foot into the still-wet desert, carrying everything they will need for the season—including all their food and potable water. They build huts to live in for the next six to eight months, set up equipment, and prepare for the harvest.

The work starts with drilling down to the briny groundwater that the flooding has left behind and pumping it up to the surface. Then they manually dig ten to twenty rectangular pans in the mud and fill them with the groundwater until it's the ideal level of salinity for farming (the women told me they can tell when it's right by the taste). Over the next month or two, the water slowly evaporates. The farmers spend that time raking or plowing the pans up to twelve times a day to bring small crystals to the surface where they can grow larger. Finally, after months of raking, the big salt crystals are ready to be carried away in arms or on top of heads in big metal pans. And they do all this in scorching desert heat.

After they finished raking, one of the women showed me a crystal of salt. Another said it was difficult to get water to drink during the day. They showed me blisters on their feet and hands from the heat and salt. I listened carefully, wanting to remember everything.

There are few places where the urgency of the climate crisis is more evident than the salt flats at Little Rann and few people more impacted by rising global temperatures than the farmers who labor there.

I was in India that winter to announce a $50 million climate resilience fund for women. What better place to do it than where climate change is impossible to ignore? I'd heard about the punishing working conditions in the salt flats and wanted to see them for myself. The women I met in the desert that day offer a preview of the challenges ahead for many millions of people around the world and the determination that will be needed to meet this crisis.

I was also there because I believe that to understand a complex policy problem you need to understand the people most affected. You need to listen to their stories, see their struggles, and hear their hopes.

A lot of good people go into public service to "change the world." I certainly did. We dream about finding big solutions to big problems. Reality is often more prosaic. You make whatever progress you can, whenever you can. Still, there's a magnetic pull toward lofty goals and ambitious plans, the kinds of accomplishments that history remembers. Sometimes, though, if you're too focused on grand strategy and transformative policies, you can lose sight of the very people you meant to help in the first place. When you're at the pinnacle of power, negotiating treaties or writing legislation, the everyday experiences of regular people can feel awfully far away.

That's why I wanted to meet the women salt farmers. It's not enough to read about the impact of climate change or even to talk to scientists and activists. The salt farmers in Little Rann are on the front lines of the crisis. They are enduring—and adapting to—the extreme consequences of our warming planet. Throughout my career, as a lawyer, First Lady, senator, and secretary of state, I've learned that showing up is how you learn. You have to talk with people face-to-face. It's also how you show that you take their concerns seriously.

There was a moment in Bill's first campaign for president in 1992 that dramatized how important a personal touch can be. It came during a town hall–style debate with President George H. W. Bush, the Republican incumbent, and Ross Perot, an independent. A woman stood up to ask the three candidates a question: "How has the national debt personally affected each of your lives? And if it hasn't, how can you honestly find a cure for the economic problems of the common people if you have no experience in what's ailing them?" Bush was a good man with a big heart, but he was also reserved and patrician. He had been president for nearly four years, grappling every day with the arcana of policy and details of diplomacy. If you're not careful, you can forget how far the White House is from people's kitchen tables. On the stage that night, Bush had trouble remembering how to talk in simple, human terms about the concerns of families who were hurting in a tough recession. But that was where Bill excelled. When it was his turn, he walked over to the woman and asked if she knew people who'd lost their jobs and lost their homes. He said that as the governor of a small state, "when people lose their jobs there's a good chance I'll know them by their names. When a factory closes, I know the people who ran it. When the businesses go bankrupt, I know them." The contrast between the two answers helped win the election.

Bill's slogan in that campaign was "Putting People First." It's an ethos both of us have tried to hold to ever since. When I was a senator, I spent countless days crisscrossing rural Upstate New York, stopping in tiny towns, touring factories and farms, and visiting far-flung military bases. I wanted to stay connected to my constituents and to understand how the challenges we debated in Washington affected their lives, from war and peace to the economy and climate change. Were the men and women of the Tenth Mountain Division getting the right kind of body armor when they deployed to Iraq and Afghanistan from Fort Drum outside of Watertown? What would it take to help small businesses in the Finger Lakes and Adirondacks get online and into e-commerce for the first time? How could we make sure firefighters in New York City received the medical care they needed in the years after 9/11 as they became sick from the toxic fumes at Ground Zero? The details mattered because the people mattered.

When I became secretary of state, I often found myself in glittering palaces and marbled halls. But I also made time to talk with activists and dissidents and to get out of capital cities and meet people in small villages. Veteran diplomats scratched their heads when I insisted on talking about everyday problems like how smoke from open fires and dirty stoves was poisoning people (especially women and children) across the developing world. That wasn't the kind of thing secretaries of state usually worried about. But I knew that household air pollution was responsible for more than twice as many premature deaths as malaria and tuberculosis combined. And I believed that if America put people first, the world would notice. So we organized a public-private partnership that distributed millions of clean cookstoves to families across the world. On a visit to Chennai, India, in 2011, a group of women showed me what a difference the new stoves made. They burned hotter, needed less fuel, and produced far less dangerous smoke than the old stoves. It was a small detour in terms of global diplomacy but a big deal in the lives of these women.

Like so many lessons, this is one I learned from Eleanor Roosevelt. She was an accomplished diplomat and led the negotiations in Paris that produced the Universal Declaration of Human Rights in 1948. She wrangled representatives from fifty-eight nations through hundreds of meetings and thousands of hours of haggling over the text. It was so grueling that at one point, a negotiator from Panama reminded his colleagues that diplomats had human rights, too. The result was a historic diplomatic accomplishment. But Eleanor never forgot that human rights only meant something if they extended from the halls of power to the homes of people. "Where, after all, do universal human rights begin? In small places, close to home," she said. In "the world of the individual person; the neighborhood he lives in; the school or college he attends; the factory, farm, or office where he works."

A highlight of my trip to India was the fiftieth anniversary celebration of the Self Employed Women's Association (SEWA), an organization I've supported since I first visited India in 1995 as First Lady. Both a trade union and a women's movement, SEWA was founded in 1972 by Elaben "Ela" Bhatt, one of the twentieth century's most effective political and labor organizers. After obtaining her law degree, Ela decided she could do more good as an organizer than by practicing law. She organized thousands of self-employed textile workers who, because they worked from home, were not protected by India's labor laws. And because they were women, they were often oppressed, disrespected, and lacked bargaining power over wages and working conditions. She encountered stiff opposition from powerful men but kept pressing her mission, becoming known as the "gentle revolutionary."

SEWA members were some of the poorest, least educated, and most shunned women in India. Some had entered into arranged marriages and lived in purdah—strict isolation within their own homes, never seen by men outside the immediate family—until their husbands died, were disabled, or left, and the women had to shoulder the burden of supporting their families. Many struggled day-to-day to survive. SEWA offered these women modest loans to enable them to earn their own income, taught them how to read, and gave them lessons in running small shops and businesses. This model became known as "microloans."

In person, Ela was soft-spoken, which belied her forceful advocacy for the women of SEWA. She was a practitioner of Gandhian nonviolence and always stressed the importance of peaceful struggle against injustice. I quickly grew to consider her a friend—and role model. As secretary of state, I was thrilled to present her with an award honoring individuals who contribute to justice and equality around the world. She often said, "Poverty and violence are not God made, they are man made," and she believed that we could unmake them.

During my first visit to SEWA's headquarters, Ela showed me stacks of enormous ledgers in SEWA's small one-room office. They contained the meticulous records that she and a few other staff members kept of the SEWA loans and repayments. As I looked at the columns of tidily handwritten numbers, I imagined the small business that each represented. Each number, so small and simple on the page, contained a wealth of new possibilities for a woman and her family.

Ela told me about the women she'd met who, thanks to SEWA's microfinancing programs and education resources, were for the first time able to achieve financial independence from their husbands' families. By coming together to share resources and find power in solidarity, they were gaining security and freedom. Their work and expertise were being respected and valued for the first time.

Ela and I immediately connected. We shared a commitment to putting people first. We recognized in each other a determination to keep fighting for every small step forward, every tangible but unglamorous difference we could make in individual lives. Over the years, I've been overjoyed to see the organization she founded grow in size and evolve to include self-employed women from many different trades.

There have been setbacks, as there always are when you're trying to make meaningful change in difficult circumstances. As SEWA has grown in size and reach, government officials and business leaders (mostly men) have sometimes felt threatened and pushed back. While SEWA successfully petitioned the International Labour Organization to expand the definition of labor to include home-based work, it has not yet convinced many governments in South Asia to ratify the change. Reema Nanavaty, SEWA's director and Ela's daughter-in-law, calls them "constructive struggles." Reema is a serene, whip-smart woman in her early sixties who always has a quick smile and expansively gesturing hands as she talks.

Ela's passing in 2022, at age eighty-nine, was a great loss. It can be hard for a group to maintain momentum after its founder is gone. But there is a SEWA saying: "Every woman is Elaben." The organization that Ela started has grown into a broader women's movement, able to carry on her spirit of determination and resilience. It has inspired other SEWAs in South Asia, southern Africa, and Latin America. When I first visited SEWA in 1995 it had 140,000 members—today that number is nearly three million.

Over the past three decades, I've seen a whole new generation of women grow up and join this movement. They're bringing their own energy and ideas to old problems and new ones. SEWA's members have valuable insights into the challenges that poor women—and men—are facing and the solutions that would make a real difference in their lives. In Cape Town, South Africa, I met with women who came together to transform their position as squatters into home-ownership and community leadership. In Mumbai, I visited a store run by SEWA women textile workers who brought their labor together to create a brand that would connect their artisan members to a global market for greater income security. In New York, I try to see Reema when she visits, and I was thrilled to welcome her to Little Rock in December 2022 to speak about SEWA's successes at the Clinton Presidential Center's Women's Voices Summit.

I have also partnered with SEWA through the Clinton Foundation and the Clinton Global Initiative (CGI). The climate resilience fund I announced in Little Rann came out of a CGI partnership with SEWA, the Atlantic Council, and other organizations. The fund focuses on the needs and perspectives of women experiencing extreme heat and provides resources to protect them from the economic and health effects. Among other things, it provides heat insurance, so women like those salt farmers don't lose income on days when it's too hot for them to work safely.

The climate crisis is already harming people all over the world, both men and women. But women generally are getting the worst of it. Physically, women are more susceptible to heat-related illness and death. Extreme temperatures have adverse effects on neonatal and maternal health. Women also continue to be employed less and paid less than men. So when temperatures rise and it's unsafe for them to work, or they miss a shift because their town is flooding and they have to move their kids to higher ground, or a prolonged drought makes them climate refugees, women's lives become even more economically precarious. Because women are often holding families together, the impact ripples out to children and across communities. Globally, women and girls represent 80 percent of climate refugees—and that number is sure to grow in the years ahead. When women are displaced, they are at increased risk of violence, human trafficking, and stalled education and employment opportunities.

To the salt farmers in Little Rann, climate change is not abstract—and it's not a problem of the future. It's here now, making their already brutal work increasingly untenable. But the women I met with also told me how they're adapting. Until recently, the pumps that brought groundwater to the surface were all powered by diesel fuel. The generators were dirty and required diligent monitoring not to overheat. Most important, they required the purchase of diesel fuel to run all season.

Diesel has always been expensive, cutting into the salt farmers' profits. But in recent years costs have risen steeply, requiring them to take out loans at the start of the season to buy enough to keep the pumps running. As a result, families were ending the season in debt. Think about that: After months of grueling work in the purgatory between sun and salt, after keeping their children out of school, after sacrificing the skin of their hands and feet and faces to the abrasion of brine and wind, families still owed money to the diesel distributors and salt merchants who fronted them loans to pay for fuel.

That's why, several years ago, NGOs including SEWA began developing solar-powered pumps designed to suit the needs of the salt farmers and the unique landscape of the Rann. These pumps have more horsepower to lift brine, which is heavier than water, and a flexible stand for the solar panels to optimize the amount of sunlight they can use. But solar-powered pumps designed for the salt flats were useless if the salt workers couldn't afford them. So SEWA worked with one of India's largest banks to develop low-cost loans for their purchase. SEWA also convinced the state government to offer subsidies for families wanting to buy them.

The solar panels themselves harness the one natural resource— besides salt—that the desert of Little Rann has in abundance. They relieve salt farmers of their obligations to fuel merchants and predatory loans, allowing them to come home from a season of hard work with meaningful profits to invest back in their families and communities. And in the offseason, many women carry these panels back to their villages. There, the possibilities multiply. On their own, the panels provide energy that lights homes after sunset for kids to study at night. Many women share the output of the panels with their communities for a small fee. They may also sell output to the grid for additional income or create their own microgrids with other local residents.

All this was possible because SEWA took a people-first approach to solving problems: They asked what members needed and how they could make their lives a little better. No idea was too small. The women I spoke to were hopeful and happy about the new

opportunities to put away some money that would have gone to diesel fuel. "I get to make money. It's my money," one woman told me
triumphantly.

In late 2023, I arrived in another desert. Instead of sweating beside
sunbaked salt pans, in Dubai I was cocooned in the air-conditioned
conference rooms of the UN Framework Convention on Climate
Change (UNFCCC) annual meeting, also known as Conference
of the Parties, or COP. Since the first COP in Berlin in 1995, global
leaders have come together once a year to discuss the climate crisis
and commit to taking action, including reducing carbon emissions,
accelerating a clean energy transition, and helping countries adapt
and build resilience. This one was COP 28.

It's a diplomatic Rubik's Cube. The policy trade-offs are brutal
and so are the politics. Representatives from small island nations
like the Maldives warn that they are literally going to be washed
away unless the world takes bold action. But oil-producing states like
Saudi Arabia and Russia don't want to give up on fossil fuels. And
it's true that if energy costs rise it will disproportionately hurt poor
people around the world. Ahead of a COP conference in Copenhagen in 2009, the Indian environment minister made an impassioned
plea to me: Addressing climate change should be the responsibility
of wealthy, industrialized countries like the United States that had
been pumping carbon dioxide into the air for centuries, not developing nations like India that still needed to lift millions out of poverty.
There's a moral logic to that argument, but it runs up against immov-
able math. It will be impossible to stop a global climate catastrophe
if big countries like India and China don't curb their emissions. And
this really is a crisis that threatens us all. About 40 percent of people
on Earth live within sixty miles of a coast. Extreme weather, rising
seas, and soaring temperatures know no borders.

Crafting a global consensus with real commitments to action

takes creative and persistent diplomacy. Sometimes that even means barging into closed-door meetings uninvited, as President Obama and I did in Copenhagen, when we found out China was trying to stop, or at least dilute, an agreement we were trying to broker. Chinese guards literally tried to bar the door, to no avail. *Newsweek* later described us as "a diplomatic version of Starsky and Hutch."

I was attending COP 28 not as secretary of state but as the Adrienne Arsht-Rockefeller Foundation's global ambassador for heat, health, and gender, in partnership with the Atlantic Council and CGI. My goal was to call attention to the growing impacts of extreme heat on women and girls in vulnerable communities across the globe. As world leaders discussed how and if it was possible to limit global warming to 1.5 degrees Celsius, I thought of the immediate impact that every half degree of warming has on the daily lives of the salt rakers in Little Rann and women all over the world.

Since I'd left India, the United States had sweated through its hottest summer on record. When I added salt to tomatoes or eggs, or passed a shaker to someone, I remembered the woman who had given me a handful of crystals, fresh from the salt pans, and the amount of work that goes into every teaspoonful. At COP, I strove to remind government ministers, scientists, and wealthy philanthropists of the human face of our discussions. I told them about the women I'd met and the harsh conditions they endured. In every meeting room, there were lush floral arrangements and tables of cold beverages, a stark contrast to the desert in Little Rann, with no vegetation or shade anywhere to be found.

In meeting after meeting, I pitched CGI's climate resilience fund and efforts to support women across the Global South adapting to rising temperatures, including scalable innovations like replacing small diesel engines with solar as the salt farmers were doing. The wealthy and powerful investors (primarily men, as you might have guessed) I talked to cared about climate change, but they wanted to fund big, high-profile projects that generate headlines and financial returns. That reflects the reality of climate investing today, not only by the private sector but also by governments and multinational funds. According to the UNFCCC, only 0.01 percent of global finance supports projects that respond to the needs of women. In the United States, less than 2 percent of all philanthropic giving is to organizations that serve women and girls.

I've been working for women's causes for half a century, so maybe I shouldn't be surprised anymore when they get marginalized. Still, over the years as I've sought support for SEWA, for other women-led businesses and organizations, and for investment in climate action focused on women, I've been shocked and disappointed at how little interest many people have in supporting women and girls. And that's not just bad for women—it's holding us all back.

Fundraising wasn't the only frustration. Many climate activists objected when Dubai was chosen to host COP 28—and when it was reported that the head of the conference, an Emirati oil executive, said that there was no science to suggest eliminating fossil fuels would help us reach the 1.5-degree goal.

Still, two things happened in Dubai under Emirati leadership that gave me reasons to be reassured and hopeful: It was the first COP to end with an explicit call for nations to transition away from fossil fuels and the first to include both a Gender and Climate Day and a Health and Climate Day—an acknowledgment that we can't talk about climate change without putting women and girls at the forefront. As I reminded delegates in Dubai, women are not just victims of climate change; they are driving the adaptations we need to survive.

Just look at SEWA. Since its inception, SEWA has pursued collaborative, creative approaches that reflect the needs and ideas of its women members, who prove the old saying "If you want something done, ask a busy woman to do it." I've traveled all around the world and talked to women from all different backgrounds who recognize the truth of that—and the power of women working together.

Whether we're starting a business, fundraising for local schools, organizing a meal train, running for office, or creating a three-million-member collective of women artisans and workers to fight for better wages and health care, women roll up their sleeves and get to work.

It's not that women are born with superpowers. But around the world, in the face of oppression, inequality, and misogyny, women have become resourceful. Women find solutions because we have to. We work together because that's how we survive.

The women of SEWA have been adapting and innovating since the beginning. They've revolutionized how women in India work and how their work is valued. For example, they saw that traditional banking was inaccessible to poor, informally employed women. So they, like the Grameen Bank and BRAC in Bangladesh, pioneered a microfinance model with their SEWA cooperative bank, which is funded, owned, and run by SEWA members and offers microloans as well as financial counseling to poor women. They ran a campaign to ensure that waste recyclers in Ahmedabad were recognized as a vital part of the urban ecosystem. SEWA helped them get better and safer working conditions, like negotiating with waste producers to designate clean waste-pickup sites.

Part of SEWA's mission is to win recognition of the vital role that "informal" work plays in the life of a village, a city, a region, a nation. The International Monetary Fund defines the informal economy as "activities that have market value and would add to tax revenue and GDP if they were recorded." This can mean anything from working off the books for a family business to doing garment piecework from home to unregistered domestic work. Informal work exists in every country, but it is particularly prevalent in low- and middle-income countries, where it makes up about a third of the economic activity. In two out of three of those countries, women are more likely than men to be in informal employment—and to have the lowest income.

I have never liked the term "informal sector." If you're picking up one-off construction work, tending a market stall in the midday sun, raking salt beds with an implement taller than you are, or sewing garments at home for sale, that's real work. It's work that keeps families, communities, and entire nations going. All that makes it informal is its lack of recognition.

SEWA has made informal work visible, so its members are seen and their voices are heard. That has allowed them to pursue better working conditions, better pay, better opportunities. They are approaching the climate crisis in the same way. They, and so many women around the world, don't have the luxury of despair over climate change. They are finding and facilitating solutions—like the solar pumps, like resilience funds to compensate workers for days they can't work because of extreme heat. These aren't substitutes for strong national and global policy changes to limit emissions and make major investments in clean energy. But they're part of how people are going to survive on a warming planet.

Decades into a career in public service, I continue to remind myself that if we're going to successfully change the world, we can't lose sight of the reason we wanted to change it in the first place. Changing the world means nothing if it's not changing individual lives for the better. That's why each time I visit SEWA, I find my determination and energy renewed by the joy and grit of the women who greet me. Our conversations remind me that the struggles we as women face look different based on our backgrounds, our races, our religions, our nationalities, our ages, but we share a common fight for equality and opportunity. They remind me that we make change one microloan, one child's education, one solar panel, and one resilience fund at a time.

Shortly before she passed away, Ela Bhatt planted a sturdy banyan tree in a park across the road from SEWA's headquarters in Ahmedabad to commemorate the spot where the seeds of SEWA were first sown. Her hope was that the younger generation of workers would nurture it so that they could celebrate SEWA's hundredth anniversary in 2072 beneath its branches. I always think of Ela like that tree:

quiet, enduring, deceptively powerful, still watching over the women of SEWA and protecting them from the sun.

I stood under the banyan tree when I was welcomed back in 2023. As I looked at the faces around me—young and old, many weathered by the sun, all jubilantly smiling—I wished Ela could have been there. The power of SEWA is not just that it provides women workers the opportunity to improve their lives. It is that every day, each of those women shows the rest of the world exactly what's possible when we stand together and take care of one another and the planet we share.

CARE PACKAGE

In 1971, the same year I met Bill at Yale Law School, Congress passed legislation to create federally funded public childcare centers across the United States. I wasn't a mom yet (Chelsea would arrive in 1980), but I'd heard plenty of working mothers lament the nightmare of hunting for day care or a space in a preschool for their child. I'd seen friends and colleagues drop out of the workforce, reduce their hours, or miss out on promotions because they had to be home with their families. I hoped the bill would bring much-needed relief to working parents, particularly moms.

The time was right. Women's participation in the workforce was rising. Researchers had established the importance of early childhood education to brain development. And the national Head Start program created under President Lyndon Johnson was already showing benefits for preschool-aged children from low-income families. The National Education Association had recently proposed universal schooling beginning at age four, and a Library of Congress report noted that childcare and development needs of American families were not being met. By 1971, five million preschool children had working mothers, yet day-care services were available to only an eighth of these children.

Walter Mondale, then a Democratic senator from Minnesota and later Jimmy Carter's vice president, was paying attention to these trends. He sent a letter to Marian Wright Edelman, the anti-poverty activist and children's advocate, asking for help developing a national childcare program. I had interned for Marian the previous summer and would go on to work for her at the Children's Defense Fund. She is a force of nature. Nobody is more passionate about helping poor kids or more astute about what it takes to drive real change. Marian was the first Black woman to pass the bar exam in Mississippi, and she became a civil rights lawyer for the NAACP in Jackson and helped create the Child Development Group of Mississippi, which ran Head Start programs when the state refused federal funding.

Together, the senator and the activist convened a large coalition including education, labor, women's, and civil rights groups. They spent several months hammering out a proposal that would provide universal childcare and incorporated educational, nutritional, and health services. Mondale and Congressman John Brademas, a Democrat from Indiana, rounded up bipartisan support for the bill in both chambers of Congress. Even twenty-four Senate Republicans voted for it, that's how good the plan was.

Then it went to President Richard Nixon's desk. During the 1968 campaign, he had promised to prioritize early childhood development and care. But now, he vetoed the bill. He said the creation of universal childcare would harm families by promoting communal child-raising. He also argued that such a "radical piece of legislation" shouldn't be enacted without a national debate. That was absurd. Congress had just debated it! And there had been plenty of conversations about the need to support working families going as far back as 1919, when the revolutionary International Congress of Working Women descended on Washington to call for childcare, paid leave, pregnancy care, breastfeeding breaks—even counting housework as part of the eight-hour workday. Nixon's own White House had declared childcare a priority the previous year.

So what happened? Privately, aides like the young conservative zealot Pat Buchanan had whispered in Nixon's ear that universal childcare would lead to the Sovietization of American children. A well-coordinated letter-writing campaign by conservative evangelicals and ultra-right-wing groups like the John Birch Society also pressured the president to kill the bill. They claimed government involvement in childcare would threaten the American family and encourage women to enter the workplace instead of staying home. A determined minority overwhelmed a relatively complacent majority. The political scientist Andrew Karch quoted one insider as saying, "It was the right wing that mobilized, and the liberal coalition supporting child development did not. No public outcry ensued. . . . [Supporters spent] too much time talking to each other and not enough time in finding ways to mobilize and inform public opinion." As he faced reelection, Nixon made a political calculation: courting vocal conservative voters was more important than keeping his promises to working families.

Nine years later, as a new mom in Little Rock, I came to better understand the impact of Nixon's veto and our country's lack of support for working parents. As the first woman partner at the Rose Law Firm, I had to make my own parental leave plan. I was more fortunate than many women to be given that time with my child, but since my salary largely depended on generating legal fees, four months at home meant a significant reduction in pay. When I returned to work, I often felt frustrated with the demands of balancing my law career with my family responsibilities. I remember one morning I was due in court for a trial. Chelsea, then two years old, woke up with a fever and was throwing up. Bill was out of town, the babysitter called in sick, and no relatives lived nearby. Frantic, I called a friend who came to my rescue. I had a pit in my stomach all day. I called home at every break in the trial and rushed back as soon as it was over. When I opened the door, I saw my friend reading to Chelsea, who was thankfully feeling better. For the first time all day, my heart stopped aching. That was one day for me, but for so many moms and dads, that ache is with them every day.

As I grew into motherhood, became First Lady of the United States, and then ran for office myself, I advocated for more assistance to help overstretched families. In 2008, I became the first presidential candidate to put forward a proposal for paid family leave. Part of why I ran was to push these issues from the margins of the political debate right to the top of the agenda. In 2016, I proposed an even more ambitious plan to guarantee up to twelve weeks of paid leave so workers could care for a new child or an ill family member, cap the cost of childcare, provide tax relief for caregivers, and much more. My paid leave plan would have included workers at small businesses who currently have little or no access to even unpaid family leave. But, importantly, it would not have imposed any additional costs on businesses or added to the federal budget deficit, because it would have been paid for not by employers but by closing tax loopholes and making the super rich pay their fair share.

I didn't get the chance to execute on these proposals, but I was glad that many of my longtime policy advisors served in both the Obama and Biden administrations, bringing along our shared passion for improving the lives of working families and providing more support to parents and kids.

Today, care is a conversation at every kitchen table in America. It's a universal need—for moms and dads of young children but also for anyone with aging parents or sick loved ones. Too many working people are cutting back on hours (if they can), using vacation time (if they even have it), or leaving the workforce altogether to take care of themselves or loved ones. Demographic shifts are compounding these challenges. Each day, approximately ten thousand babies are born in America and another ten thousand people turn sixty-five. Americans today live longer than previous generations, which means the number of people living with disabilities and chronic illnesses will continue to grow, and the overwhelming majority (90 percent) want to age at home or in their community. This puts more pressure on the "sandwich generation," those caring for aging parents and children at the same time (most of whom are women). Despite the extraordinary care they provide, care workers (like home health aides, childcare providers, and nurses) are often invisible and among the lowest paid of any occupation. Nearly half live in households that depend on public assistance, and many are undocumented immigrants without strong networks of support. The median annual income of home care workers in America is $33,530 per year. That's not nearly enough for workers to care for themselves and their loved ones and live in dignity—and it leads to high turnover and unmet care needs.

A big part of meeting the needs of working families and our aging population is bolstering the care workforce. We should be valuing the people caring for our kids and our parents. That's why, as a candidate for president, I proposed launching a Care Workers Initiative to improve opportunities for care workers to build sustainable careers and earn fair wages.

Ai-jen Poo, leader of the National Domestic Workers Alliance and Caring Across Generations, calls investments in the care workforce "triple dignity investments." They benefit care workers by providing them with training, livable wages, and dignified jobs. That benefits the people they're hired to care for, who receive quality, consistent care. And *that* benefits family members, who are free to pursue their own careers outside the home. It's a win-win-win.

On top of investing in the care workforce, we need to invest in new parents. The United States is the only developed nation in the world that doesn't require paid leave for new mothers. Many offer parental leave for mothers *and* fathers. That means a lot of moms and dads in the U.S. can't stay home with their newborns because they can't afford unpaid time off. The consequences of this failure fall particularly hard on women. One in four new moms in the United States returns to work within two weeks of giving birth, potentially sacrificing her health and her baby's. On top of that, many families are forced to choose between spending a significant portion of their income on childcare (the cost has more than doubled in the last decade while wages remained mostly stagnant) or abandoning paid work altogether to become a full-time caregiver.

Critics say a care agenda is too expensive, but that's a scarcity mindset that never seems to get in the way of another tax cut for billionaires or subsidies to big corporations. And not investing in care comes at a cost to the wider economy. Businesses lose an estimated $12.7 billion annually because of their employees' childcare challenges. If American women earned minimum wage for their unpaid caregiving work in 2019, they would have made $1.5 trillion a year— exceeding the combined revenue of the fifty largest companies on the Fortune Global 500 list, including Walmart, Apple, and Amazon.

The COVID-19 pandemic made all this worse. As schools and childcare centers closed, working moms left the workforce in droves. And although the workforce now reflects pre-pandemic parity levels, the return-to-work rates for women lagged significantly behind those for men.

Despite the clear needs, every attempt to make progress has faced implacable opposition, mostly from Republicans but regrettably from some fellow Democrats as well. Here's a quick story to give you a sense of what we've been up against: In 1994, after Republicans won a majority in Congress, the new Speaker of the House, Newt Gingrich, proposed taking children away from moms on welfare and sticking them in state-run orphanages. Gingrich and his allies were especially keen to go after the kids of unmarried women under the age of twenty-one. The idea was to send the kids—babies, really—to orphanages and the mothers to group homes. I have heard politicians spout a lot of horrible and heartless ideas over the years, but this was one of the worst. After decades of working on children's issues, I can tell you that the evidence is clear: Kids are almost always better off with their families, unless there is real abuse or neglect. And parents, including single moms, deserve support, not scapegoating. Republicans claimed to be the party of "family values," yet they were cavalierly talking about breaking up families and victimizing children.

Listening to that nonsense helped convince me to write a book pulling together everything I'd learned from years of working with children and families and from being a mother myself. My goal was to explain the responsibility we all have to help create a healthy, nurturing community for children. I called the book *It Takes a Village.*

Republicans, after having just proposed taking kids away from parents, now turned around and accused me of wanting to destroy families and put the state in charge of raising children. Senator Bob Dole, the Republican nominee for president in 1996, even devoted part of his acceptance speech at the Republican National Convention to these charges. (In fairness, the country was enjoying so much peace and prosperity under my husband's leadership that Dole struggled to find targets for his ire.)

Throughout my career advocating for children and families, I've been called a socialist, a "nasty woman," and much worse. Other women who have run for office and championed these family issues have faced similar attacks. That's just what happens when women seek to gain power and use it on behalf of other women. And that's the key. In 1971, we didn't have enough power to overcome Nixon and the Birchers. We had staunch allies like Mondale, but women were still easy to ignore politically. In the decades since, we've made gains—but not enough. And where we've fallen short, it usually comes down to power: who has it and who doesn't.

Let me tell you the story of another important piece of legislation designed to help working parents and why this one succeeded where the childcare bill failed.

In the early 1980s, the Women's Legal Defense Fund (now the National Partnership for Women and Families) wrote the first draft of a proposal to provide guaranteed family and medical leave across America. A federal district court had recently struck down California's maternity leave law as sex discrimination against men, and women across the state and around the country were furious. The new proposal would provide unpaid leave to both moms *and* dads. Like the team behind the childcare bill in 1971, advocates built a big (and un-likely) coalition of partners. Women's groups were joined by organized labor because the plan was good for workers. Senior citizens groups like AARP joined and pushed to include elder care. The U.S. Cath-olic Conference backed it (even though it was drafted by pro-choice organizers) because it supported nurturing babies. Later, some Re-publicans would get on board, too, because they hoped parental leave would reduce abortions if women didn't have to choose between their careers and caring for a newborn. (Like I said, unlikely allies.) In the end, a total of 239 groups and organizations joined the coalition.

In 1985, Pat Schroeder, the irrepressible Democratic congress-woman from Colorado, formally introduced what would become the Family and Medical Leave Act (FMLA). It made it through only two House subcommittees before stalling. Despite the broad coalition of support, most of the powerful leaders in Congress (all men) had other priorities. Over the next nine years, the bill was repeatedly re-introduced, debated, and amended. Congress argued over the length of leave that should be provided, the amount of time the worker must be employed to qualify for leave, the minimum size of the company to be held to the new legal requirements, how much these benefits would cost businesses, and whether leave should be paid. Mean-while, supporters worked with states to develop pilot programs to demonstrate that the concept worked. Nearly forty states adopted some type of family leave policy.

It wasn't until 1991 that the FMLA finally passed Congress with bipartisan support. Once again, a Republican president sat in the White House. And once again, when legislation to help working par-ents came across his desk, he vetoed it. This time it was President George H. W. Bush. He said he supported family leave policies but thought they should be voluntary, not mandatory. The bill's sup-porters tried again the following year, but Bush vetoed it again. This time, he said it would hurt the economy.

Then came the Year of the Woman. At the same time voters sent

Bill to Washington in 1992, they also elected a record-breaking four women as senators and twenty-four women as representatives in Congress. Many of these new female leaders ran because they were appalled by the all-male Senate Judiciary Committee's mistreatment of Anita Hill during the Supreme Court confirmation hearings for Clarence Thomas in 1991. Hill testified that Thomas had sexually harassed her when they worked together at the Equal Employment Opportunity Commission. Like millions of women across the country, they wondered whether Hill would have been treated more respectfully if there were women senators on the Judiciary Committee. So, they ran. They won. And they got to work resurrecting the FMLA. Like Eleanor Roosevelt once said, it's up to the women.

I was thrilled to be joining so many energetic new women leaders in Washington and to have powerful new allies in the fight for family leave. During the 1992 campaign, Bill and I met countless Americans struggling to choose between their job security and family emergencies. Friends of ours had missed critical time bonding with their newborns after birth because they couldn't miss work. I reminded Bill that most other advanced countries provided parental leave to all citizens and this was the right thing to do. He didn't need convincing. We both believed that other parents should have the same priceless opportunity we'd had to care for Chelsea.

On February 5, 1993, Bill went to the Rose Garden at the White House and signed his first piece of legislation as president. It was the Family and Medical Leave Act. The new law granted millions of American workers access to twelve weeks of job-protected leave for family emergencies like welcoming a newborn or caring for a sick relative. It was a glorious day. Later, Bill told me he was thinking in the Rose Garden about the first few months after Chelsea's birth. How inconsolable she could be when she cried, no matter how much we rocked her. How easily her smile made us forget how much sleep we weren't getting. And what a blessing and a necessity that time was as we learned how to be a family of three.

Today, the FMLA has been used nearly 463 million times. I'll never forget the mail we received at the White House from Americans who took advantage of the law's protections and discovered the profound difference it made in their lives. A woman in Colorado wrote to me to say that her husband had recently died of congestive heart failure after several years of illness. Under the FMLA, she had been able to take time off from work to transport him to doctor appointments and hospital visits and to comfort him at the end. She did not have to spend the critical last months of her husband's life worrying that she would not have a job after he died. The FMLA may not be perfect—it applies only to employers with fifty or more workers, and it doesn't guarantee the time off is paid—but it was an important step toward building an economy that supports working families. And it was only possible when women and our allies gained power and used it.

In September 1995, I agreed to speak in Beijing at the United Nations' Fourth World Conference on Women. On the flight, my friend Madeleine Albright, then the U.S. ambassador to the United Nations, asked me a simple question: "What do you want to accomplish with this speech?" My answer was equally simple: "I want to push the envelope as far as I can on behalf of women and girls."

I have long believed—supported by mountains of evidence—that relegating women's health, education, and economic participation to the margins of foreign and domestic policy is ruinous not just for women but for entire nations. The Beijing conference represented a rare opportunity to focus the world's attention on the status of women and girls. I wanted to argue that it was no longer acceptable to talk about human rights and women's rights as separate. They were one and the same, and I was determined to make people hear this. "If there is one message that echoes forth from this conference," I said, "let it be that human rights are women's rights and women's rights are human rights, once and for all."

As I delivered my speech, each line was translated in real time into dozens of languages, creating a gap between me and the audience. Hundreds of delegates stared back blankly. This was my chance to change the way the world thought about women, and it didn't seem to be going well. But when I finished speaking, the room erupted in cheers. The delegates rose, giving me a standing ovation, a rarity at buttoned-up UN gatherings. As I left the hall, women hung over banisters to grab my hand. Some had tears in their eyes. The declaration of a simple, obvious message should perhaps not have had such a galvanizing effect. But in 1995, it caused shock waves.

Since 1995, the phrase "women's rights are human rights" has appeared on tote bags, cell phone cases, needlepoint pillows, and T-shirts. I'm happy about this. But the work is nowhere near done. As we make progress in some areas and continue to struggle in others, what's become clear is that simply embracing the concept of women's rights, let alone enshrining those rights in laws and constitutions, is not the same as achieving full equality. Rights are important, but they are nothing without the power to claim them.

Not long after the 1995 conference, I was on a Voice of America radio program when a man called in to ask what I meant by my speech. As I recall, he was phoning in from Iran. I asked him to close his eyes and picture all the rights men have: the right to earn an income, the right to an education and a job, the right to vote and hold elective office, the right to be heard and valued in their families and communities. "We want the same rights," I explained. He burst out: "That's impossible!"

Nearly two decades later, as secretary of state, I sat across the table from presidents and prime ministers and watched their eyes glaze over when I raised the issue of women's rights and opportunities in their countries. It was only when I showed them hard data and pointed out what nations were losing economically by excluding half their population from full participation that some of them started to listen. When women and girls participate in their economies and societies, the benefits ripple out. Women leaders, for example, are more likely to increase budgets for health care and education.

Yet, even though women are now running for office—and winning—in unprecedented numbers, progress has been slow. We've risen from 12 female heads of state in 1995 to just 29 today. Only 13 countries out of 193 have parity in their national cabinets. The share of women in parliaments is only 26.5 percent on average. As I write this, only five countries in the world have achieved parliamentary parity.

So what's holding us back? Although overt discrimination and structural barriers are in many places no longer legal, they're still very much with us, embedded deeply in our culture and psychology.

Mary Beard, a renowned classics professor at Cambridge University and one of the smartest women I know, dedicated an entire book to this subject. In *Women & Power: A Manifesto*, she explores the misogyny that has shaped our world for centuries. From our earliest example of Western literature (Telemachus silencing his mother, Penelope, in Homer's *Odyssey*), to Shakespeare (Lavinia's tongue is cut out in *Titus Andronicus* after she's raped, borrowed from the ancient myth of Philomela), to depictions of Donald Trump as a triumphant Perseus holding my decapitated head as if I were Medusa—the overwhelming message is that women should be silent. Submissive. Powerless. As a result, we've been conditioned to think of women as interlopers in public life. Even the metaphors we use to describe women gaining power—"'knocking on the door,' 'storming the citadel,' 'smashing the glass ceiling,' or just giving them a 'leg up'— underline female exteriority," Mary writes. As if by assuming or seeking power women are taking something that doesn't belong to us. And when we do, the backlash is swift and severe. We pay a high price for making ourselves heard.

Mary urges readers to be more reflective about what power is, what it is for, and how it is measured. That means rejecting the notion of power as a zero-sum game. If power is seen as a tool only a few people can wield at a time, within systems designed by and for men, women will forever be excluded from it. Instead, she suggests, why not look at power more comprehensively? We should think of it as "the ability to be effective, to make a difference in the world, and the right to be taken seriously, together as much as individually."

It's a beautiful vision of what collective power might look like. But right now in America, power still is held by only a relatively few people, most of them men. And too many of those men (mostly Republican, but not always) love to dismiss childcare and paid leave as "women's issues" instead of the economic imperatives they are. They dismiss the contributions women make to our economy and ignore the obstacles that prevent us from contributing even more. And that's bad for everyone, not just women. We can't build an economy that's strong and fair if we leave half our talent on the sidelines. Women who want to work should be able to do so without worrying every day about how they're going to take care of their child or what will happen if a family member gets sick. That's not a luxury, and it's not a "women's issue"—it's a necessity. It's a growth strategy. This isn't complicated: When you shortchange women, you shortchange families. And when you shortchange families, you shortchange America. If the people in power can't see that, then we need to spread that power around to people who can.

Here's one more story about what it takes to make real change—and why we desperately need more women in power.

Joe Biden kicked off his campaign for president in the midst of a deadly pandemic and an economy in crisis. During lockdown, Americans experienced firsthand the loss of both jobs and support, like childcare. Advocates started making the argument that care policies should be part of relief and recovery investments. They published a "Care as Infrastructure" paper with support from women-led groups working in childcare, paid leave, elder care, and workers' rights.

Throughout the pandemic that coalition kept growing, building grassroots support, and informing Biden's campaign agenda while he was running for president. They made the case that if the definition of "infrastructure" is that which enables commerce and economic activity, then care policies were as important as roads and bridges.

Then, in the lead-up to the Democratic National Convention in August 2020, Biden delivered a speech laying out his economic recovery agenda. He called it "Build Back Better"—a once-in-a-generation investment in infrastructure, combatting climate change, and expanding the social safety net. It was an exercise in setting ambitious goals and advancing many long-cherished priorities. The third plank of Biden's four-part plan was a $775 billion overhaul of the nation's caregiving system. The proposal was historic for its size and for its place in his campaign agenda. Biden wasn't relegating care to a sub-bullet under "women's issues." He was making affordable quality childcare, paid family medical leave, access to aging and disability care, and good care jobs the core of his economic recovery agenda.

After defeating Trump and entering the White House, Biden and Vice President Harris worked with Congress to quickly pass the American Rescue Plan, a massive fiscal package to stabilize the economy and provide resources for beating COVID. I was delighted that it also included historic support for parents by funding childcare centers and expanding the Child Tax Credit.

Previously, families had to wait until they filed their taxes every year to claim the benefit, and the poorest parents were excluded. But Biden made the Child Tax Credit more accessible and equitable, applying lessons from the success of the Earned Income Tax Credit for working families, which my husband dramatically expanded in the 1990s and which helped lift millions of low-wage workers out of poverty. For the first time, working- and middle-class parents started receiving monthly Child Tax Credit payments of up to $300, usually through direct deposit, that they could use to help pay for diapers, groceries, childcare, or any of the many expenses that come with having kids. Biden's expanded Child Tax Credit covered 88 percent of American kids and helped cut child poverty nearly in half—a historic achievement. (At least until Republicans later blocked an extension of the credit and allowed those kids to fall back into poverty.)

The Biden administration next began planning how to pass the rest of its ambitious economic agenda. As negotiations got underway for the sweeping new legislation that became known as the Build Back Better Act, policymakers and advocates were jostling to have their favorite issues included: paid leave, childcare, tax cuts for electric vehicles, affordable housing, broadband internet, reducing prescription drug costs. Not since the New Deal in the 1930s and the Great Society and War on Poverty in the 1960s had an American president proposed such sweeping legislation.

To make sure the package met the needs of American families, the administration talked to legislators, advocates, and activists with a long history of championing paid leave and childcare. Leaders like Ai-jen, Connecticut congresswoman Rosa DeLauro, New York senator Kirsten Gillibrand, SEIU president Mary Kay Henry, Washington senator Patty Murray, and Paid Leave for All director Dawn Huckelbridge. Women who have spent decades fighting for these issues, amassing political power, and building the coalitions needed to finally get this done.

In the House, Nancy Pelosi, in her fourth term as Speaker, worked hard to usher the bill to passage. I've always thought Nancy is one of the shrewdest, smartest, and most effective politicians in Washington. She has a spine of steel, deftly builds and holds consensus in the ranks, and knows better than anyone how to count votes. She also proudly declared in a press conference while advocating for Build Back Better that as a mother of five children, she's changed more diapers than anybody in Congress. Republicans have demonized her for years because they know she gets things done. She deserves enormous credit for marshalling the votes for the 2010 Affordable Care

Act. In fact, when I called President Obama to congratulate him on its passage, he told me I really should call Nancy since she had made it happen. So I did. Now, I was keeping my fingers crossed that she and the Democrats could pull off Build Back Better, too.

But the Senate, with its fifty-fifty split and obstinate personalities, was another story. A single Democratic defection would sink the bill, and two had yet to explicitly endorse it: Senators Joe Manchin of West Virginia and Kyrsten Sinema of Arizona. Manchin was troubled by some of the bill's best provisions. He hated the Child Tax Credit expansion in Biden's rescue package and falsely claimed it discouraged work and rewarded laziness. He also opposed providing paid family and medical leave. Democrats had already scaled back the paid leave provision from twelve weeks to four weeks as they worked to shrink the cost of the bill to appease Manchin. "We just can't be spending so much money," he told one reporter. "I can't put this burden on my grandchildren," he told another. He also griped about the scope of the bill. Throwing "everything under the sun, and major policy changes . . . in a bill that no one participates [in] except one party" was wrong, he said. It was infuriating. Just when our country was finally getting close to passing much-needed legislation to support working women, Manchin was standing in the way. Senator Patty Murray, who joined the Senate in 1993 and had been pushing for paid leave ever since, said during the negotiation process, "We're not going to let one man tell all the women in this country that they can't have paid leave."

President Biden and Senate Majority Leader Chuck Schumer tried to negotiate with him. Nancy Pelosi did, too. In a moment that went viral, she was seen animatedly talking on her cell phone at the congressional baseball game behind the dugout at Nationals Park. On the other end of the line was Manchin. I tried to reason with him as well. Worried about the bill's uncertain future, advocates asked if I'd appeal to him directly. I was eager to try, because we were friends and he vigorously supported me in 2016, at political risk to himself. But when I got the senator on the line and explained why I was calling, he just handed the phone to his wife, Gayle. That told me everything I needed to know.

In the end, after months of playing coy and extracting concessions, Manchin reluctantly agreed to support a differently named, less sprawling legislative package—but only if paid leave and the Child Tax Credit were left out. It was a bitter pill, but Biden and congressional Democrats had no choice but to swallow it. They secured the most important climate legislation in history and investments in many key priorities. But once again, "women's issues" were left on the cutting-room floor.

In 2022, American women lost constitutional rights that we've counted on for decades. An ultraconservative majority on the Supreme Court is poised to continue ripping away progress we've made for women and families. Right now, it can feel like all we can do is play defense and fight like hell to claw back what we've lost. But that's right where they want us. Lowering our sights. Limiting our ambitions. Yes, we need to regain the ground we've lost. But it's also crucial to stay on offense. Keep dreaming big about how to build a better, fairer country. We need a "yes, and" approach. Yes, Democrats must do everything possible to defend and restore legal abortion—*and* we must also champion investments in childcare and education. Yes, stop attacks on maternal health—*and* keep advocating for paid family and medical leave. Yes, fight back against attempts to deport millions of immigrants that will decimate America's care workforce—*and* push to give care workers better pay and benefits. We might not achieve all this tomorrow or even in the next four years. But it's important to set lofty goals that people can organize around and dream about, even if it takes generations to achieve them.

That's what happened with universal health care. For a hundred years, Democrats campaigned on giving all Americans access to affordable, quality care. Bill and I tried to get it done in the 1990s, and we succeeded in creating the Children's Health Insurance Program to cover children in working- and middle-class families with parents who worked jobs without employer-provided health insurance but made too much to qualify for Medicaid. It wasn't until Obama was swept into office with a supermajority in the Senate that we could finally pass the Affordable Care Act in 2010. Even then, it was a hodge-podge of imperfect compromises. But that historic achievement was possible only because Democrats had kept universal health care as our North Star for decades.

We also simply need to elect more women who will fight for working parents. History has shown that unless women have the power to drive these reforms they won't happen. Men should understand that these are their issues, too, and the smart ones do. That's why Bill signed the FMLA, Obama passed the Affordable Care Act, and Biden made such ambitious proposals. But too many men, even Democrats, don't prioritize these issues.

It's important to note that it's not just men who oppose care policies. Plenty of Republican women are against them, too. As Nancy Pelosi was trying to pass paid family leave through Congress in 2021, Colorado representative Lauren Boebert (bizarrely) explained she was against it because she allegedly gave birth to one of her children in her truck: "I delivered one of my children in the front seat. . . . Because, as a mom of four, we got things to do. Ain't nobody got time for two and a half months of maternity leave." (Actually, they do.) And in response to Governor Gretchen Whitmer's push to improve paid leave, Christina Doerr, a spokesperson for Michigan House Republicans, published a memo criticizing Whitmer's plans to support hardworking families by calling paid leave a "summer break for adults." As my friend Madeleine

Albright said, there's a special place in hell for women who don't help other women.

At a 2024 rally hosted by a coalition of organizations, advocates, and caregivers called Care Can't Wait, Biden proposed historic care laws, including national paid family leave, affordable childcare, investments in early childhood education, and extending the Child Tax Credit. He was joined on-stage by hardworking Americans whose lives have been impacted by our country's lack of these policies—people like Crystal Gail Crawford, who lost her job as a nanny when COVID hit, was injured in a car accident a few months later, and relied on her mom to care for her during her recovery. "That's when I realized in a whole new way how important care is," she told the crowd. "It's a constant in my family."

It's a constant in Sylvia Liang's family, too. Sylvia quit her job to care for her autistic son full-time because she couldn't find anyone to help care for him. And Tiffany Mrotek, who struggled with postpartum depression, said she "desperately needed paid time to come back to myself and find my identity as a mom." She went on to say that even though she had some maternity leave through her employer, it hadn't been nearly enough. "I am heartbroken for parents who don't get that privilege. We want all women and new parents to get the opportunity to have that pause and be present."

Each of their stories affirms the importance of the policies Democrats are fighting for. It's just one of the many reasons to be excited about the 2024 election and what it could mean for our future. We're not just voting against Donald Trump; we're voting for a future where families thrive, our economy prospers, and women can actually balance family and work. To do that, we need what the 1971 childcare coalition did not have but has steadily been building ever since: a mobilized majority of voters seizing power and applying political pressure. We need all of *us*.

Franklin Roosevelt famously told a group of activists who sought his support for bold legislation on civil rights, "You've convinced me. Now go out and make me do it." Movements succeed with political pressure from both outside and within. That's why advocacy groups are so important. Why voting is so important. Why making our voices heard in every legislative fight is so important. We haven't won them all, but we're getting closer and closer.

DOBBS AND DEMOCRACY

On a hot August day in 2022, the nation's eyes were on the reliably conservative state of Kansas. Across the state, Kansans stood in long lines to vote in the first referendum on abortion rights since the U.S. Supreme Court overturned *Roe v. Wade* two months before, ending the constitutional right to abortion nationwide. The question was whether to amend the state constitution to remove the right to an abortion, which had been affirmed by the Kansas Supreme Court in 2019. If the measure passed, it would allow Republicans in the legislature to ban abortion statewide. If it failed, then women in Kansas would keep both their freedom to choose and their right to access needed health care despite the fall of *Roe*.

The outcome was anything but certain. Though Kansas had been the first state to hold a referendum on women's suffrage, the first state to elect a female mayor, and one of the first states to ratify the Equal Rights Amendment, it had a long history of hostility to abortion rights. Lawmakers had repeatedly tried to ban the procedure. Thirty years ago, abortion opponents staged a "Summer of Mercy" in Wichita that was anything but merciful. They lay down in front of cars to prevent women from reaching clinics and getting the care they needed. In 2009, Dr. George Tiller, an abortion provider whose clinic was bombed in 1986 and who survived an assassination attempt in 1993, was shot dead while serving as an usher at his Wichita church by an anti-abortion extremist. And Donald Trump, who promised to appoint Supreme Court justices who would overturn *Roe*, had won the state by fifteen points over Joe Biden in 2020. So there were plenty of reasons to expect Kansas voters would embrace an amendment to end abortion rights in their state.

But after *Roe* was overturned, the ground seemed to shift. The week after the ultra-right-wing majority on the U.S. Supreme Court announced their decision, voter registration in Kansas increased by over 1,000 percent. More than 70 percent of those newly registered voters were women. Was this a political earthquake or a blip? It was hard to tell. Registered Republicans still far outnumbered Democrats statewide, and going into Election Day, polls showed voters narrowly divided.

As temperatures reached the triple digits that August day, more than nine hundred thousand Kansans showed up to the polls—the biggest turnout for a primary (or referendum) in the state's history. The last voter, a woman in Wichita, cast her ballot at 9:45 p.m. after waiting in line for nearly three hours.

Kansans held their breath (I did, too) until the result was announced around midnight. Unexpectedly strong support for abortion rights from independent voters led to a landslide victory of 59 to 41 percent. Fourteen counties that went for Trump in 2020, as well as all five that went for Biden, voted against the amendment and *for* reproductive freedom. Abortion rights were safe in Kansas—for now.

I was relieved but painfully aware of how much work remained and how much suffering lay ahead. Earlier that summer, when I read the Supreme Court opinion authored by Justice Samuel Alito striking down *Roe*, I thought about the women whose health or lives were saved because they had access to a safe and legal abortion. I'm old enough to remember life in the United States before *Roe*, when thousands died from botched, illegal abortions and untold numbers of women had no choice as to whether they became mothers— regardless of their personal situations.

I've also seen what it's like when the heavy hand of the state reaches into women's lives and bodies, robbing them of autonomy and liberty. I have visited countries around the world where governments forced women to bear children against their will or made them terminate pregnancies they wanted to keep. I will never forget meeting survivors of the brutal dictatorship in Romania, which strictly outlawed abortion. Every month, women were subjected to humiliating examinations in their workplaces to check if they were using contraception or pregnant, in which case the secret police would monitor them to make sure they delivered (something Trump has proposed allowing states to do if he's reelected). In China, I met women who endured similar government intrusion with the opposite goal: The Communist Party forced them to have abortions or be sterilized in order to limit population growth. I knew that without the shield of *Roe*, many American women who had long taken our freedoms for granted would now face a dangerous future.

Since then, it's been chilling to watch Republican lawmakers race to propose new state laws to criminalize abortion, sometimes without exception—not for rape or incest or, in some cases, even to save a woman's life. Never mind that doctors have recounted delivering babies to young girls forced to carry to term, including one who clutched a teddy bear while in labor. Never mind that women with high-risk pregnancies are dying from lack of access to lifesaving abortion care—like Yeniifer Alvarez-Estrada Glick of Luling, Texas, who died at age twenty-seven from serious, life-threatening complications during pregnancy just weeks after Texas enacted its harsh new abortion ban. Multiple experts who reviewed Yeniifer's case said that her death was preventable, that an abortion would have likely saved her life, but her doctors denied her medical information and treatment. One in three women of reproductive age in the United States now lives under an abortion ban. This has devastating consequences. Women in states with laws that limit or ban abortion in most cases are up to three times more likely to die during pregnancy, childbirth, or soon after giving birth. Infant mortality goes up, too. For example, after Texas banned abortions after six weeks, the state's infant death rate increased and more babies died of birth defects. And an Everest of evidence shows that when women are forced to carry unwanted pregnancies, it negatively impacts their health, lives, and safety. Abortion bans also have a chilling effect among doctors. Ninety-three percent of OB-GYNs in states that have banned or severely restricted abortion say they have been unable to follow standards of care because of abortion laws. Abortion bans are driving doctors out of hostile states (Idaho lost nearly a quarter of its practicing OB-GYNs since *Roe* was overturned, including more than half of the state's high-risk doctors). And medical students are less likely to apply for residency in states with abortion bans.

We're also seeing the criminalization of pregnancy outcomes, like when a woman named Brittany Watts in Ohio faced criminal charges for miscarrying a pregnancy at home. I was grateful those charges were later dropped, but data shows that upward of 1,200 women have been arrested for pregnancy outcomes post-*Roe*. These arrests are usually in the South and typically target poor Black pregnant women.

The zeal with which some right-wing extremists seek to punish women and doctors, including proposing classifying abortion as homicide and giving prosecutors the power to seek the death penalty, echoes the ugly misogyny of foreign dictators. Think of Russia's Vladimir Putin decriminalizing domestic violence, or Iran's religious authorities assaulting, imprisoning, and killing young women for removing their headscarves, or the Taliban stoning women in Afghanistan. Misogyny is hatred of women. It's the rage that makes men confuse cruelty for morality—that makes them think they should own women's bodies and dictate women's choices.

This dark reality is what I feared would eventually happen when George W. Bush nominated Alito to replace Sandra Day O'Connor on the Supreme Court in 2005. O'Connor was a true conservative, appointed by Ronald Reagan, and I disagreed with her about many things—especially her complicity in the truly egregious decision in *Bush v. Gore* that handed the 2000 election to the Republicans. But

O'Connor stood up for civil liberties and fundamental freedoms at key moments, including the right to a safe and legal abortion. By comparison, Alito struck me as an angry, unconstrained ideologue, and as senator from New York I strongly opposed his confirmation. "This nomination could well be the tipping point against constitutionally based freedoms and protections we cherish as individuals and as a nation. I fear that Judge Alito will roll back decades of progress," I warned on the Senate floor, adding, "*Roe v. Wade* is at risk; the privacy of Americans is at risk; environmental safeguards; laws that protect workers from abuse or negligence; laws even that keep machine guns off the streets. All these and many others are in peril." I take no pleasure in having seen what was coming.

In his *Dobbs v. Jackson* decision, Alito claimed that overturning *Roe* would "allow women on both sides of the abortion issue to seek to affect the legislative process." "Women," he wrote, "are not without electoral or political power." Translation: *Stop complaining. If you don't like us taking away your rights and turning the clock back on women's equality, just try to stop us. You'll find that we Republicans will beat and block you at every turn.* Which of course misses the whole point that having a constitutional right means that it's yours wherever you live, whether it's popular or not.

To what I can only imagine is the great surprise and consternation of Alito and his ilk, women did, in fact, rise up and seize that political power. The Kansas referendum was the first big sign that a wave of anger and activism was building that could remake the political landscape. The results—and the depth of support for abortion rights—shocked Republicans and, frankly, a lot of Democrats, too. Since then, we've seen that Kansas was no fluke. Women (and a lot of men) have voted to enshrine reproductive freedom in overwhelming numbers at virtually every opportunity. They've done it in reliably blue states like Vermont and California, swing states like Michigan, and even red states like Montana, Kentucky, and Ohio.

For a lot of voters, this goes beyond politics. It's visceral and personal. It's fundamental. Abortion bans are a denial of women's citizenship and humanity. There is no freedom without bodily autonomy—and no autonomy without full reproductive health care.

Watching women and men rise up for abortion rights in places like Kansas and Kentucky reminded me of a great line from Shirley Chisholm, the first Black woman to be elected to Congress and to run for president. "The law cannot do it for us," she said. "We must do it for ourselves. Women in this country must become revolutionaries." Amen.

All of this terrified Republicans, turning their long-sought holy grail into a poisoned chalice. Alito's patronizing comment about women's political power had come true in ways they never expected. They needed to do something or risk disaster. Would they moderate their policies? Seek compromise? Listen to voters? To women? Of course not.

Instead, Republican leaders across the country made a strategic decision. If people were going to vote for abortion rights, then they just had to make it harder for them to vote at all.

In 2023, Republican lawmakers introduced fifty-eight proposals intended to make it harder for ballot measures to come before voters. This was not a coincidence. They're trying everything they can think of to make it harder for grassroots abortion rights campaigns to succeed, from requiring more signatures across a district for an initiative to reach the ballot (known as "geographic distribution requirements") to raising the bar for passage and requiring large supermajorities. The Brennan Center for Justice rightly noted this is "part of a larger anti-democracy blueprint—yet another example of state officials trying to manipulate the rules of elections and obstruct the will of voters."

The Ohio secretary of state, a Republican named Frank LaRose, said the quiet part out loud: "It's 100 percent" about keeping abortion off the ballot.

I've paid particular attention to what's been happening in Arkansas, where a near-total abortion ban threatens to make already-high maternal mortality rates even worse. When I gave birth to Chelsea in Little Rock in 1980, Arkansas's maternal and infant mortality rates were among the highest in the country, in large part because of lack of access to quality health care. Many rural hospitals did not offer labor and delivery services for expectant mothers. I saw this firsthand as chair of a state task force on rural health care. As governor, Bill made it a priority to provide better care for pregnant women and infants. He ran public awareness and educational campaigns across the state and invested heavily in rural hospitals. I was proud of the progress we made in Arkansas, and the lessons we learned later informed our push for national health care reform. So it breaks my heart that women in Arkansas are again losing ground.

The state's draconian abortion ban means that women are being denied essential health care services. Sixty percent of rural hospitals still do not offer labor and delivery services and Black women are more than twice as likely to die from pregnancy-related causes than white women. A 2023 report found that 92 percent of pregnancy-related deaths in Arkansas were likely preventable. To keep abortion inaccessible and prevent Arkansas voters from improving access to reproductive health care, Republican governor Sarah Huckabee Sanders tripled the number of counties where signatures must be gathered for proposed initiatives to qualify for the ballot. She did this even though, in 2020, Arkansans rejected a measure that sought to add hurdles by increasing geographic distribution requirements, instituting a 60 percent supermajority, and eliminating the opportunity to fix any problems with voter signatures. In 2022, they again voted down a supermajority requirement. Sanders and Republican legislators pushed through the changes anyway, ignoring the state's motto, *Regnat populus*, "The people rule."

Undaunted, Arkansans gathered signatures to put a constitutional amendment on the ballot to reverse the state's abortion ban
and limit government interference in health care decisions. By July
2024, they had enough to overcome the state's hurdles. But the secretary of state is now challenging their paperwork to keep abortion
off the ballot. We don't know the final outcome as of now, but Arkansans are fighting back. John Brummett of the *Arkansas Democrat-
Gazette* wrote, "However it turns out, and it may turn out well, this
abortion petition effort, amid intimidation without outside money
or manpower and against all odds, is heroic." I'm proud to support
the Arkansans working on this effort through Onward Together, an
organization I launched in 2017 to empower those working for democratic progress. I'm hoping that in November we'll see a repeat of
what happened in Kansas.

A similar story has played out in a number of Republican-
controlled states. The attorney general of Montana tried to stop a
constitutional amendment to protect abortion access from going
before voters. The state's supreme court ruled against him, and supporters are gathering the sixty thousand required signatures needed
to put it on the November ballot. In Missouri, where abortion rights
advocates are trying to amend the constitution, Republicans have
repeatedly attempted to change the rules so that any amendment
would have to receive not only a majority of the vote statewide but
also a majority in five of eight congressional districts (five of which
are deeply conservative). In Mississippi, which already bans most
abortions, state lawmakers are trying to pass an initiative that would
make it impossible to change abortion laws through statewide elections. In Florida, which recently banned abortions after just six
weeks, Republican attorney general Ashley Moody asked the state
supreme court to block a proposed abortion rights initiative from
reaching voters, saying that the language would "hoodwink" them.
The state's supreme court ruled that the initiative could proceed, and
advocates collected enough signatures to put an amendment on the

ballot this November. And after voters in Ohio approved a constitutional right to abortion in 2023 (overcoming a new supermajority
requirement), Republican legislators are now trying to prevent the
courts from enforcing it.

It's been infuriating but not surprising to watch anti-choice
Republicans—who for years repeated the talking point that abortion policy should be left to the states and the democratic process—
suddenly change their tune. Now, many are all in for a federal abortion
ban. And the last thing they want is for Americans to be able to vote
on any of this. They've learned the hard way that voters overwhelmingly support reproductive freedom and oppose government over-
reach. Don't just take my word for it. Former Republican senator Rick
Santorum complained, "Pure democracies are not the way to run a
country. . . . You put sexy things like abortion and marijuana on the
ballot and a lot of young people come out to vote." (Yes, Rick. That's
how democracy works—voters cast ballots for issues they care about.)

But make no mistake, abortion will be on the ballot this November, and reproductive rights are very much at risk even in the bluest
states. If Trump returns to the White House, he and his allies will
seek to ban abortion nationwide. We shouldn't be fooled that the
braggart who crowed about "terminating" *Roe* is now trying to minimize backlash by obfuscating his position on the issue. One week
he promises to sign a national abortion ban. The next, he says states
should decide, including whether to monitor women's pregnancies
and prosecute those who seek illegal abortions. Then he says he's
personally for protecting the life of the mother and for exceptions for
rape and incest, but he wants states to have the power to ban those
exceptions and even jail women who disagree. He can't be trusted.

What we know is that if he wins in 2024, his whole administration will be filled with people doing everything they can to erase
reproductive rights, full stop. On day one he could also sign an executive order canceling the Food and Drug Administration's approval of mifepristone and misoprostol (used to induce abortion and

essential for treating miscarriages) without congressional approval. He could categorize abortion medication as controlled dangerous substances like Louisiana legislators did in May 2024, criminalizing women and anyone who helps them obtain these drugs. He could enforce the Comstock Act, a long-dormant 1873 law that criminalizes the mailing of any materials used in an abortion, including abortion pills and medical equipment used in surgical abortions. That would likely force many clinics in the country to close. He could reverse the Biden administration's requirement that federally funded hospitals perform lifesaving abortions, even in the sixteen states with near-total bans. In April 2024, Idaho argued before the Supreme Court that its ban (which only allows abortion to prevent a woman's death) doesn't conflict with the federal law—even if denying an abortion means the loss of reproductive organs, future fertility, or other organs. As writer Jessica Valenti put it, "It's pretty discouraging to watch the nation's highest court hear arguments over just how sick you have to be, or just how many organs you can lose, before hospitals are legally required to give you care." The Court later dismissed the case on a legal technicality, essentially kicking the can down the road while anti-choice extremists are doing everything they can to control women's bodies.

It's not just abortion that's at risk. In 2024, some clinics in Alabama briefly stopped offering in vitro fertilization (IVF) services after the state supreme court ruled that frozen embryos are people. (No one knows better than a woman undergoing IVF that an embryo is not a child.) The blowback was intense, and the Alabama legislature scrambled to pass a temporary fix. But Republicans in Congress blocked Senator Tammy Duckworth's efforts to protect IVF nationwide. Tammy, who had both of her children with the help of IVF, said, "IVF made our family. It made my heart whole. It made my life full." In a second Trump administration, this vital treatment could disappear everywhere. Reproductive rights groups are worried about so-called fetal personhood bills, which lawmakers in more than a dozen states are considering and which could be used to prosecute pregnant people for miscarrying or potentially for undergoing IVF. Trump would also likely ban fetal stem cell research. And don't be surprised if they come for contraception next. House Republicans voted overwhelmingly against federal protection for birth control after *Dobbs*, and extremists on the Supreme Court want to revisit *Griswold v. Connecticut*, which legalized contraception for married couples in 1965.

Trump doesn't talk much about abortion on the campaign trail. He knows all this is deeply unpopular. But he brags to his base that he's the president responsible for finally killing *Roe*, and it's true. If given the chance, he'll go even further next time. As Vice President Harris has said in rally after rally, another Trump term means "more bans, more suffering, and less freedom." I believe voters will ultimately see through his lies, recognize the threat, and stand up for their rights, just as they did in Kansas. Despite right-wing efforts to silence voters and shut down the democratic process, we still have a voice and a vote. It's imperative we use both.

Panicky Republican efforts to restrict direct democracy to prevent voters from protecting abortion rights brings together two issues at the heart of the 2024 election: *Dobbs* and democracy. Yet the truth is abortion rights and democracy have always been entwined, even if before the fall of *Roe* it was rarely framed that way. Democracy is about voting and fair elections and majority rule (all of which are now under assault)—and it's also about civil rights, individual freedoms, and protections for minorities that should not be subject to the whims of the majority. Nearly thirty years ago I caused a bit of a stir when I said that women's rights are human rights. They still are. A country can't be a true democracy if women are denied the right to make decisions about their own bodies and their own health care.

It's not a coincidence that the decades-long right-wing campaign against abortion rights was led by forces deeply hostile to democracy and civil rights. Around the world, women's rights are often among the first things authoritarians target, usually cloaked in the mantle of traditional family values and religious piety. We've seen this in Russia, Hungary, Iran, Afghanistan, and many other countries. These attacks are like the proverbial canaries in the coal mine.

In the United States, the Republican Party was not always opposed to abortion. When I was growing up, in the pre-*Roe* era, abortion wasn't really a polarizing political issue, and many Republicans cared more about protecting individual freedom than imposing a particular cultural agenda. That was true of my dad, a World War II veteran and anti-communist Republican. It was also true of Senator Barry Goldwater, the conservative's conservative.

Since I followed my dad's politics in those days, I was an enthusiastic "Goldwater Girl" in the presidential election of 1964, even wearing a straw cowboy hat with the slogan AUH_2O (the periodic table symbols for "gold" and "water"). In retrospect, Goldwater was wrong about many things. But he was right to support abortion rights. And he wasn't alone. In the late 1960s and early 1970s, prominent Republican governors like Spiro Agnew, Nelson Rockefeller, and even Ronald Reagan signed bills legalizing abortion in their states. Surprising, isn't it? But abortion wasn't a red or blue issue. In fact, in 1972, the year before *Roe* was decided, a Gallup poll asked voters if they believed abortion should be a matter left to a woman and her doctor—not the government. Two-thirds of Republicans said yes. (Even more surprising is that the Southern Baptist Convention supported "legislation that will allow the possibility of abortion" in certain cases. The convention reaffirmed that position post-*Roe* in 1974 and again in 1976.)

In that same era, however, several key factors came together to turn the Republican Party against both abortion and democracy itself. This may feel older than the dinosaurs, but it's worth understanding because it helps explain the threats we face today. Let's look briefly at three big, mutually reinforcing drivers: money, race, and religion.

First, follow the money. The Republican Party has always been the party of Big Business and a vehicle for the super rich to advance their economic agenda. Everything else is secondary. And by the early 1970s, right-wing business leaders were losing patience with democracy. They hated paying taxes to fund programs they opposed and even some they didn't. They also hated new laws to protect consumers and the environment and restrict abuses by corporations. In 1971, Lewis Powell, whom Richard Nixon was about to appoint to the Supreme Court, wrote a memo for the U.S. Chamber of Commerce laying out a strategy for corporate interests to take control of American politics "aggressively and with determination—without embarrassment." That's exactly what happened. Corporate political spending skyrocketed. And a small number of ultra-wealthy right-wing families—including the Kochs, Scaifes, Olins, and Coorses—contributed astronomical sums of money to help create a web of organizations and initiatives to reshape the political landscape at every level. The Heritage Foundation, Cato Institute, American Legislative Exchange Council (ALEC), and many others emerged from this effort. Later, Rupert Murdoch and former Nixon advisor Roger Ailes created Fox News to give the Far Right a powerful national media platform.

Undermining democracy was at the heart of this decades-long project. These forces invested heavily to restrict voting rights, remove restrictions on corporate money in politics, and prevent the moderate majority of Americans from stopping their extreme agenda. Paul Weyrich, a key leader of these interlocking right-wing groups, put it bluntly in 1980: "I don't want everybody to vote. . . . Our leverage in the elections quite candidly goes up as the voting populace goes down."

Another important element of their strategy was to use divisive social issues to mobilize blue-collar white voters who might otherwise not have supported right-wing economic ideas—even persuading them to vote against their own economic interests.

That brings us to race. I won't belabor this, but it's important.

After Lyndon Johnson signed the Civil Rights Act of 1964, he accurately predicted that white working-class Americans, especially in the South, would abandon the Democratic Party and move to the Republicans. Goldwater and other conservative leaders made a cynical decision to welcome racists into their party. He voted against the Civil Rights Act and infamously advised Republicans to "go hunting where the ducks are," meaning appeal to supporters of segregation looking for a new political home. Over the decades that followed, Republicans pursued what became known as the "southern strategy" but was really an aggressive appeal to white backlash voters all across the country. They used coded racial appeals on issues such as school busing, crime, and welfare. When in office, they gutted civil rights enforcement and anti-poverty programs that disproportionately aided people of color. They also campaigned relentlessly to make it harder for Black people to vote.

All this was fundamentally at odds with the principles of democracy. When the Republican Party became the party hostile to civil rights, it was inevitable that it would become more anti-democratic. You can't be both the party of freedom and the party of repression. (In 2005, Ken Mehlman, then the chairman of the Republican National Committee, who would later publicly come out as gay, formally apologized for the southern strategy. But the party only accelerated efforts to restrict voting rights targeting people of color.)

Two things can be true: Deep-pocketed factions stoked backlash to the achievements of the civil rights, women's rights, and gay rights movements to advance their own ideological and economic interests, *and* there was a genuine rise in reactionary fervor among social conservatives who had previously been less engaged in politics, especially evangelical Christians.

Here's where religion—and abortion—enter the story. The Supreme Court's 1973 decision in *Roe* inflamed Christian conservatives who opposed abortion on religious grounds and gave opportunistic right-wing leaders a chance to channel that anger into a broader movement that would reshape politics and end up consuming the conservative movement and the Republican Party. At the vanguard of this backlash were people who believed that Christians should take control of American government, business, and culture: activists like Anita Bryant, who launched a nationwide crusade against gay rights; anti-feminist Phyllis Schlafly, who helped derail the Equal Rights Amendment; and Moral Majority co-founder Jerry Falwell, who declared war on homosexuality, abortion, and direct democracy (the name was a phrase coined by the same Paul Weyrich who said, "I don't want everybody to vote").

Today, extremists who believe God has called certain Christians to exercise dominion over every aspect of American life are often called "Christian nationalists." They believe that there should be no separation between church and state and that their white supremacist version of Christianity should trump the Constitution. House Speaker Mike Johnson, a Republican from Louisiana who displays a Christian nationalist flag outside his office on Capitol Hill (the same flag carried by many insurrectionists on January 6 and flown by Justice Samuel Alito's wife at the couples' New Jersey vacation home), said the separation of church and state is a "misnomer." That's a dangerous claim that is hostile to pluralism, liberty, and democracy.

Christian nationalists are particularly hostile to women's rights and empowerment, some even vocally envisioning an America where women don't vote and are subservient to their husbands, stay home to rear children instead of pursuing an education or career, and have their most personal medical decisions dictated by biblical edicts. For them, the dystopian Gilead of The Handmaid's Tale isn't a cautionary tale; it's an aspiration.

They're not even trying to hide it: North Carolina's Republican nominee for governor, Mark Robinson, said at an event hosted by the Republican Women of Pitt County that he wants "to go back to the America where women couldn't vote." (Interesting electoral strategy, Mark.) While advocating for an anti-abortion bill in Oklahoma,

Republican state legislator Justin Humphrey said pregnant women's bodies aren't their own because they are "hosts." Steve Pearce, a former congressman and current chairman of New Mexico's Republican Party, published a book in 2014 in which he declared that a "wife is to voluntarily submit" to her husband. These ideas all fit together. In the Christian nationalist worldview, women should know their place, and it's not to have a career or a say in the direction of the country; it's to serve men and procreate. That's it.

Now, I want to be clear that I'm not saying that the majority of churchgoing, God-fearing Christian Americans are Christian nationalists, racists, or authoritarians. As a Christian, I believe strongly that Christian faith and teaching are not themselves at odds with democracy. Quite the opposite. Much of our most significant progress in American history has been inspired by Christian advocacy and led by big-hearted, open-minded people of faith, including the abolition of slavery, civil rights, and women's suffrage. My own Methodist faith influences my belief in equal rights for all and doing all the good we can for all the people we can.

But we should not be shy in saying that Christian nationalism is not what I was taught in Sunday school, not what my reading of the Bible teaches me, and not what I believe Jesus preached in his short time on earth. Instead, this selective, partisan version of Christianity is a naked power grab using religion to impose political control. Just look at how Michigan state senator Mallory McMorrow was smeared by Republican opponents as a "groomer" for supporting LGBTQ+ rights. I loved her impassioned speech at the state capitol when she said her mother taught her faith is "about being part of a community, about recognizing our privilege and blessings and doing what we can to be of service to others—especially people who are marginalized, targeted, and who had less, often unfairly."

People with religious convictions and deeply held moral beliefs have every right to decide for themselves whom to marry, whether to seek abortion care, or if they want to send their kids to a secular public school or a private religious one. But it is anti-democratic and anti-freedom to impose your religious beliefs on everyone else, especially at the expense of other people's rights and freedoms.

As Christian nationalists gained power within the conservative movement, old-school conservatives like Goldwater were appalled by what they had helped unleash. "To see the party that fought Communism and big government now fighting the gays, well, that's just plain dumb," he said near the end of his life. He also said abortion was "a decision that's up to the pregnant woman, not up to the pope or some do-gooders or the Religious Right."

Ronald Reagan managed to hold together both strands of conservatism, despite the contradictions, claiming big government was at the root of our nation's problems while empowering Christian nationalists who wanted to use the government to impose their authoritarian cultural agenda. Trump—no one's idea of a devout Christian—ended up reconciling this tension by abandoning the GOP's traditional skepticism of state power and fully embracing Christian nationalism as a means to consolidate his own power. A growing number of Trump's Christian followers believe he was appointed by God to rule America and frame the 2024 election as a battle over our spiritual destiny.

We should take seriously and literally that Trump is amplifying this dangerous rhetoric, that his supporters want to twist the federal government to their purposes if he's reelected, and that a Supreme Court dominated by extremists who don't represent the majority of Americans may continue their crusade by overturning same-sex marriage, IVF, and even the right to contraception.

To see how all these pieces fit together, pay attention to people like Cleta Mitchell, a lawyer and activist who likes to call herself the "consigliere to the vast right-wing conspiracy." Mitchell has worked closely with everyone from the National Rifle Association to Ginni Thomas, the right-wing activist and wife of Supreme Court justice Clarence Thomas. Mitchell is an outspoken critic of the women's movement and abortion rights, and she has helped lead the American Legislative Exchange Council, co-founded by Paul Weyrich and funded by the Kochs and other corporate backers, which teaches state legislators how to draft new abortion bans and other laws to restrict freedom and deregulate corporations. She is an architect of the Right's long assault on voting rights, pushing restrictions that disproportionately impact people of color, young people, and poor people all over the country. She was also deeply involved in Trump's effort to overturn Biden's free and fair victory in the 2020 election. She was an active participant in the phone call after the election in which Trump tried to bully the Georgia secretary of state into "finding" enough votes to reverse the outcome. "All we have to do, Cleta, is find 11,000-plus votes," Trump said.

Mitchell's line about "the vast right-wing conspiracy" is meant as a joke, but it's not a funny one. That phrase is something I said back in the late 1990s when I was trying to describe the web of dark-money-funded political groups that was not yet widely understood or recognized as a threat. I was mocked for being hyperbolic, even hysterical. But events have shown my words to be accurate. There *is* a vast right-wing conspiracy that seeks to advance an extreme agenda at the expense of everyone else. They succeeded in overturning *Roe* and stripping away abortion rights from American women. Democracy itself is in their crosshairs. This is no laughing matter. It's deadly serious.

There's a passage in Elaine Weiss's book *The Woman's Hour* about the struggle for women's suffrage where she writes, "Everything the Cause had accomplished—every state won, every piece of legislation, every change of heart and shift in policy—was once considered utterly impossible. Until it wasn't."

That's how I feel about the struggle ahead of us. Our rights are vitally important, but they are nothing without the power to claim them and defend them. The other side understands power. They're obsessed with it. We need to be equally clear and determined about what's at stake and how to effectively build and wield power.

History tells us that a well-funded, highly motivated minority (in this case, Christian nationalists) can prove more politically potent than a complacent majority. That's why we must vote and win in overwhelming numbers, just like Kansans did. It seemed impossible at the time. But what started as five people strategizing in the public library in Lawrence to protect abortion access turned into a multimillion-dollar campaign and coalition of longtime activists, first-time voters, Christians and atheists, and people across the political spectrum protecting the constitutional rights of Kansans. They knocked on doors, wrote postcards to get out the vote, fundraised, and phonebanked. They talked to neighbors, parishioners, coworkers, family members, and friends, urging one another to vote for freedom. One of those changemakers was Colleen Boeding, a seventy-three-year-old Catholic woman who volunteered for the Democratic Party for the first time in her life. She even planted a VOTE NO sign in her yard—her first public stance on abortion rights. "For a lot of us," she said, "it was more than abortion. It was them wanting to rule our bodies and tell us what to do."

A year later, two million Ohioans from across parties and geography went to the polls for many of the same reasons. "This is about so much more than abortion," said Katie Paris, the founder of Red Wine and Blue, a group of suburban women mobilizing voters. "It's about more than reproductive rights. This, too, is about: 'Will the majority be able to be heard?'"

Republicans, no doubt, will keep trying to silence us. So here's what we do: We defeat Trump and elect more women who believe in the Constitution. Is it any surprise that states with the most restrictive abortions laws also have the least women in statewide and legislative office? We must also call on Congress to codify the protections of *Roe* into federal law, defend medication abortion, and strengthen access to IVF and contraception—all policies the Biden-Harris administration supports—and add the Equal Rights Amendment to the Constitution so women's rights are once and for all enshrined. And while we mobilize to remove barriers to abortions nationwide, we must work to ensure that patients who self-manage abortions or obtain abortions in states where it's illegal are not criminally prosecuted. And finally, we must stay engaged and informed. It can sometimes feel overwhelming, but it's more important than ever that we stay focused on anti-democratic efforts in our back yards and across the country so we can organize quickly to thwart them.

It's hard to have hope in a moment like this. But we have come through dark times before. When I was growing up, American women couldn't open bank accounts in their own name or take legal action against sexual harassment, let alone legally access birth control or abortion. My mother was born before American women could vote. They were completely powerless to determine the laws that impacted them. All that changed because brave and determined Americans recognized that women's rights, opportunities, and participation in our economy and society are crucial to our democracy, and they fought hard to make the dream of equality a reality.

Reproductive freedom has never been about reproduction alone. It's about power. Power over women's bodies, yes, but also over our dreams, careers, and how expansive and fulfilling our lives are. So if you find yourself tired, or discouraged, or filled with anger, remember: We're not just fighting *against* these attacks on our rights. We are fighting *for* a future where everyone has access to the care they need, to free and fair elections, and to the power and freedom they deserve to determine their futures. That's a future worth fighting for.

TEACHING CRISIS

"This isn't a Taylor Swift concert." I'm not often compared with the nearly six-foot-tall blond pop star, but twenty minutes into my first class at Columbia University, my teaching partner, Dean Keren Yarhi-Milo, stopped our lecture because students were snapping photos and recording videos like we were performing "Cruel Summer." She reminded them that they were there to learn and gave everyone a five-minute grace period to take all the photos they wanted, then put their phones away.

To be fair, I was as excited as the students. It was my first time back in the classroom since I joined the University of Arkansas School of Law faculty in the 1970s. For many of us, no matter how far we get from our own school days, autumn is blank notebooks and sharp pencils. The promise of a new start. That was true for me in September 2023 as I returned to teaching for the first time in fifty years. And just like millions of students around the country, I was meeting new people, making friends who would shape my perspective, and learning new things.

Our classroom was an auditorium, the largest in Columbia University's School of International and Public Affairs (SIPA), on West 118th Street in Manhattan. At the front was a stage with two white armchairs in the center, a lectern on either side, and a blue backdrop. To the side was a big screen. As Keren and I walked on-stage that first day, students applauded. Every seat was filled. Keren and I were both a little giddy; the class we'd been envisioning for months was finally a reality. The energy in the room was electric.

My journey back to teaching started in 2017, when Lee Bollinger, then president of Columbia University, invited me to an event at his house, a stately brick building across from campus. That night it was filled with Columbia professors and all kinds of interesting New Yorkers. We discussed a range of issues affecting the university and whether I would be interested in some kind of affiliation. Of course, I knew a little bit about teaching at Columbia, because Chelsea, who has her PhD in international relations with a focus on global public health from Oxford and co-authored a textbook in the field, taught for twelve years at the Mailman School of Public Health. I admired her dedication, academic rigor, and concern for her students who introduced themselves to me all over the world to tell me Chelsea had been their professor.

My discussion with Lee continued on and off for the next few years, and then in the fall of 2022, he introduced me to a woman with dark hair and impeccable style. "I thought you two should meet," he said, with a twinkle in his eye. It was Keren Yarhi-Milo, dean of SIPA and a globally recognized scholar on the psychology of leaders facing crises. I had read one of her books and was glad to have the chance to talk to her about her research and insights. What I couldn't anticipate was how fast we would click.

Holed up in Lee's library, we talked about everything from Kim Jong Un to the protest movements of the Arab Spring. Keren's career was in academia and mine in public service, but we found that we shared similar experiences. We'd both been the only woman in many rooms. We were both frustrated by conversations about peace and security, international economics, or climate change that excluded women. And yes, we bonded over Taylor Swift, but only Keren is a true Swiftie.

We shared a desire to see greater connections between academia and the real-world policymaking process. Over my years in government, whether debating legislation in the Senate or steering diplomacy as secretary of state, I'd seen that the latest research and ideas from academics rarely get the attention they deserve. Some politicians stigmatize anything that comes from the "ivory tower" and reject expertise altogether. Others just don't have the bandwidth to seek out or absorb dense academic writing. It doesn't help that many scholars do not work at the speed required by policymakers facing fast-moving crises. And too often, their research is hard to translate for lay readers—even for experienced practitioners. Neither politicians nor professors have all the answers to the increasingly complex challenges we face as a country and an international community, but we'd be better off with more dialogue in both directions.

As Keren and I talked, the seeds of a plan were sown. I would join SIPA as a professor of practice in January 2023. We would teach together and launch a new Institute of Global Politics. It would be a place where we could convene some of the smartest people in academia and politics to talk about shared challenges and train the next generation of leaders.

Keren and I recruited people I knew like former New Zealand prime minister Jacinda Ardern and former Google CEO Eric Schmidt to participate. We organized events and public discussions around the war in Ukraine, the crisis in the Middle East, human rights, artificial intelligence, and more. And, most exciting of all, we designed a course to co-teach.

Keren's academic specialty is crisis decision-making, and I'd logged many hours inside the White House Situation Room managing crises and watching leaders make the hardest decisions imaginable. There was so much to talk about. We decided to call the class Inside the Situation Room. In the context of Keren's studies, crises are defined largely as situations where leaders have to decide whether to take military action, overt or covert. Based on my experience, I thought we could define "crisis" more broadly for the purposes of the class, to include issues like the climate crisis and crackdowns on human rights. So that was the first merging of our academic and practical experiences as we began to hammer out the approach we would take. We started lesson planning in earnest in the spring of 2023, and by early summer we had an outline for all thirteen class sessions.

Each session would center on a theme, whether a concept like reputation and credibility of governments or a set of challenges like digital threats to democracy. Keren—and her incredible team of teaching assistants and aides—started to put together the academic writings that we would include in the syllabus. My memoir of serving as secretary of state, *Hard Choices*, became a teaching tool because it provided case studies to illustrate the theories. We're now working on an edited academic book that combines the work of scholars and practitioners who have studied or lived and led through crises in the United States and other countries.

Keren and I met regularly the summer before our class began. In person and over Zoom calls, we talked through class outlines and lecture drafts. I carried around an enormous binder full of materials we would assign to students, my lecture notes, and documents from Keren.

As summer turned to fall, I got excited thinking about all that we'd teach our students and all I was learning from Keren along the way. I eagerly read the academic articles that she added to the syllabus. One that I found fascinating was from Daniel Kahneman and Amos Tversky's 1979 paper "Prospect Theory: An Analysis of Decision under Risk" that posited that people feel the pain of losses more intensely than the pleasure of gains. When applied to leaders and decision-makers, that insight reshaped how foreign policy analysts interpret international threats and leaders' behavior (and it earned Kahneman a Nobel Prize in Economics).

I thought of Vladimir Putin, my old adversary. One could see him as motivated primarily by what he seeks to gain: power, territory, riches, respect. But I believe Putin is motivated more by loss. He's obsessed with Russia's lost empire and its perceived humiliations. He's also terrified of losing what he has—not just his power but his head. The "color revolutions" of the 2000s—the popular uprisings that toppled authoritarian regimes in several former Soviet bloc countries—made him intensely paranoid. He reportedly frequently rewatched a gory video of the deposed Libyan dictator Muammar al-Qaddafi being pulled from a drainage pipe and beaten to death in 2011. Reading Kahneman and Tversky confirmed my view that Putin did not invade Ukraine and crack down on dissent at home because he felt strong; he did it because he felt scared. This is one of many examples where the class's syllabus of scholarly analysis enhanced my understanding of a leader's actions.

Keren is a world-class expert in explaining the sometimes erratic behavior of leaders. As an academic, she's written extensively about the irrational decisions of everyone from Neville Chamberlain to Saddam Hussein. As a teaching partner, she was a wonderful counterpoint. We bounced ideas off each other in preparation for lectures, came at problems from different angles, and felt comfortable enough to disagree with each other respectfully. My experience going "back to school" would not have been the same without her.

In many ways, this was a very different experience from the last time I taught at the University of Arkansas School of Law in the '70s. For one, every class session Keren and I taught was filmed so that the students we couldn't fit in the auditorium could watch the lectures online, and soon the online class will be open to nonstudents as well. The teaching technology was certainly different, too. Fifty years ago, we pretty much just had a chalkboard and a slide projector. Now, Keren and I used a big screen for presentations, we had microphones so we could be heard clearly in the room and on tape, and students could scan a QR code to respond to questions on their phones in real time. Each time we stood at our lecterns on the stage, we looked out at a sea of laptops and phones being used to take notes.

But in other ways, teaching was refreshingly familiar. When Keren and I planned our lessons and delivered our lectures, I enjoyed the camaraderie of a true partnership, and it reminded me of the wonderful friends I found teaching in Fayetteville all those years ago. In class, I felt the old thrill of helping young minds expand and make connections. You could almost see the synapses firing. And, to my delight, I was learning every day, too—from Keren, from the readings, and from the students who asked probing questions and challenged me to see the world through their very different eyes.

My favorite part of every class was when Keren and I would leave our lecterns, sit in the two chairs in the center of the stage, and take questions. Each week, students who had arrived early to get a seat along the aisles would rush to the microphone for their turn to speak. I've been in public service longer than they've been alive, and I was often surprised and delighted (and occasionally confounded) by topics that interested them. They asked about wars they're too young to remember, about gender disparities in foreign policy and the double standard women face. They asked about the potential role of artificial intelligence in diplomacy, about regulating social media. Often they'd share a bit about their backgrounds and how their lives were shaped by global policy decisions—sometimes decisions I had been involved in or ones made by leaders I'd known well.

There was the student who shared that as a child she dreamed of becoming a journalist in Mexico, but now she was reconsidering because of how many reporters there had been killed and harassed with impunity. (Thirteen journalists were killed in Mexico in 2022 alone, and Latin America was consistently one of the deadliest regions in the world for journalists.) How could she find the courage to persevere in her dream when there was so much danger and so little accountability from her government or the international community?

It was a timely question because that day we were fortunate to have as a guest lecturer the brilliant Filipino journalist, scholar, and crusader for press freedom Maria Ressa. Maria smiles easily, with bright eyes and an open face that looks much younger than her sixty years. She can just as quickly crack a joke as deliver a thoughtful treatise on disinformation campaigns around the globe. Her youthful energy and sense of humor belie the fact that over her thirty-seven-year career as a journalist, she has been repeatedly targeted by intimidation campaigns and viciously attacked online. For her courage and determination to fight for free expression, Maria received the Nobel Peace Prize in 2021.

Who better to answer this difficult but important question? Maria's response was characteristically pragmatic and wise: This is a real problem, and unfortunately many governments around the world do not respect freedom of the press. Too many target journalists or turn a blind eye to harassment and violence. But the work of journalists, especially journalism that holds the powerful to account, is too important to give up. Journalists need to stand together, she said, to share the dangers they face, protect one another, and hold bad actors accountable. That's why press freedom organizations like the International Center for Journalists, Committee to Protect Journalists, and Reporters Without Borders are so important. There is safety in numbers, and these organizations often provide legal funds and support. That's no substitute for responsible governments and the rule of law, but it helps. It was an answer that only she could give with such authority and credibility, because she has lived the challenges and dangers that the student was asking about.

This discussion brought me back to my time as secretary of state. Mexico's secretary of foreign affairs at the time was Patricia Espinosa, a career diplomat who became one of my favorite colleagues. We certainly talked about human rights and the challenges facing journalists, but the overriding priority was how to work together to stem the drug-related violence plaguing border cities such as Tijuana and Ciudad Juárez and threatening to spill into El Paso and other nearby American communities. We also focused on important economic issues and challenges around immigration. Because of our shared border, a good relationship with Mexico is vital for America's security and prosperity, but it's difficult for our two countries to strike the right balance of cooperation without crossing into interfering.

I could see how to this student and others, it looked like the American government should be able to do more to protect journalists and stop Mexican drug gangs from getting away with murder. Those jobs belong to the Mexican government, and what we can do is offer help; they decide whether to accept it. The trade-offs in diplomacy are never easy. That's why I called my book *Hard Choices*.

Another student's question forced me to consider an even harder choice. During our class on women and decision-making, she came to the microphone with a high ponytail and big glasses. She told us that she was from China and had been born a second child in violation of China's one-child policy, which imposed strict limits on family size. Her father had bribed the local authorities to "buy her life" when her mother was pregnant because he was hoping for a son. "And sorry for him, but lucky for me, he didn't throw me away."

On visits to China over the years, I have heard terrible stories from women about abuses perpetrated under the one-child policy, which sought to limit the country's population growth. Starting in the early 1980s, local Chinese Communist Party authorities closely monitored women's menstrual cycles and use of contraceptives. They needed to get permission to have a child. Once they had their allotted one baby, they could be sterilized against their will. Women who got pregnant a second time could be forced to have an abortion and faced steep fines, imprisonment, and other punishments. Draconian limits on family size and a cultural preference for boys led to widespread "gendercide." Baby girls were killed or abandoned because their parents wanted a boy.

This is why, in my speech about women's rights in Beijing in 1995, I made a point of saying, "It is a violation of human rights when women are denied the right to plan their own families, and that includes being forced to have abortions or being sterilized against their will."

I had heard these stories and worked on these issues for decades, but now in this Columbia classroom, I was face-to-face with a young woman whose very existence was an act of defiance against this brutal policy. Her parents had risked everything to conceive and keep her. She grew up knowing that as a second child and a girl, she was alive by the narrowest chance. Yet here she was, not just alive but thriving, receiving a world-class education at Columbia University.

Her question for us that day was about the double standard women in politics face. But as Keren and I took turns answering, all I could think about was the courage and determination it took to make it so far. And I appreciated that after all these years, I was still learning about the resilience of women and the persistence of the human spirit.

Midway through the semester, a new crisis exploded—one as complex and challenging as any in our syllabus. On October 7, 2023, Hamas, the extreme Islamist terror group that ruled the Gaza Strip, attacked Israel and murdered 1,200 people. Hamas fighters slaughtered babies, raped women, and kidnapped more than two hundred hostages. Israel retaliated by bombing and invading Gaza to destroy Hamas. The conflict devastated the densely populated Palestinian enclave, killed thousands of civilians, and created a humanitarian disaster.

In the days after October 7, Columbia's campus was tense with shock and grief. Keren's and my first priority was to engage our students with empathy, respect, and information that would help them make sense of the complex situation in the Middle East. I was focused on being a good partner to Keren, for whom the situation was particularly fraught. She balanced two difficult emotional realities: her responsibility as dean to nearly 1,400 American and international students, and her concerns for her family in her native Israel, where she had fulfilled her mandatory service in an Israel Defense Forces intelligence unit.

I understood the intense emotional reactions so many felt to this conflict. I have grieved with Israeli families whose loved ones were abducted or killed in terrorist attacks. I have held the hands of the wounded in their hospital beds. In Jerusalem, I visited a bombed-out pizzeria and will never forget it. I have also been to Gaza and the West Bank and talked with Palestinians who have suffered greatly for many years. They dream of peace, a state of their own, and an end to the humiliations of occupation. I met women using microloans from the United States to start new businesses and become breadwinners for their families, including a dressmaker who—because she was finally able to buy a sewing machine—could send her two daughters to school. My decades of experience in the region taught me that many Palestinian and Israeli parents may say different prayers at worship, but they share the same hopes for their kids—just like Americans, just like parents everywhere.

Keren and I understood that the events of October 7 and the war that was about to start would change a lot of things for the rest of the semester. The material and topics of the class would become more relevant, and we knew the students would engage with both through the lens of what was unfolding in the Middle East. Even more important, we recognized that this class was a huge responsibility and opportunity to expose them to relevant history and analysis.

When our class met on October 11, Keren and I decided to allot twice our usual time at the end of class for student questions. We anticipated emotions would be high. We had several Palestinian and Israeli students and knew that many others were outraged, upset, and searching for answers. Keren spoke first, telling the class that she hoped our community would exercise compassion and empathy toward each other. If anyone disagreed with someone else, and we expected some might, we hoped they would do so in a respectful, civil way.

Students wondered what the path forward might look like, whether peace was possible, and how the United States could help. They asked about empathy in leadership. One student who came to the microphone was a young Israeli journalist who had taken a leave of absence from her job at a left-wing publication to study at Columbia. She had advocated for Palestinian rights in her career, but she also told us about students from her school who had been kidnapped by Hamas and relatives of loved ones who had been murdered. She asked about the possibilities for diplomacy to avoid ground warfare in Gaza but also asked what the U.S. response would be if we were similarly attacked by terrorist forces from a neighboring area, like Canada. I was moved and impressed by her respect for all the parties involved and her understanding of the complicated history of the region.

But other questions from students troubled me, like why was Hamas considered a terrorist organization but not the IDF? I was also surprised by some of the blank stares I received when I told the students that if Yasser Arafat had accepted the deal offered by my husband in 2000 for a state that the Israeli government was prepared to accept, the Palestinian people would be celebrating their twenty-third year of statehood.

In the weeks and months that followed, I was struck by how little history of the region most of our students had been exposed to. In a survey taken shortly after October 7, less than 25 percent knew who Arafat even was. (He was the longtime leader of the Palestine Liberation Organization who agreed to put away his guns, recognize Israel's right to exist, and negotiate toward a two-state solution, although he could never bring himself to say yes to a final deal.)

In the early days of the conflict, pro-Palestinian protests popped up on campus. Students and outside allies pitched tents at the center of campus and refused to leave. They occupied and vandalized Hamilton Hall, the main administration building, and refused to leave. The protesters were an eclectic group; some knew a lot about the Middle East and others knew very little. For some it was about the suffering in Gaza, and for others it was an excuse to chant anti-Semitic slogans. Most seemed earnestly heartbroken by the violence. We don't have to agree on every policy point to respect the anguish they feel.

Students began chanting and raising signs in classrooms, at convocations, and across college lawns. They organized sit-ins and walkouts—including from our class, although only a small percentage of the 375 students actually left. Some of the protests were respectful and focused on concrete goals, such as convincing the U.S. government to stop providing unconditional military assistance to Israel. Others were not. They were disruptive, disrespectful, uninformed, unfocused, and often plainly anti-Semitic.

One student declared on video, "Zionists don't deserve to live." All this fueled fierce debates on campus and across the country about free speech, anti-Semitism, and universities' loss of control. Columbia's brand-new president, Nemat "Minouche" Shafik, faced intense pressure and eventually was forced to cancel the university's main graduation ceremony. The presidents of Harvard and the University of Pennsylvania were forced to resign. (It wasn't lost on me that the first college presidents being scrutinized most by politicians, the press, and the public were women.)

I was troubled that "From the river to the sea" became a popular phrase for protest signs I saw on campus, which suggested Palestinian sovereignty between the Jordan River and the Mediterranean and an end to the Jewish state, but most students, according to surveys done at various campuses, couldn't even name the river or the sea they were referring to. They also chanted "We don't want two states; we want all of that." Did they realize that their slogan is seen by many as calling for the destruction of Israel?

How many of the young people demanding Israel immediately halt its response understood that Hamas had repeatedly broken previous ceasefires in recent years, including the one in place on October 7, and that leaving it in power in Gaza would allow the bloody cycle of violence to continue? Were they aware that Hamas deliberately placed military installations in and below hospitals, schools, and refugee camps because it was trying to maximize, not minimize, the impact on Palestinian civilians for its own propaganda purposes? And did they understand the fragility of international support for Israel given a mounting humanitarian crisis? Did the vocal supporters of Israel's military campaign know the history of failed attempts to defeat radical ideology through force alone, from the French in Algeria to the United States in Iraq and Afghanistan and many other examples around the world? It's hard to win a war when you don't have a plan to build peace.

History matters. Context matters. Especially in such a difficult and complex crisis, where nothing is black and white and enmities go back decades if not millennia. If we don't educate ourselves—and not just through propaganda or snippets of video served up by an algorithm controlled by the Chinese Communist Party (CCP) on TikTok—we can't form good judgments or advocate effectively for smart policies. That's not just true for young people; it's true for all of us, including policymakers in Washington and other capitals. Nobody in any of our classes ever said anything as uneducated and insensitive as the Republican congressman from Michigan who said Gaza should be handled "like Nagasaki and Hiroshima." While students in our classes and across campus were confused about the dynamics at play in the Middle East, many showed a deep compassion and a willingness to hear each other. They shared their own experiences and approached painful subjects with open minds. Keren and I hosted webinars, private events, and public gatherings with Americans, Israelis, and Palestinians to discuss how to move humanitarian aid in greater amounts more quickly into Gaza to relieve the suffering of civilians and what could be done the day after the conflict stopped.

On campus and off, I did what I could to share my long experience working for peace in the Middle East, including negotiating a ceasefire between Israel and Hamas in November 2012. In an interview on *The View* on ABC, I tried to explain some of the historical context that had been missing from recent debates. In an essay in *The Atlantic*, I examined how and when ceasefires can be effective and argued that Israel needed a new strategy and new leadership. In an interview on MSNBC, I was more explicit and said that Israeli prime minister Bibi Netanyahu was untrustworthy and needed to go.

As the conflict continued, I met with families of hostages and prayed and advocated for their swift return. I agonized over the mounting Palestinian death toll, particularly the deaths of thousands of women and children. I was heartbroken when seven aid workers from World Central Kitchen, the humanitarian organization run by my friend José Andrés, the celebrated chef, were killed in an Israeli airstrike. War is always terrible, but this conflict was causing unimaginable pain.

If my class had been in session the spring semester as the crisis escalated, it would have been a real-time opportunity to apply lessons from our syllabus. After all, we were teaching how to make good decisions in a crisis—something that seemed in short supply all around.

For example, I've seen leaders falter because they failed to set firm boundaries and enforce them or because they made threats that they couldn't or wouldn't back up. So I wished that campus administrators at top American universities had set out clearer rules around protesting earlier and enforced them more consistently. I don't think free speech gives anyone the right to harass or threaten others or vandalize property. Universities and students everywhere deserve better than that. Stronger statements and policies against anti-Semitism in the immediate aftermath of October 7 would also have helped. Instead, too many universities sent mixed messages and had to scramble later on to control events.

I also found myself thinking back to my experience during and after the Egyptian revolution of 2011. Massive protests, led as they so often are by young people, brought down the longtime Egyptian dictator Hosni Mubarak. But the protesters had no plans beyond toppling Mubarak. When I met with a group of students in Cairo who had helped organize the demonstrations in Tahrir Square, I asked about their plans to move from protests to politics: How were they preparing to influence the writing of a new constitution and contest the upcoming elections? They had no plans and didn't seem interested in making any. "Have you considered forming a coalition and joining together on behalf of candidates and programs?" I asked. They stared at me blankly. Not surprisingly, they achieved virtually none of their goals other than deposing Mubarak, and Egypt ended up with a Muslim Brotherhood president who was later removed by the army and replaced with another military dictator just as before.

A lesson for students at Columbia and other universities is that the most effective protest movements do their homework, have clear goals, and build coalitions rather than alienate potential allies. Just look at the mass marches in Israel in 2023 that helped block Netanyahu's ultra-right-wing government from gutting judicial independence.

Another lesson is that peaceful protests can drive progress, but violence and vandalism can set it back. I saw this when I was a student myself in the turbulent Vietnam War era. I was in Chicago's Grant Park when an anti-war protest outside the 1968 Democratic National Convention turned into a riot. I narrowly missed being hit by a rock thrown by someone in the crowd. I was against the war, but I worried about causing a backlash that would help elect Richard Nixon and prolong the war. Subsequent academic research has found that the looting and riots in cities after Dr. King's assassination and those in Chicago did help swing enough votes to hand the race to Nixon.

Even back then, I understood that protesting is only effective if it's part of a broader strategy to drive real change. At Wellesley, I ran for student government president because I thought I could convince college administrators to make reforms through negotiation rather than disruption. I never lost my belief that political dissent is an important part of democracy, but I learned from seasoned activists like Marian Wright Edelman, the founder of the Children's Defense Fund, that to make real and lasting change requires more than protests and political stunts. You have to do the work, step-by-step, year by year, sometimes even door by door. Yes, you need to stir up public opinion and put pressure on political leaders. But to shift policies and resources you also need to win elections. You need to change hearts *and* change laws.

So, I must admit, I don't have much respect for disruptive heck-lers who shout down teachers or speakers, especially when all they're doing is screaming about imperialism or colonialism. I have zero tol-erance for those who may not even be able to locate Gaza on a map and yet insist that Israel has no right to exist.

I also have little patience for the grandstanding of politicians seek-ing to exploit events on campus for their own political gain. When Mike Johnson, the Republican Speaker of the House, rushed to Co-lumbia and demanded that President Biden send in the National Guard, it was a transparent stunt. It's hard to take the outrage seri-ously when it comes from a party that has trafficked in anti-Semitic tropes for years, from Republican congresswoman Marjorie Taylor Greene's nonsense about space lasers controlled by Jews to Trump posting Nazi memes featuring the Star of David over a sea of money.

The tumult on campus attracted so much attention that at times it seemed to blot out the news from the real crisis unfolding in the Middle East. That's where most of my attention was focused. I held long talks with intelligence and military experts and retired as well as serving diplomats and decision-makers about ideas for the "day after" and a path to an enduring peace that would provide security and dignity for both Israelis and Palestinians. The issues are incredi-bly thorny, and the trauma on both sides from this latest round of the conflict only makes them harder to resolve. But there is no alterna-tive but to keep working for peace.

As the war in Gaza continued, I found myself thinking back to wise leaders I'd known in the region and wondering how they would have handled the current situation.

Bill and I were privileged to call former Israeli prime minister Yitzhak Rabin a friend. Watching Rabin and Arafat—two former enemies—shake hands on the South Lawn of the White House on September 13, 1993, was one of the best days of Bill's presidency.

Rabin's assassination on November 4, 1995, was one of the worst. Rabin was a warrior who understood that making peace can take more strength than making war. He felt deeply the human toll of violence on all sides of the conflict in the Middle East. He used to say, "A destroyed house can be rebuilt, a burned-down tree can be replanted, but a young life cannot be replaced." We could use more of that kind of wisdom and empathy today.

I also think about Golda Meir, another former Israeli prime minister. As a young woman, I admired Meir, who took office the same year I graduated from college. She mixed humor and gravitas, chain-smoked her way through meetings with senior generals, and brought great humanity to everything she said and did. Not bad for a grandmother from Milwaukee!

Meir was prime minister in 1973 when Egypt caught Israel by surprise with the start of the Yom Kippur War. As my teaching partner Keren has written, Israeli intelligence received warnings about the invasion from a spy close to Egyptian president Anwar Sadat but discounted the reports out of a "failure of imagination." Meir and her advisors could not conceive of Sadat taking such an "irrational" risk—an error in decision-making that Keren's research shows is common to many leaders. She has pointed out that Netanyahu similarly misread Hamas in the run-up to the October 7 attack.

Yet in an important way, Netanyahu is nothing like Meir. She accepted a commission of inquiry into the failures that led to the Yom Kippur War and resigned from office. Netanyahu, by contrast, has taken zero responsibility and refuses to call an election, let alone step down.

A lesson of Keren's research, and of my experience returning to the classroom at Columbia, is the importance of keeping an open mind and questioning our assumptions. As Margaret Mead said, young people keep our imaginations fresh and our hearts young, and they keep us on our toes. My students did that for me. I came to Columbia to teach and am grateful to have been taught in return.

THE KIDS ARE NOT ALRIGHT

Having a child to love, wonder at, and worry about is one of life's greatest gifts. Being a parent is the most important job one can ever have—and also the hardest and most nerve-racking. I wrote a book about that, *It Takes a Village*, back in 1996. I quoted the writer Elizabeth Stone, who said that having a child is like letting "your heart go walking around outside your body." When Bill and I welcomed Chelsea into the world in 1980, I desperately wanted to protect her from anything that might harm or disappoint her. As every parent knows, that's mission impossible—but the urge never really goes away. Now that I'm a grandmother of three, I'm watching Chelsea and her husband, Marc, experience the same mix of joy, worry, and wonder that Bill and I did. They're fantastic parents, and nothing makes me happier or prouder.

I also know that parents today, including my daughter and son-in-law, face more complicated challenges than previous generations. At the top of the list is technology—especially the toxic combination of smartphones and social media—which has profoundly changed childhood and adolescence in ways we're just starting to understand. The data is blaring code red: The kids are *not* alright.

Today, 95 percent of teens in the United States have smartphones, and nearly half say they use the internet "almost constantly." That includes an average of nearly five hours a day on social media platforms and video apps like TikTok, and far more for the most intense users.

Some young people find the friendship and affirmation online that they don't get in real life, which can be especially important for those who are marginalized or bullied in school, including LGBTQ+ kids. But for most teens, many of those hours online are spent scrolling through impossibly perfect photographs of unattainable bodies on platforms like Instagram, which unsurprisingly encourages social comparison and damages self-esteem. Internal research from Meta, Instagram's parent company, confirmed in 2019 that "we make body image issues worse for one in three teen girls." Many boys are also spending countless hours on violent video games and online pornography.

This isn't just an American problem. One study found that almost 10 percent of young people across nearly thirty countries suffer from "problematic social media use" that bears all the hallmarks of addiction. Like with addictive drugs, heavy social media and video game use creates dopamine spikes that bring abnormal highs, followed by withdrawal that brings anxiety, aggression, and depression.

All-consuming immersion in screens and social media is having devastating consequences for young people's mental health and well-being. They're sleeping, exercising, reading, and dating less than previous generations. And research shows that young people who spend more than three hours each day on social media are twice as likely to experience depression and anxiety. This helps explain why depression, anxiety, loneliness—and, ultimately, self-harm and suicide—have reached epidemic proportions in recent years. A survey conducted by researchers at Dartmouth found that the number of young women who said every day of their lives is a bad mental health day doubled from 2010 to 2022. The suicide rate among people in their early twenties surged by more than 60 percent from 2001 to 2021. For ten- to fourteen-year-olds, it increased by more than 115 percent. These are numbers that should shake us to our core.

My three grandchildren are too young to experience the worst of this. Still, I can't help but think about how they and their friends and classmates will soon be exposed hour after hour to whatever content some hidden algorithm decides to promote. And artificial intelligence is creating new risks for parents to worry about. Disturbing deepfake pornography is starting to make its way into high schools, sometimes as part of cyberbullying. AI chatbots are providing tips on how teens can mask the smell of alcohol and pot. There are new tools that can help students cut corners on homework or cheat on tests. This is all just the tip of an iceberg that's heading straight at families and schools—not to mention virtually every other aspect of American life, from our jobs to our elections.

I am deeply worried about our children's mental health and their sense of perspective and reality—their connections to one another and our larger society. My heart breaks for parents who don't know where to turn for help making sense of this new world. I also fear that the consequences are far-reaching, threatening our broader social fabric and the health of our democracy.

Tackling these challenges isn't easy. We're not just grappling with rapidly evolving, difficult-to-understand technology. We're also up against powerful multinational corporations determined to block regulation and keep people addicted at all costs. Plus there are political actors exploiting the dark side of social media and gaming to stoke anger and alienation and advance an authoritarian agenda. Despite it all, I believe that Americans can pull together to protect our kids and our democracy, but we must act now.

I want to raise the alarm but also offer hope. I've been advocating for children and families my entire career, and I know that it's possible to make progress on challenges that may appear intractable, that it's possible to mobilize parents and communities to defeat industry lobbyists and make a real difference in the lives of vulnerable kids. In the 1990s, when I was First Lady, we took on two of the biggest threats to the health and well-being of young people: smoking and teen pregnancy. The tobacco industry spent millions to stop reforms that would help kids but hurt its bottom line. Critics said there was no way we could bring people together to drive real change on such hard problems. The cultural trends we were fighting were too entrenched and our politics—even then—too polarized. But we did. Rates of teen smoking and pregnancy plunged. Millions of young people lived healthier lives as a result.

Today's youth mental health crisis is an even bigger challenge. I don't pretend to understand every aspect of the technologies harming our kids. But I do know that it's possible to build a movement for change. I see it happening. Many parents and young people are taking back control of their lives. Schools are creating new policies to help. There are good ideas for reforms that could make a real difference. So I hope you will read this as a call to arms and, if nothing else, take comfort in the fact that you are not alone in this fight.

The technology may be new, but the roots of today's crisis go back decades. In the '90s, when I was not just First Lady but also the mother of a teenage girl, I feared that American life had become frantic and fragmented for many people, especially stressed-out parents. Social, economic, and technological trends seemed to be pulling us apart rather than lifting us up.

I was concerned that hours spent in front of the television and video games were taking children away from what they needed most: meaningful time with family and friends, unstructured play, and activities that engaged them physically, emotionally, and intellectually. I also took seriously what the experts were saying: TV and video games were desensitizing young people to violence. I invited Hollywood filmmakers, TV programmers, and other media leaders to the White House to talk about shielding younger audiences from harmful images and advocated for a better ratings system to give parents the information they needed to set good boundaries. I encouraged moms and dads to turn off the television more often and tried to start a national conversation about how we could better support kids and families.

In It Takes a Village, I wrote about the responsibility we all have to help create healthy, nurturing communities for children—including protecting them from out-of-control technology. Nearly thirty years later, my concerns about violence on TV seem quaint. Few could have imagined back then how completely new technologies would reshape our kids' lives—the way phones and social media networks now inject bullying, abuse, disinformation, outrage, and anger directly into their brains. I wasn't the only person raising questions about technology and the unraveling of our social fabric. In his seminal book *Bowling Alone*, Robert Putnam described the erosion of social spaces and community ties. It ran deeper than I realized and was more dire than I could have imagined. But the prescriptions in *It Takes a Village*—putting families first, placing reasonable limits on technology, and recommitting to the core American values of community and mutual responsibility—have only grown more urgent and necessary.

Like many people, it took years for me to understand the dangers of this new era of technology. I didn't think much about Facebook or other social media until 2008, when Barack Obama's presidential campaign showed that these platforms could be powerful tools for connecting, organizing, and motivating people—especially young people. As secretary of state, I prioritized helping activists and dissidents across the world use technology to hold repressive governments accountable, document human rights abuses, and give voice to marginalized groups, including women and young people. In a speech in 2010, I defended access to a free and open internet as a universal human right.

In the years that followed, as I prepared to run for president in 2016, I grew intensely concerned about the looming mental health crisis in America driving what later became known as "deaths of despair," including suicides and deaths from alcohol and drug overdoses. At the time, Bill and I were friends with three families who had tragically lost children to opioids, and I knew that more than thirty-three thousand Americans had died from overdosing on opioids in 2015 alone. But I didn't yet connect these disturbing trends to the phones constantly buzzing in young people's pockets or the so-cial media networks that were chipping away at their self-esteem and connection to reality. It was only after 2016, when I saw how Rus-sian intelligence operatives and right-wing trolls had exploited social media to manipulate voters, spread vile conspiracy theories, and poi-son our politics that I began focusing on the new dangers lurking on-line. I talked to experts, read everything I could get my hands on, and tried to understand how Big Tech companies used secret algorithms to addict users and keep them consuming potentially harmful con-tent. The more I learned, the more alarmed I became.

I wasn't the only one. In 2023, U.S. surgeon general Vivek Mur-thy released two landmark advisories that crystallized many of my concerns. The first warned that a growing "epidemic of loneliness and isolation," fueled in part by the negative effects of social media, threatens Americans' personal health and the health of our democ-racy. The second showed how heavy social media use among teen-agers is driving the increase in depression, anxiety, and other mental health challenges. In the past, surgeons general have at crucial mo-ments sounded the alarm about major crises and drawn our attention to underappreciated threats, including smoking, HIV/AIDS, and obesity. Reading these new reports, I became convinced this was one of those moments.

I also read a remarkable op-ed by Dr. Murthy in the *New York Times*. He wrote about his own struggles with mental health, loneli-ness, and social isolation and how he relied on his family and friends to help him regain his footing after a particularly dark period. It was unusually candid for a high public official, and I thought it was quite brave. I didn't know Dr. Murthy well, but I had been impressed by him from afar. He's the grandson of a poor farmer from India, was educated at Harvard and Yale, and became President Obama's sur-geon general in 2014 at just thirty-seven years old. The National Rifle Association nearly tanked his nomination because he had the temerity—and good sense—to call guns a public health issue. After barely winning Senate confirmation, he did the job so well that President Biden brought him back for a second stint in 2021 to help lead the nation's response to COVID. Now he was raising the alarm about our youth mental health crisis and the risks of social media.

I called Dr. Murthy to talk about his findings. I also wrote an essay in *The Atlantic* to draw attention to the epidemic he identified. I did interviews on national television, recorded a podcast with Dr. Murthy, everything I could think of to make sure more people heard this important warning.

Here's what you need to know: People who use social media for more than three hours a day are twice as likely to experience loneliness and feelings of social isolation compared with those who use social media for less than thirty minutes a day. The more time we spend online, the less we interact with each other in person. In recent years, the average time young people spend in person with friends has declined by nearly 70 percent. The more we live in social media echo chambers, the less we trust one another and the more we struggle to find common ground with or feel empathy for people who have different perspectives and experiences. This is all especially dangerous for young people, whose adolescent brains are more susceptible. "Young people are not just younger older people," Dr. Murthy explained to me. "They are fundamentally at a different phase of development, of brain development, of social development." Our brains don't fully develop until around age twenty-five.

When I talk with high school students these days, they often tell me the only community they know is online. "That's not real life," I point out. "It's *our* real life," they say. "There are no places for us to go. No one for us to talk to." They feel isolated from teachers, counselors, even parents.

They tell me their parents are just as addicted, glued to their own phones, not interacting. They tell me if they have problems and go to counselors at their high schools, the counselors call their parents, who often seem incapable of or indifferent to addressing their anxieties.

All this takes a toll. "Loneliness is so much more than a bad feeling," Dr. Murthy told me, adding, "Loneliness and isolation are public health issues that should be on par with how we think about tobacco and obesity."

The data backs this up. Shockingly, prolonged loneliness has similar adverse health impacts as smoking up to fifteen cigarettes a day. When people are disconnected from friends, family, and communities, their lifetime risk of heart disease, dementia, depression, and stroke skyrockets. It's also a gateway to substance abuse. "If you think about loneliness as a deep source of emotional pain, it is not surprising that so many people may look for things to help relieve that pain," Dr. Murthy said.

Researchers have found that loneliness can generate anger, resentment, and even paranoia. It diminishes social cohesion and increases political polarization and animosity. By 2018, just 16 percent of Americans said they felt very attached to their local community. Unless we address this crisis, Dr. Murthy warned, "we will continue to splinter and divide until we can no longer stand as a community or a country."

For demagogues and authoritarians who thrive on anger and division, this dynamic is a feature, not a bug. Take Steve Bannon. Before he ran Donald Trump's 2016 presidential campaign, he was involved in the world of online gaming. He discovered an army of what he later described as "rootless white males" disconnected from the real world but highly engaged online and often quick to resort to virtual sexist and racist attacks. When Bannon took over the right-wing website Breitbart News, he was determined to turn these socially isolated young gamers into the shock troops of the alt-right, pumping them full of conspiracy theories and hate speech. Bannon pursued the same project as a vice president and board member at Cambridge Analytica, the notorious data-mining and online-influence company largely owned by the right-wing billionaire Robert Mercer. According to a former Cambridge Analytica engineer turned whistleblower,

Bannon targeted "incels," or "involuntarily celibate" men because they were easy to manipulate and prone to believing conspiracy theories. "You can activate that army," Bannon told the Bloomberg journalist Joshua Green. "They come in through Gamergate or whatever and then get turned onto politics and Trump."

In 2016, I was too slow to see the impact this strategy could have. Now we should all have our eyes wide open. As the surgeon general said to me, "It is so much easier to come in and to divide people and turn them against each other when they don't have connections with one another, when they're feeling lonely and isolated."

How did we get here? As the researchers Jean Twenge and Jonathan Haidt have documented, there is good reason to believe that the key turning point was the widespread adoption of smartphones and mobile access to social media in the early 2010s. That's when loneliness and social isolation, depression, suicide, and other mental health challenges all got dramatically worse. By 2015, nearly three out of four teens had a smartphone. "Once young people began carrying the entire internet in their pockets, available to them day and night, it altered their daily experiences and developmental pathways across the board," Haidt wrote. Haidt's bestseller *The Anxious Generation* has this telling subtitle: *How the Great Rewiring of Childhood Is Causing an Epidemic of Mental Illness.*

Social media companies like Meta (which owns Facebook and Instagram), Google (parent company of YouTube), X (formerly Twitter), and ByteDance (the Chinese company behind TikTok) have strong financial incentives to keep people watching and clicking. Their business model is simple. In 2018, when a baffled senator asked Mark Zuckerberg how his platform makes money with a free service, the Meta founder and CEO replied bluntly, "Senator, we run ads." If you want to understand any of the choices these companies make, it all comes back to that. More eyeballs for more time mean more ads.

More data collected from users means more hyper-targeted ads. Sensational and extreme content elicits strong emotional reactions and more "engagement"—and that, too, helps sell more ads. Everything about these platforms, especially their user interfaces, algorithms, and recommendation engines, is designed to advance this goal. Like tobacco companies before them, Big Tech companies know that a more addictive product is a more profitable product.

Zuckerberg and other executives love to say that social media doesn't create harmful outcomes; it just holds up a mirror to all the good and the bad in the world around us. That's like when the NRA says that guns don't kill people, people kill people. If social media is a mirror, it's a twisted fun-house mirror that shows not reality but a picture carefully calibrated to generate emotions and engagement. It's like the mirror in *Snow White* that drives the queen mad with envy and encourages her violence. Kids, with brains still developing and hormones raging, are particularly vulnerable to this kind of manipulation. Young people already struggling with mental health challenges are especially at risk.

The fact that many tech tycoons don't let their own kids use the social media platforms they profit from is telling. They know their products aren't safe. Leaked documents, whistleblowers, and lawsuits have exposed damning details. When a security expert for Meta flagged that Instagram's approach to protecting teens from unwanted sexual advances wasn't working, Zuckerberg ignored him. Zuckerberg and other senior executives have repeatedly thwarted internal initiatives designed to improve the well-being of teens on Facebook and Instagram that could have reduced profits.

In 2023, forty-one states and Washington, D.C., filed a joint lawsuit against Meta for harming young people's mental health by deliberately building addictive features into Instagram and Facebook. The lawsuit cites Meta's own research, leaked by whistleblower Frances Haugen, that the company knew about the harm Instagram can cause teenagers (especially teen girls) when it comes to mental health and body image issues. One internal study cited 13.5 percent of teen girls saying Instagram makes thoughts of suicide worse and 17 percent of teen girls saying it makes eating disorders worse. Despite being caught red-handed, Meta isn't giving an inch.

The industry marshals an army of lawyers, lobbyists, and publicists to drown out critics, bat down legal claims, and quash reforms. It's the same playbook the tobacco industry used for decades, despite knowing that smoking causes cancer. When the Federal Trade Commission determined in 2023 that Meta had "repeatedly violated its privacy promises," misled parents about protections in its Messenger Kids app, and "put young users at risk," the company responded not with remorse or a commitment to fix the problems. It dismissed the whole thing as a "political stunt."

In part because of the millions of dollars spent by tech companies to battle regulation, Congress has so far been unable or unwilling to pass meaningful legislation to protect kids online. States are stepping up to fill the gap, but they, too, are being pummeled by industry muscle. In 2022, California became the first state to pass a law to safeguard child privacy on social media. It would have required tech companies to limit data collected from kids under the age of eighteen, assess the ages of users to prevent adult strangers from contacting young people, and put other privacy protections in place. But in 2023, a tech trade association representing Google, Meta, Amazon, X, and TikTok sued California to block the law from taking effect, saying it violated the First Amendment. A federal judge agreed, and California is now appealing the ruling. When Utah adopted a parental consent law to protect children under eighteen on social media platforms and banned addictive features and data mining of minors, tech industry lobbyists decried that law as unconstitutional as well.

So long as social media platforms are raking in billions of dollars in ads aimed at revenue from kids, this is likely to continue. A Facebook employee's 2018 email tried to quantify future profits the company could expect from a young user: "The lifetime value of a

13 y/o teen is roughly $270 per teen." At a January 2024 Senate Judiciary Committee hearing on Big Tech and the child exploitation crisis, members of Design It for Us, a youth-led coalition advocating for safer social media and online platforms for teens, wore T-shirts that read WE'RE WORTH MORE THAN $270.

Some of Big Tech's most prominent defenders dress up their defense of obscene profits in high-minded, pseudo-intellectual manifestos. They call themselves "techno-optimists" and think the "Great Men" of history—inventors and investors like Zuckerberg and Elon Musk—should not be held back by the petty concerns of regular people or by pesky rules and regulations. The venture capitalist Marc Andreessen published a long list of "enemies," which included academics, environmentalists, ethicists, and corporate "trust and safety" teams that try to remove harmful content from social media platforms. Most of all, Andreessen and his allies hate the idea that government might try to regulate technology and protect users. They say it will destroy innovation, sap American dynamism, and empower rivals like China. They say we have no choice but to let technology run wild and live with the consequences.

Shake off the Silicon Valley technobabble and this is no different from what every plutocrat has said since the beginning of time. Every commonsense limit on the power of Big Business is derided as communism. Every consumer protection is attacked and undermined. You don't want children laboring in our factory or digging coal in our mine? You must hate capitalism and freedom. Stop marketing cigarettes to kids? This isn't Soviet Russia! We can't dump toxic chemicals into the air and water? This will destroy the economy.

Give me a break. The advance of technology is not an unalloyed good. It's a tool that can help or harm society depending on how we use it. Steel can be used to build bridges or tanks. Nuclear power can light up a city or destroy it. Social networks that can mobilize protests against dictators and make LGBTQ+ kids feel less alone can also fuel an epidemic of anxiety and incite violence like we saw on January 6, 2021.

Regulators don't always get it right, but we have a long and successful history of taming the worst aspects of technology so it works more for us than against us. Think about seat belts and speed limits. They didn't destroy the auto industry. They just made it safer for Americans to drive. We need to do the same thing for social media.

The first step is to better understand the data these giant companies are collecting on our kids. Many parents would be stunned by the sheer volume of it. As the Nobel Prize–winning economist Paul Romer puts it, "These firms know more about citizens of the world's democracies than the Stasi knew about East Germans." We also need to understand how that data is used to inform recommendation algorithms and design features that promote addiction. Independent researchers need access to black box algorithms so we know what we're dealing with and can figure out how to regulate it effectively.

Second, it's time to rein in surveillance advertising, through either a ban or a tax on targeted digital ads, as Romer has proposed. So long as it's highly profitable for social media platforms to target ads at kids, they'll keep doing it.

Third, we have to update our laws governing the internet and reform or repeal Section 230 of the 1996 Communications Decency Act, which gave tech companies immunity from being held accountable for the material posted on their platforms. Europe has already passed new laws to protect privacy and require consent for using personal data. As I was finishing this book, Dr. Murthy published another op-ed calling for warning labels on social media platforms, stating that they are associated with significant mental health harm for adolescents. "A surgeon general's warning label, which requires congressional action, would regularly remind parents and adolescents that social media has not been proved safe," he wrote. Evidence from tobacco studies show that warning labels can increase awareness and change behavior. Doing the same for social media would be a helpful start.

I'm glad that Congress has finally taken on TikTok, passing a law requiring the Chinese app be sold or shut down. Allowing an app controlled by the CCP to hoover up Americans' personal data and shape the content our young people consume is a clear national security risk. This isn't a question of limiting free speech—there are plenty of other platforms where Americans can post videos of themselves dancing or expressing any opinion they want—it's a matter of limiting the influence of a foreign power. Former TikTok employees have reported that Beijing exercises much more control and has access to much more data than TikTok would have us believe. If you want to see for yourself how the CCP is influencing what our kids are consuming, try searching TikTok for videos about the repression of China's Uyghurs. See how many videos you can find about the crackdown in Tiananmen Square. Compare that with what turns up in the flood of content (some of it anti-Semitic disinformation) targeting Israel or Ukraine or attacking Joe Biden. That's no accident. There's no way we'd allow Vladimir Putin to control Facebook or let Kim Jong Un buy YouTube. Allowing Xi Jinping and the CCP to keep their hands on TikTok is just as crazy.

Beyond TikTok, though, I'm realistic about the chances of sweeping legislation addressing our broader challenges with technology and social media. Waiting for Congress can be like waiting for Godot. And waiting. And waiting. But there's a lot that families, schools, and communities can do to protect our kids while we push for national reforms.

In my experience, to make progress on complex social problems you need the three-legged stool: responsive governments, responsible business leaders, and active civil society. You need grassroots movements of parents, teachers, civic organizations, faith leaders,

activists, and advocates all working together. That's how we dramatically reduced the rate of teen pregnancy in America, which Bill called
"our most serious social problem" in his 1995 State of the Union address. The National Campaign to Prevent Teen and Unplanned
Pregnancy (now Power to Decide) brought together Democrats and
Republicans, groups like Planned Parenthood worked alongside
Catholic Charities, and parents led the way. Most of all, we started
listening to teenagers—really listening—and designing programs
to address their needs and lift up their hopes. As a result, teen pregnancy fell to an all-time low, and millions of women and girls had the
chance to get an education, pursue a career, follow their dreams, and
start a family when they were ready.

How can we drive similar change today? In his book *The Anxious
Generation*, Haidt offers these four simple suggestions for parents
and schools grappling with how to manage technology and support
kids: No smartphones before high school. No social media before
age sixteen. No phones in schools. And more independence, free
play, and responsibility in the real world. There's no one-size-fits-all
answer that will be right for every family, but these are ideas worth
exploring.

Studies show that delaying unlimited internet access until after
puberty (the years when social media use is most likely to be cor-
related with poor mental health) can protect kids from the worst
impacts. But some advocates point out that easily circumvented age
restrictions may be less effective than requiring tech companies to
design products so they're safer for children. Groups like Accountable Tech and Common Sense Media have specific ideas for how to
do that, and several states are considering legislation. They say that
instead of fighting a losing battle to keep kids off the internet, we
should focus on protecting them on the internet. These are the right
debates to be having.

When kids do go online, parents, caregivers, and schools must
teach them the skills they need to safely navigate their digital lives.

Families should think about setting ground rules for using smartphones, laptops, and video game consoles to prevent overuse. Parents should also talk candidly about the realities of mental health challenges and the dangers of unmitigated use of devices and social media. Organizations like Thumbs Down. Speak Up. and the Jed Foundation have tool kits and resources to start important conversations.

Unsurprisingly, students who text or use social media during class tend to learn less and get worse grades. According to UCLA researchers, sixth graders who went five days without glancing at a smartphone, television, or other digital screen did substantially better at reading human emotions than sixth graders from the same school who continued to spend hours each day looking at their electronic devices.

Thankfully, many schools are already testing out screen bans and using lockable phone pouches from companies like Yondr. Take Illing Middle School in Connecticut, for example. After deploying phone pouches, students focused and engaged more in class, but there were other positive side effects, too. Social media–fueled fights ended, group vaping sessions decreased, and more friendships were made. Where once the lunchroom was filled with kids silently hunched over their screens, the room was now filled with the hum of genuine conversation. One study across four hundred schools found that phone bans decreased bullying incidents by 43 percent. Girls' visits to the doctor because of mental health challenges dropped by 29 percent. And GPAs rose—most especially for girls in lower-income families. These are all signs of successful policymaking in my book, and more schools and districts should take notice. Some already are. In June 2024, the Los Angeles Unified School District's board of education voted to ban cell phones and social media during the school day starting in 2025, and are considering using cell phone pouches and designated lockers.

I'm encouraged by signs that many young people are looking for healthier ways to use technology more responsibly, too. For example, more people are buying old-fashioned flip phones. Trendy "dumb phone" companies are selling out models that encourage users to spend less time on their devices. And "Luddite clubs" that promote socialization without social media or technology are popping up in schools across the country.

It's also important to consider what screen time is replacing. Convincing young people to step away from their phones is about offering better alternatives—like exercise, socializing in person with friends, and spending time outdoors. There is so much that digital natives can teach older generations about how to master new technology, but there is also a lot we can share, too. We have only so much time left in which generations that lived a majority of their lives without the internet can share firsthand wisdom with people who have never lived a day without it. This is a moment when we shouldn't discount the value of a kind of intergenerational diplomacy for the oldest generations and youngest generations to learn from each other.

Dr. Murthy told me he thinks about this a lot. "It's just as important for our kids to learn how to understand their emotions, how to build healthy relationships, how to manage conflict, how to have real conversations, especially when we disagree, but do so respectfully," he said. "It's just as important for them to build those skills, I believe, as it is for them to learn how to read and to write and to learn about history and economics."

He argues that we can all do more in our own lives to nurture relationships with friends, family members, and neighbors and seek out opportunities to serve and support others. On a tour of college campuses, he proposed what he called the 5-for-5 Connection Challenge. He asked his audiences to take one action a day for five days that gives them the experience of connection. "You can either express gratitude to someone, you can extend support to someone, or you can ask for help," he explained. It's simple, but the result is meaningful. "There are all of these rays of hope that have just gone out into the world. People are going to receive those messages. . . . They're going to feel appreciated. They're going to feel connected. And it's going to feel good to know that you helped create that feeling."

I want my grandkids and future generations to know that there is so much more to life than social media and screens. In a moment like this, I'm reminded of the words of Annie Dillard: "How we spend our days is, of course, how we spend our lives." We were made for so much more than screens. We shouldn't lose sight of that, and we should remind our kids of that every chance we get.

PUTIN'S REPUBLICAN PARTY

On the evening of May 26, 1940, Americans gathered around radios in living rooms and kitchens all over the country to listen to one of President Franklin Roosevelt's fireside chats. War was raging in Europe, and it was going badly.

"Tonight over the once peaceful roads of Belgium and France millions are now moving, running from their homes to escape bombs and shells and fire and machine gunning, without shelter, and almost wholly without food," the president said. "They stumble on, knowing not where the end of the road will be."

This was not yet America's fight. Pearl Harbor was still more than a year and a half away. But Roosevelt understood that the advance of fascism in Europe threatened America's security and the future of democracy everywhere. He would not sit idly by while Hitler's armies swept across the continent and crushed the forces of freedom. That did not yet mean joining the war directly, but he was determined to make the United States the "arsenal of democracy" by sending aid and arms to defend Britain and others fighting the Nazis. But to do that, Roosevelt had to convince the American people to care about a war thousands of miles away. He had to persuade them to turn away from the isolationists in Congress and the media who shouted "America First" and opposed any involvement in the conflict.

If that sounds familiar, it's because "America First" has once again become a rallying cry on the Right. Donald Trump has proudly adopted the slogan despite—or perhaps because of—its association with fascism. Once again, isolationists in Congress blocked

American aid while a murderous dictator made war in Europe. We may not be on the brink of world war, but once again, the future of democracy depends on whether the United States will lead or retreat.

In October 2023, President Biden sent Congress an urgent request to provide weapons and funding to help Ukraine's fragile democracy fend off Russia's brutal invasion, along with support for Israel, civilians in Gaza, and Taiwan. Egged on by Trump, Republicans in Congress balked. Month after month, as they refused to even bring this critical aid up for a vote, Ukraine paid the price. The Ukrainian army ran short of ammunition and troops. Russia stepped up its aerial bombardment. Putin's troops overran the eastern city of Avdiivka and pressed their advantage. Every day that went by, the outgunned and outmanned Ukrainian defense forces wondered how much longer they could survive without American aid. In the Kremlin, Putin crowed that he'd been right all along about the weakness of the West.

Finally, in April, under intense pressure, the House of Representatives, led by Speaker Mike Johnson, who at the last minute bucked Trump, approved $60 billion for Ukraine. It was a lifeline for the embattled nation, but the delay caused serious damage, and it remains to be seen whether this belated support will be too little, too late.

How did the party of Reagan become the party of Putin? It's worth going back to Roosevelt and his fireside chat on that May evening in 1940. Roosevelt explained that the America First isolationists of his era fell into three groups, and his analysis provides a useful primer for understanding what we're up against today as well.

In 1940, the most dangerous group was comprised of Nazi sympathizers or, worse, "spies, saboteurs and traitors," who were sowing discord in the country and exploiting "prejudices through false slogans and emotional appeals." Roosevelt was withering in his criticism of those who spread foreign propaganda and sought to create conflict and political paralysis in the United States. "These dividing forces are undiluted poison," he said. They were a "Trojan Horse," a "Fifth Column that betrays a nation unprepared for treachery." This was not hyperbole. In

February 1939, more than twenty thousand American Nazis rallied in Madison Square Garden beneath a giant portrait of George Washington flanked by swastikas. They booed Roosevelt, chanted "Heil Hitler!," and fantasized about the end of American democracy.

Not all isolationists were Nazi puppets. Some were simply blind partisans "who have deliberately and consciously closed their eyes because they were determined to be opposed to their government." If Roosevelt was for something, they were knee-jerk against it—even if that meant playing into Hitler's hands.

Then there was a third category—maybe the largest in number—those who were well-meaning but deeply misguided. They believed sincerely that what happened in Europe was none of America's concern, that the oceans and a policy of neutrality would protect us. This was a view that stretched back to the nation's founding and President Washington's warning about avoiding entangling alliances. But it was dangerously outdated in a world where bombers swept across the skies and submarines stalked the seas. Washington never confronted an enemy as evil as Hitler, nor could he have imagined the power and reach of the Nazi war machine. In a speech on June 10, 1940, Roosevelt derided the "obvious delusion" that the United States could safely be "a lone island in a world dominated by the philosophy of force."

Delusion or no, it was a potent political force. Hundreds of thousands of isolationists signed up with the America First Committee. One of them, the most prominent isolationist of all, was Charles Lindbergh, who had become an American hero and a major celebrity after making the first solo flight across the Atlantic in 1927. Lindbergh was dashing, brave, and a repulsive anti-Semite. In 1936, he visited Germany and palled around with Hermann Göring, Hitler's demonic number two. On his tour with Göring, Lindbergh oohed and ahhed over Nazi warplanes and arms factories. He extolled the "genius" of Nazi Germany and the "great intelligence" of its policies. Joseph Goebbels, Hitler's propaganda chief, could hardly have scripted it better himself. Two years later, on another visit, Göring presented Lindbergh with one of the Third Reich's highest honors, the Service Cross of the Order of the German Eagle. Lindbergh wore the medal, complete with four swastikas, pinned to his chest.

Back home, Lindbergh did his part. He railed against U.S. support for Britain and suggested Hitler could be America's friend. He also blamed the Jews for pushing America into war and undermining its national strength. "A few Jews add strength and character to a country," he wrote in his diary in 1939, "but too many create chaos. And we are getting too many." In a speech for the America First Committee just months before Pearl Harbor, Lindbergh declared, "The three most important groups who have been pressing this country toward war are the British, the Jewish [sic] and the Roosevelt Administration." Instead of worrying about Nazi aggression, Americans should be worried about the Jews. "Their greatest danger to this country lies in their large ownership and influence in our motion pictures, our press, our radio and our government," Lindbergh said.

Roosevelt saw the pilot turned pundit for what he was. "I am absolutely convinced that Lindbergh is a Nazi," he told friends. Yet much of the public still adored and trusted Lindbergh, and his words carried real weight. If the attack on Pearl Harbor had not forced America into the war, it's quite possible that Lindbergh's view would have prevailed. The novelist Philip Roth sketched out this scenario with chilling realism in his book *The Plot Against America*. In Roth's all-too-plausible alternative history, Lindbergh runs for president on an "America First" platform, defeats Roosevelt, and makes peace with Hitler. Anti-Semitism surges, fascism takes root in the United States, and soon Jews and political dissenters face widespread persecution.

After the 2016 election, Roth was asked if he saw parallels between Lindbergh and Trump, who after all had adopted the same slogan. The key difference, Roth said, was that Lindbergh, "despite his Nazi sympathies and racist proclivities," was a man of substance and accomplishment. "Trump is just a con artist." It's a fair point. But in the years since, the similarities have piled up. Trump, like Lindbergh before him, admires dictators and disdains democracy. His devotion to Vladimir Putin seems to have only grown since Russia invaded Ukraine and began murdering civilians and abducting children. He doesn't bother to hide his hostility toward NATO and America's democratic allies. And like Lindbergh, Trump exploits prejudices against minorities at home to derail aid to allies abroad. That's why Trump's acolytes in Congress are always trying to divert attention from the very real invasion of Ukraine by heavily armed Russian troops to the ginned-up "invasion" of America by destitute Central American migrants, many of them women and children. It's xenophobic three-card monte, and the American people are the marks.

Generally speaking, today's "America First" crowd opposing aid for Ukraine falls into the same three categories as it did in Roosevelt's time.

There is a core group close to Trump that is unabashedly pro-Putin. Some may well be on the Kremlin's payroll. In 2016, Kevin McCarthy, then Republican House majority leader and later Speaker of the House, was recorded telling his colleagues, "There's two people I think Putin pays: Rohrabacher and Trump." He was referring to Representative Dana Rohrabacher, a Republican from California who was defeated in 2018. We know that others, like Trump's former national security advisor Michael Flynn, have been paid by RT, Russia's state-run propaganda outlet. And without a doubt many parrot Russian talking points, whether it's Trump praising Putin's "genius" (the same thing Lindbergh said about the Nazis), Tucker Carlson slobbering over the dictator in a soft-focus interview and regularly trashing the Ukrainians, or the ultra-MAGA congresswoman Marjorie Taylor Greene asking, "Why doesn't anyone in Washington talk about a peace treaty with Russia?"

A few honest and appalled Republicans have admitted publicly what's going on. "Russian propaganda has made its way into the United States, unfortunately, and it's infected a good chunk of my party's base," said Representative Michael McCaul from Texas, the Republican chairman of the House Foreign Affairs Committee. His colleague Michael Turner from Ohio, chairman of the House Permanent Select Committee on Intelligence, agreed. "We see directly coming from Russia attempts to mask communications that are anti-Ukraine and pro-Russia messages—some of which we even hear being uttered on the House floor," he said. As in the run-up to World War II, our adversaries want to divide and distract us—and they're finding too many stooges ready to help. As Roosevelt said, it's a Trojan horse. It's undiluted poison.

Many Republicans have no love for Putin, but they follow Trump's lead because partisanship too often eclipses patriotism. In April, 112 House Republicans voted against aid for Ukraine, defying their own Speaker and the pleas of top military and intelligence officials. They're not all pro-Kremlin extremists. They're just partisans in thrall to Trump. There are also still misguided "realists" who oppose arming brave Ukrainians because they fear they can't win, or they don't want to further antagonize Putin, or they still believe the "delusion" that America can be an island with no care about what happens to the rest of the world. We don't need speculative works of fiction to imagine what the result will be if these arguments carry the day. Ukraine will fall. Russian troops will roll forward and be in a position to threaten NATO allies like Poland, Estonia, Latvia, and Lithuania. Around the globe, autocrats will be emboldened and democracies will waver. The world will be more dangerous and America will be less secure. If we let that happen, if we are persuaded by cowards and demagogues to abandon Ukraine, then that surely will metastasize into wider threats to our security.

It's important to understand that the Russians are already meddling in our politics, stirring up division, and undermining American democracy. They've been doing it since 2016.

Now, you may have heard that Russian interference in 2016 was a "hoax" or that Trump was exonerated of any complicity. That's dead wrong. The investigation by Special Counsel Robert Mueller found conclusive evidence that "the Russian government interfered in the

2016 presidential election in sweeping and systematic fashion." The Senate Intelligence Committee summed it up in a bipartisan report:

> Russian President Vladimir Putin ordered the Russian effort to hack computer networks and accounts affiliated with the Democratic Party and leak information damaging to Hillary Clinton and her campaign for president. Moscow's intent was to harm the Clinton Campaign, tarnish an expected Clinton presidential administration, help the Trump Campaign after Trump became the presumptive Republican nominee, and undermine the U.S. democratic process.

It still makes me angry just reading this.

The impact of Mueller's findings was blunted and distorted by Trump's attorney general, Bill Barr, who released his own misleading summary in advance to shape the public reception. But Mueller did secure thirty-seven indictments and seven guilty pleas or convictions. He documented how the Russians attacked election infrastructure in at least twenty-one states, including voter registration databases. Mueller also discovered "numerous links between the Russian government and the Trump Campaign." Trump associates lied to investigators, and Trump himself obstructed justice repeatedly. He was not charged because of a long-standing Justice Department policy against indicting a sitting president. There was no exoneration. The only hoax was Trump claiming this was all a witch hunt.

As part of their "information warfare," the Russians created fake groups on Facebook with deceptive names like "Tea Party News" and "Stop All Immigrants" and reached 126 million people with 80,000 fraudulent posts. Fake Twitter accounts posted more than 175,000 tweets spreading lies and propaganda—much of it then amplified by Trump allies. This operation was run by Putin's confidant Yevgeny Prigozhin, who later played a key role in the invasion of Ukraine as head of a private army called the Wagner Group that recruited

Russian convicts and sent them to kill Ukrainians. After Prigozhin staged a short-lived rebellion against Putin in 2023, he died in a not-so-mysterious plane crash. I shed no tears.

None of this is fake news. I wish it were *old* news. But it's still happening. Now. In 2024.

The Russians are actively using bots, fake social media accounts, and fraudulent news websites with names like "D.C. Weekly" and "New York News Daily" to spread disinformation designed to hurt Democrats and help Trump. Artificial intelligence has the potential to make this operation much more effective, including with the use of deepfake audio or video and more sophisticated targeting. We saw a glimpse of the dangers ahead when an AI-generated robocall impersonating President Biden targeted thousands of voters in New Hampshire in early 2024 and discouraged them from voting in the upcoming Democratic primary. In that case the culprit was a rogue political consultant, but the same tools could be used by foreign adversaries with devastating effects.

The Microsoft Threat Analysis Center has warned that the Kremlin "remains the most committed and capable threat to the 2024 election," which it sees as a "must-win political warfare battle." U.S. security officials worry that the Biden-Harris administration's strong support for Ukraine could prompt the Russians to step up their election interference. Making matters worse, China is following Russia's example. FBI director Christopher Wray has said that China's army of hackers is bigger than that of all major countries combined. Intelligence officials and disinformation experts say China is ramping up efforts to meddle in the 2024 election and damage the Democrats.

U.S. officials like Wray and General Paul Nakasone, the former director of the National Security Agency, have warned Congress and the public that this threat is urgent. But Trump and Republican allies have conducted an aggressive, well-funded, and successful campaign to prevent any real action to protect our elections from foreign interference. They've bullied tech companies, sued government agencies, harassed academic researchers, and blocked reforms. As the *New York Times* reported, "Waged in the courts, in Congress and in the seething precincts of the internet, that effort has eviscerated attempts to shield elections from disinformation."

Republicans in Congress haven't just left us exposed; they've actively amplified Russian propaganda. Most egregious is the case of Alexander Smirnov, the star witness in the GOP's pathetic attempt to impeach President Biden. Republicans trumpeted allegations from Smirnov that a Ukrainian energy company had paid millions of dollars in bribes to Biden and his son Hunter. This was supposedly a smoking gun proving Biden's corruption. Except it was false information Smirnov had received from Russian agents. In February 2024, federal prosecutors indicted Smirnov for lying to the FBI about Biden. They said he met with Russian intelligence officials and then started "actively peddling new lies that could impact U.S. elections." Smirnov admitted that "officials associated with Russian intelligence were involved." In other words, it sounds like he was a plant and this whole thing was based on Kremlin disinformation.

When I hear stories like this, I think about how in 2016, the Republican Senate leader Mitch McConnell strong-armed Obama administration officials into staying quiet about intelligence on Russian interference in the election because he wanted to protect Trump. It was shameful and should stain the legacy of "Moscow Mitch" forever. Yet in some ways, what Republicans in Congress are doing now is even worse. They know vastly more about Russia's campaign against American democracy than anyone did in 2016. And they're still putting naked partisanship ahead of national security and American democracy.

"Please do not feel sorry for us," Olga Rudneva told me. "We know what we are fighting for. We are fighting for our freedom, independence, and the right to be a country. So please be proud of us."

Olga runs a remarkable program in Ukraine that provides pros-
thetic limbs to badly injured victims of Russia's invasion. She and
her team have helped thousands of wounded civilians and soldiers
begin to rebuild their lives and regain their mobility after losing legs
or hands in this terrible war. She's seen the horrendous toll of Putin's aggression—bodies shredded by shrapnel, ripped apart by land
mines, and blown to bits by artillery shells. Yet instead of shrinking
from this horror, she and so many others have thrown themselves
into the work of helping in every way they can.

I met Olga in September 2023 at the Clinton Global Initiative in
New York, where she and I helped launch the CGI Ukraine Action
Network, a coalition of aid organizations and philanthropies. Olga
talked with me matter-of-factly about the terrors inflicted by Putin's
army. She told me how the Russians target medics and ambulances
at the front lines and that, as a result, it often takes many hours for
wounded soldiers to receive medical care. The long wait increases
the likelihood of amputation, as even minor wounds become serious.

There aren't enough prosthetics for everyone who's been maimed
and few rehabilitation services. Battlefield medics and clinics like
Olga's triage as best they can, focusing on the most difficult and
complex cases. I have some sense of the enormous effort this takes
because of my experience working with John McCain to raise money
for the Intrepid Fallen Heroes Fund, which helped build a state-of-
the-art rehab facility in San Antonio to treat seriously wounded service members coming home from Iraq and Afghanistan. But Olga
and her team are not working in a gleaming building in Texas; they're
working in the middle of a war zone.

Listening to her stories, I was amazed by the resilience of a people subjected to so much brutality. Olga told me about a double
amputee who the doctors said would never walk again. The man refused to accept that fate. Now Olga sees him walking every day. "I
see him planking!" she told me, adding, "He is absolutely amazing."
It reminded me of my old friend Danny Inouye, a Medal of Honor

recipient who lost his arm during World War II and then represented Hawaii in the Senate for nearly fifty years. I'll never forget Danny telling me about the painful rehabilitation process he endured and how he made it through that dark time. "I could have not just lost an arm but lost my life even if I'd stayed alive," he told me. "But the people who took care of me, who gave me support, who taught me how to dress myself and how to do day-to-day activities, they gave my life back to me." That's what Olga and her team are doing every day. Not just for soldiers, but also for many civilians caught up in the indiscriminate destruction rained down by Russian bombs. And thankfully, American philanthropists like Howard Buffett have helped Olga and her team build and equip a world-class facility in Lviv to treat the wounded and provide prosthetics.

The bravery of the Ukrainians' resistance has inspired the world, including me, as they defied the odds and fought the far larger Russian army to a standstill. But it's difficult to sustain heroism day in and day out, especially when the world's attention wanders, America's support wavers, and the killing continues mercilessly and relentlessly. "Olga, what gives you hope for the future of your country?" I asked. "These people that I see every day. . . . They give me hope," she told me. Patients learning to walk. To exercise. To live. Average Ukrainians continuing their lives despite everything. Mothers delivering babies. Children going to school. Workers showing up on the job no matter what. "We didn't give up," Olga said, "and that's enough hope to keep moving. When you see that we are still alive? It gives you energy to keep living."

It doesn't surprise me that Trump doesn't care about Olga or the people she helps—that he doesn't care about Ukrainian democracy, the security of Europe, or the future of the transatlantic alliance. He doesn't care about anyone but himself. Beyond Trump, however, there are still Republicans who take a Reaganesque view of America's role in the world and talk a good game about defending freedom. And I believe many of them genuinely believe it. They say the right things about deterring Russia and competing with China. But with embarrassingly few exceptions, these GOP hawks are undercutting those goals—and the values they claim to cherish—by aiding and abetting Trump's attacks on America's democratic institutions. The hard truth is that if Republicans won't stand up to Trump, they can't stand up to Putin or Xi Jinping.

Republican leaders are abandoning core tenets of American democracy even as the stakes in the global contest between democracy and autocracy are clearer and higher than at any time since the end of the Cold War. They are defending coup plotters and curbing voting rights at a moment when Russia and China are eager for any evidence that liberal democracy is a decadent failed experiment. Republicans are largely going along with the Trump-led attack on American democratic institutions and legitimacy at precisely the time when we need to set an example for the world. Some of them may be genuinely attracted to authoritarianism and disdainful of pluralism and equality. But most are making a Faustian bargain to preserve their own power at the expense of fundamental democratic norms and institutions—a move as cynical as it is shortsighted.

Think of them as the hypocrisy caucus.

Trump's secretary of state Mike Pompeo declared in a major speech about China in July 2020 that "free nations have to work to defend freedom." Yet a week after Joe Biden's victory in a free and fair election that November, Pompeo said, "There will be a smooth transition to a second Trump administration." Whether he believed that statement doesn't matter. Coming from the secretary of state standing at the State Department podium, it was a performance of authoritarian mendacity that would have made North Korean propagandists blush.

Senator Josh Hawley of Missouri rails often against China and has said the United States should confront a Chinese Communist

Party that is "a menace to all free peoples." Yet Hawley led the effort in Congress to overturn the 2020 election, and the image of his raised fist saluting insurrectionists on January 6 is an indelible memory of that dark day for American democracy. His reelection campaign sold coffee mugs with the photo for twenty dollars.

Senator Marco Rubio, the ranking GOP member on the Senate Intelligence Committee, urged his colleagues to stand up to China and "prove our democracy can work again, our system of government can function. That it can solve big problems in big ways." Yet he helped lead a filibuster to defeat the John R. Lewis Voting Rights Advancement Act, which would have strengthened a cornerstone of American democracy, and also blocked a bipartisan commission from investigating the January 6 insurrection.

One of the ringleaders of the effort to challenge the 2020 election results, Senator Ted Cruz of Texas, later said what was obvious to everyone who watched the assault on the Capitol that day: It was a "violent terrorist attack." That was enough to make him an apostate in Trump's Republican Party, and Cruz had to beat an embarrassing on-air retreat on Fox. To regain his standing, he started pushing a bizarre and baseless conspiracy theory that the insurrection may have actually been a false flag operation planned by the FBI. Even for Cruz that was embarrassing.

Senator Mitch McConnell has no love for Trump, supports Ukraine, and has called January 6 a violent insurrection. Yet McConnell still blocked a bipartisan 9/11-style commission to investigate it. More broadly, McConnell and his allies have pushed power politics to the breaking point in a way that has eviscerated the norms and trust that democracies need to function—most infamously with Republicans' abuse of the filibuster and preventing President Obama from filling a Supreme Court vacancy. Under McConnell's leadership, every single Republican in the Senate—every one—has consistently blocked legislation to restore the Voting Rights Act, while Republican-led states pass ever more draconian restrictions on voting that disproportionately affect people of color, young voters, and poor people. Political scientists say that while these legislative tactics may lack the dramatic images of an insurrection or a coup, their effect on democracy can be devastating.

Sometimes it seems as if Liz Cheney is the only prominent Republican able to see how undercutting democracy at home makes it harder to defend it abroad. She's a conservative Republican and the daughter of former vice president Dick Cheney. Over the years, she's said harsh things about me and advocated for policies I opposed. But she's got her eyes wide open about the danger facing our democracy and has shown courage in telling the truth about Trump and his acolytes. Liz has paid a high price for putting patriotism ahead of partisanship, getting drummed out of office by angry Republicans loyal to Trump. But, as she told me when we met for a long conversation in the spring of 2024, democracy has to come first. Liz's moral clarity stands in stark contrast to McConnell and many other Republicans who condemned Trump but then fell meekly back in line as he secured the GOP presidential nomination in 2024. Even Nikki Haley, Trump's rival in the primaries, who described him as dangerously "unhinged," said she would vote for him. So many profiles in cowardice.

Back in 2021, just before Republicans ejected her from the House leadership, Liz warned that "attacks against our democratic process and the rule of law empower our adversaries and feed communist propaganda that American democracy is a failure." That's exactly right. Chinese and Russian propagandists jump at every opportunity to denigrate American-style democracy as leading not to freedom and opportunity but to gridlock, instability, and ultimately national decline. By contrast, they claim that their authoritarian systems, which they describe as the "true" democracies, produce better results. For example, when President Biden organized a major international summit for democracies, the Chinese Ministry of Foreign Affairs countered by putting out a report that promised to "expose the deficiencies and abuse of democracy in the U.S." and specifically highlighted the January 6 insurrection. "The refusal of some U.S. politicians to recognize the election results and their supporters' subsequent violent storming of the Capitol building have severely undercut the credibility of democracy in the U.S.," the report crowed. The Chinese and Russian ambassadors published a joint op-ed assuring the world, "There is no need to worry about democracy in Russia and China," while warning that "certain foreign governments better think about themselves and what is going on in their homes."

The autocrats know we are in a global debate about competing systems of governance. People and leaders around the world are watching to see if democracy can still deliver peace and prosperity or even function, or if authoritarianism does indeed produce better results. This is more than a popularity contest. It's a debate that could well determine whether Ukrainians, Poles, and Hungarians save their democracies or slip into an authoritarian sphere of influence dominated by the Kremlin. It could lead countries across Asia and Africa to reject China's financial coercion and maintain control of their resources and destiny. Or it could result in Beijing remaking the global order to its own design, writing rules of the road that suit its ambitions for new technologies like artificial intelligence and erasing universal human rights long enshrined in international law.

These are the stakes of the argument between democracy and autocracy. And when Republicans undermine American democratic institutions and trash our democratic norms, they make it harder to win that argument. They make it harder for the United States to encourage other countries to respect the rule of law, political pluralism, and the peaceful transfer of power. Those values should be among America's most potent assets, inspiring people all over the world and offering a stark contrast with authoritarians whose power depends on squashing dissent and denying human rights. Instead, America has shown the world the ugly sneers of the insurrectionist and the conspiracy theorist.

To take just one example, think about the repeated, totally un-
necessary crises over the debt ceiling. Republicans in Congress have
consistently voted to raise the debt ceiling with little drama when
a fellow Republican is in the White House—including three times
under Trump. But during Democratic administrations, they have
threatened to allow the United States to default on its debts in order
to extort policy concessions and budget cuts. This kind of reckless
brinkmanship sends the message to our allies and our adversaries
alike that America is divided, distracted, and can't be counted on.
That we are no longer a serious country.

It's worth noting that the debate over the debt ceiling is not about
authorizing new spending. It's about Congress paying debts it has already incurred. Refusing to pay would be like skipping out on your
rent or mortgage, except with global consequences. And because of
the central role of the United States—and the dollar—in the international economy, defaulting on our debts could spark a worldwide
financial meltdown.

I was secretary of state during the debt ceiling crisis of 2011, so
I saw firsthand how this partisan posturing damaged our nation's
credibility around the world. I vividly remember walking into a
Hong Kong ballroom that July for a conference organized by the
local American Chamber of Commerce. Congressional Republicans
were refusing to raise the debt ceiling, and the prospect of a default
was getting closer by the day. I was swarmed by nervous businessmen from across Asia. They peppered me with questions about the
fight back home over the debt ceiling and what it would mean for
the international economy. The regional and global stability that
America had guaranteed for decades was the foundation on which
they had built companies and fortunes. But could they still trust the
United States? Were we really going to spark another worldwide financial crisis? And the question that no one wanted to ask out loud:
If America faltered, would China swoop in to fill the vacuum?

I tried to reassure those businessmen the same way I did when

I spoke with anxious foreign diplomats throughout that summer, confidently promising that Congress would eventually reach a deal. I repeated a quip often erroneously attributed to Winston Churchill: You can always count on Americans to do the right thing, after they've tried everything else. Privately, I crossed my fingers and hoped it was true.

Later that day, I headed to a villa in mainland China for a meeting with my counterpart, State Councilor Dai Bingguo. Over the years, I had heard monologues from Dai about America's many supposed misdeeds, his criticisms at times bitingly sardonic but usually delivered with a smile. So I was not surprised when he, too, turned the conversation to the debt ceiling, barely containing his glee at our self-inflicted wound. I was not in the mood for lectures. "We could spend the next six hours talking about China's domestic challenges," I told Dai.

Fortunately, Congress and President Obama finally reached an agreement to raise the debt ceiling before careening into the fiscal abyss. But the S&P 500 still fell 17 percent, consumer and business confidence nosedived, and the government's credit rating was downgraded for the first time ever.

Fast-forward a decade, with Biden now in the White House, and Republicans once again played the same game. Except this time, the risks were even higher. Russia and China are eager to disrupt the dollar's dominance as the world's reserve currency. Every time we go through this nonsense with the debt ceiling, their argument gets stronger.

Over the years, Republicans have often invoked Reagan's Cold War dictum "weakness only invites aggression"—usually to argue for less diplomacy, bigger defense budgets, and more military intervention. Yet they seem blind to how their attacks on American democracy and the effectiveness of our institutions make our country look to our adversaries. Whether Putin continues testing NATO's resolve and whether the trajectory of our competition with China veers toward conflict will in part be driven by Russian and Chinese perceptions of America's decline or resilience. When our democracy looks weak, our country looks weak, and as Reagan said, that only invites aggression.

At the end of George W. Bush's presidency, Chinese leaders watched carefully as the financial crisis devastated the U.S. economy and the wars in Iraq and Afghanistan drained American resources and resolve. For decades, Chinese foreign policy had been constrained by Deng Xiaoping's direction to "hide capabilities and bide time" waiting for the "international balance of power" to shift toward China and away from the United States. With America on its heels, President Hu Jintao announced in 2009 that China was no longer content to hide and bide but now would aim to "actively accomplish" its goals. It started making more aggressive moves in the region, testing how hard it could push—accelerating a naval buildup and asserting claims to wide swaths of water, islands, and energy reserves in the South and East China Seas. China's belligerence in the region and beyond accelerated greatly under Xi Jinping, along with a lurch toward tighter authoritarian control and persecution at home. Xi's aggression not only reflects his personal ambition but also stems from a perception of accelerating U.S. decline. Rush Doshi, a scholar who has closely studied decades' worth of CCP documents and pronouncements, has observed that the combination of Brexit, Trump, and the coronavirus pandemic convinced Chinese leaders that the time was right to challenge the U.S.-led international order like never before. The January 6 insurrection helped convince Xi that, as he put it shortly afterward, "time and momentum are on our side." The sack of the Capitol, and the democratic disarray it represented, reinforced the notion of a "period of historical opportunity" for China to seize the mantle of global leadership.

After the 2020 election, when Trump was whipping up his followers to reject the results and oppose the peaceful transfer of power, a senior Republican official explained to the *Washington Post* why party leaders were doing nothing to stop him: "What is the downside for humoring him for this little bit of time?" With the United States competing against a powerful adversary adept at playing the long game, Americans cannot afford to be so painfully shortsighted. And the argument is exactly the one German politicians and businessmen made about Hitler, whom they thought they could control.

We need to once again put America before partisanship. When I was secretary of state, people around the world asked me how I could serve with President Obama after the long, difficult campaign we had waged against each other for the 2008 Democratic nomination. People were especially surprised in countries where losing an election might lead to exile or prison, not a seat in the cabinet. My answer was simple: We both loved our country. The good of our democracy comes first.

Sometimes I wonder what my dad, an old-school Republican, would think about his preferred party spouting Russian propaganda and weakening our nation on the world stage. Before Pearl Harbor, Hugh Rodham was more or less an isolationist who thought we should mind our own business and stay out of foreign affairs. He was certainly no fan of Franklin Roosevelt. But when America was attacked, he enlisted in the Navy. He became a chief petty officer responsible for training thousands of young sailors before they shipped out to sea, mostly to the Pacific theater. Years later, he told me how sad he felt when he accompanied his trainees to the West Coast to join their ships. He knew some of them wouldn't survive. They probably knew it, too. But still, they went to serve because they knew their country needed them.

After the war, Dad returned to his small business in Chicago. The last thing he wanted to hear from politicians in Washington was that hardworking American taxpayers, who had already sacrificed so much, should shoulder the responsibility of rebuilding our former adversaries in Germany and Japan as well as our allies in Europe. That's what George Marshall, Harry Truman's secretary of state, was proposing, and Dad thought it was nuts. So did many members of Congress. They described the plan as a "socialist blueprint" and "money down a rat hole." So Marshall went to see Senator Arthur Vandenberg, a Republican from Michigan, who chaired the Foreign Relations Committee. Like my dad, before Pearl Harbor, Vandenberg had been a classic isolationist, deeply skeptical of expensive foreign adventures and highly allergic to taxes and government spending. Marshall made his case to Vandenberg and spent so much time with the senator that, as he put it, "we could not have gotten much closer unless I sat in Vandenberg's lap or he sat in mine." Marshall, a former five-star general and a hero of World War II, explained why America's future security and prosperity depended on having capable allies who would share our interests and buy our goods. And even more important, he argued, America had a responsibility and an opportunity to lead the world. He appealed to Vandenberg's patriotism and asked for his help. This would only work, Marshall said, if it was a truly bipartisan national effort. Vandenberg, once the most vocal of isolationists, became a champion of the Marshall Plan and deserves a share of the credit for its eventual success. He said it was necessary to put "national security ahead of partisan advantage."

That made a big difference to my dad, and to a lot of Americans. His generation knew real hardship, from depression to world war, and they accepted the responsibility of global leadership because they realized it was the best chance to give their kids—kids like me and my brothers—a future with freedom and security. That's still true today.

THIS OLD HOUSE

Our red-brick house at the end of Whitehaven Street is vacant more often than not these days. If Bill, Chelsea, Marc, or I have a meeting or speech in Washington, D.C., we'll come with overnight bags for a day or two, greeted in the front hall by framed family photos in which we haven't aged. On the occasions when we host gatherings at the house—like the fifty-year reunion I threw in May for all of us still around who worked on the Richard Nixon impeachment inquiry—the front drive will be blocked by catering trucks, and the back patio will come alive with chatter, laughter, and the clinking of glasses. But the hummingbird feeders, flower beds, and koi fish—anything that needs regular attention—are no more.

It feels like a lifetime ago that I first fell in love with the place.

In the busy blur that was the end of 2000, Bill was wrapping up his second term as president and preparing to relocate full-time to our new home in Chappaqua, New York, an hour's drive from his new office in Harlem, where he would plan his presidential library and launch the Clinton Foundation. Me? I had just been elected to the Senate and was hosting my final round of White House holiday festivities, packing up our things in the White House residence, figuring out where I would live while Congress was in session, and already mapping out the work I wanted to do for New York State as its junior senator. House-hunting, which would normally be fun for me, was one more thing on the to-do list. But then my real estate agent brought me to Whitehaven Street. At the far side of a dead-end off-shoot of Washington's Embassy Row, the house was neo-Georgian in style on the outside and, on the inside, very much stuck in 1951, the year it was built. An "*Ozzie and Harriet* interior" is what my friend Rosemarie Howe, an interior designer, called it. I was skeptical. It would take a lot of work and time I didn't have to update the 1950s kitchen and bathrooms. But with six bedrooms, we would have plenty of space for Chelsea, my mother, and guests. The quiet street without through traffic was promising for privacy. I climbed two narrow staircases to the third floor, looked down at the gardens in the back yard, then out over the trees to the back of the British embassy. It was like being in old-time London. I was sold. The house was ours by New Year's Eve, the perfect time to close one chapter and start a new one.

My mother, Dorothy, was eighty-one when, from a seat in the Senate gallery, she watched me get sworn in on January 3, 2001. It was a celebratory day. But for Mom, it was also just a visit. I couldn't convince her to move to Washington or New York with me. She had been a widow for eight years by then and her life was still in Little Rock, in the small one-bedroom house she and my dad bought back in 1987. That was the year they relocated to Arkansas from my childhood home in Park Ridge, Illinois. Bill was governor at the time, and I was a partner at a law firm. We welcomed my parents' help raising Chelsea, who was just seven years old and already sweetly bonded to her grandparents, who had regularly visited the governor's mansion since she was a baby. Chelsea remembers whole days spent with my mom and dad, taking walks on the grounds and watching cartoons (*The Jetsons* was a favorite) and reading books with them in the attached guesthouse. Every fall, Chelsea would announce her dream Halloween costume—a vacuum cleaner one year, an ice cream cone the next—and my mother would somehow whip it together on her sewing machine. There was a special magic between grandmother and granddaughter that only grew stronger, even after we left Arkansas for the White House and my father died of a stroke less than three months later, on April 7, 1993.

With my father gone, my mother often visited us at the White House, sometimes for weeks at a time. She loved to travel and joined us on a couple of trips overseas. Air Force One was always exciting to her, and she insisted on paying her own costs. (Yes, we were billed for personal guests who flew with us.) But she refused to live at 1600 Pennsylvania Avenue. Little Rock remained her home. She was healthy and active, with a network of close friends nearby and no one trying to manage her independent and rebellious streaks. She indulged herself with the higher education she had always wanted, auditing college classes in psychology, philosophy, and other interests. A favorite day might be taking a drive, with her friend Patty Criner at the wheel, the soundtrack to *Priscilla, Queen of the Desert* blasting through the open car windows, and a thrift store or antique shop in their sights.

My mother collected things of beauty: paintings, stained glass, accent tables—anything that suited her taste and sparked joy. These were not extravagances. My father wouldn't have countenanced fanciful splurges. Instead, her thirst for art and her eye for quality led her to treasures for ten or twenty dollars at Goodwill. I think her collections were, at least in part, a sort of remedy for her miserable childhood. Born to teenagers who weren't ready to be parents, neglected as a baby, and then abandoned at age eight to live in California with her cruel paternal grandmother, my mother grew up knowing only the beauty that she discovered on her own in nature: the scent of orange blossoms and the sound of birdsong as she walked to and from school or read a book under a tree. When it came to love, she didn't even know what that *looked* like until she was a teenager, working as a live-in babysitter for a family that showed each other the kind of warm and nurturing attention she never had. The experience left her determined to create a family of her own to love and to surround us with beauty.

Going straight into secretarial work after high school (she had no money for college), my mother seized her chance at a real home and a family when she married my father. He proved an excellent provider but could be difficult to live with. My father was frugal (to put it mildly) and temperamental. Showing affection was not his thing, but he loved me fiercely and did his best to guide me. He never told me there was any difference between my aspirations and those of my brothers or the boys I played with in school. There wasn't anything I couldn't do if I studied and worked hard, but I'm sure even Dad would have been surprised that I ran for the Senate and president.

I know that he and my mother had a tense relationship. They were ill-suited for each other, but like so many couples of that era, they made a life for themselves focused on buying a house in a nice neighborhood and sending their kids to good public schools. They socialized with couples like themselves, the men talking about business and politics while the women discussed their families. I learned while writing this book that my mother, in her later years, once confided to a friend that a cold current often ran through her marriage and she thought many times of divorce. "I never knew what love was," my mother told this friend, "until I held Hillary in my arms as a baby." She thought about it but never left.

I wasn't surprised, as heartbreaking as it was to hear, because my parents were so different. I was their firstborn and would spend decades—culminating in a sixteen-day vigil at his bedside as he finally slipped away—struggling to connect with my father on an emotional level. I loved him and I was grateful for all he'd given and taught me. He had beautiful eyes and a sensitive side he kept bottled up. He was very much a man of his time—scraping through the Depression and serving in the Navy during World War II—much like the fathers of all my baby boomer friends. He taught me how to play tennis and baseball. He even threw footballs to me, as well as my brothers. We watched a lot of sports on our clunky black-and-white TV, especially when the Chicago Bears and Cubs were on. I wonder still today how much more my father and I could have had between us before he was gone.

It was different with my mom. My mother was never one of those coddling moms who ladled out "I love you"s or cooed over her children's hurt feelings. I think it was because she grew up stifling emotion. What was the use of crying if there was no one to comfort you? Instead, she showered my two brothers and me with attention and was devoted to our education. She *showed* love and found creative ways to nurture an appreciation for beauty in the wider world around us. When we were little, she would lead us through the back yard on the first day of every spring and show us the sprouting crocuses and nesting wild rabbits with their bunnies. And every Christmas Eve, she baked each of us an enormous chocolate chip cookie the size of a dinner plate. Her whole life was a lesson in resilience, how to forgive and how to tend an independent spirit and be devoted to your family at the same time. I connected with that deeply and admired her for it. No matter the pain or disappointment, she steeled herself for another day, a better day. She got up and she kept going. She kept her family whole and never wanted to be seen as a victim.

Last Christmas, someone sent me a tin of cookies made from Mom's recipe. They were just as good as I remembered them.

My mother was diagnosed with colon cancer at the end of June 2001, just after we celebrated Chelsea's graduation from Stanford. Without a second thought, Chelsea and Mom's friend Patty took up residence in my mother's Washington hospital room while she recovered from surgery. It would be another two years before my mother finally agreed, in 2003, to move to Washington. Still, she wanted her own place. She rented a two-bedroom apartment in a grand old building just a mile or two away from my house and bordering the National Zoo, telling me, somewhat ridiculously, "There's no room at your house!" I certainly had more room to offer than her apartment, which was now crowded with her dozens of paintings and antique treasures and even her baby grand piano from Little Rock. But I understood where she was coming from. The once-little girl who pined so long for a place to call home wanted now, as ever, to live in a place that felt *hers*.

I had already been thinking about making the house bigger, so after she had been in Washington for about two years—during which she suffered a minor heart attack but was otherwise healthy—she and I started brainstorming what a renovation could look like. We would extend the back of the house to add a light-filled breakfast room and solarium that opened onto the back yard. While the house was torn up by construction in the fall of 2005, I moved in with my mother at her apartment for six weeks. It was cozy (some might say cramped) and wonderful and a little surreal. After a day at work in the Senate, I would go home to my mother's apartment, sit with her on her little balcony facing the zoo, and listen for the roar of the lions.

The renovation project brought out the interior designer in my mom. She relished working with Rosemarie to select furnishings, upholstery patterns, and paint colors—a vibrant turquoise in the dining room, a rosy red in the tiled kitchen, and a "Bird of Paradise" pink for the small office off the kitchen that she would soon fancy for writing letters and paying her bills. She designed and oversaw the installation of colorful flower beds in the back garden. Best of all, she agreed, finally, to come live with me.

When the time came to bring her things over from the apartment, we had a deal: Everything could come as long as she found a place for it all. That's how the ersatz petticoat table with the faux-marble top, a piece she had designed and had made in Arkansas, ended up in our foyer, along with her piano (which she still played) beside our living room window and her paintings in just about every room in the house. For a framed piece of Wedgwood stained glass that used to hang in the family cottage built by my father's father on Pennsylvania's Lake Winola, my mother got especially creative. I came home one day to find it nailed—as if it were a skylight—to the center of our powder room ceiling. It made me laugh. It also made me reflect: No matter how dark her childhood was or how disappointing her relationship with my father was, she honored her past, held pieces of it close, and shared its stories without bitterness. She even came to find compassion for the parents who abandoned her. Whenever she talked about her parents, she said they simply were too young, too immature, and that she suspected her father might have secretly been gay. That might explain his family's cruelty toward her. Despite that, her few memories of her father were happy ones. On the rare occasion he showed up at the home where she lived with his parents in San Gabriel outside Los Angeles, he would come with gifts and take her for ice cream, before disappearing again. She didn't see her mother at all until she graduated high school and left California to visit her in Chicago with the hope of finding a home. That was a dead end, so my mother was back on her own. I don't know the truth about my grandfather. He died in 1947, the year I was born. But I've always admired how my mother was a woman far ahead of her time in her acceptance of the LGBTQ+ community.

Mom moved into a second-floor bedroom and made the new-and-improved house a real home. She was its heart and its grande dame. Every day, no matter the weather, she walked the back lawn to check the flowering plants, the bird feeders, and the koi pond. She used the pool almost every day from May to October and had visitors all the time. I would come home from the Senate—or, later, the campaign trail or State Department—to find her in her usual seat at the head of the breakfast table, where she could see the TV and also keep an eye on the finches in her garden.

If she wasn't reading or watching *Dancing with the Stars*, which was appointment television for her, she was deep in conversation with a visiting friend or her grandson Zach, who would walk a mile and a half to our house a couple afternoons each week after school. And she relished time with my brother Tony and his wife, Megan's, other little children, Fiona and Simon. Some of Mom's good friends, like Patty and Carolyn Huber, would come and stay at the house with her for weeks at a time. My mother had a finely tuned radar—and zero tolerance—for ingratiating opportunists. But for the dozens of people who offered genuine friendship, including many of Chelsea's school friends, some of whom Mom had known as children, she had unlimited time and attention. She collected friends just like she collected art, and her phone rang almost constantly with their calls to chat. She especially loved her frequent long talks with Chelsea—about philosophy, history, and literature—and reveled in being a surrogate grandma to Chelsea's big circle of friends. At her ninetieth birthday dance party, a group of them kept her swinging and twirling to the big-band music for so long that her friend and physician, Dr. Gigi El-Bayoumi, had to step in and say, gently, "That's enough now."

An Egyptian American, fellow midwesterner, and internist, Gigi did so much more than monitor my mother's health. She fed Mom's intellectual curiosity about philosophy, culture, medicine, and art. They could spend hours talking about old movies, lamenting that Hollywood stars today don't have the same elegance and glamour. My mother relished hearing about the (anonymous) cases Gigi was diagnosing and how she would treat them. And she got righteously angry when Gigi would tell her about the inequity she saw in her work in Washington, D.C. How the mostly white people in wealthy Georgetown have a life expectancy of ninety-four years, but the poor people of color in Anacostia can expect to live little better than two-thirds as long, sixty-seven years. And how Gigi could add ten years to the life expectancy of kids in Anacostia, where the high school graduation rate was a dismal 50 percent, if only she could get them to stay in school—because, she explained, education is the biggest social determinant of good health. This resonated deeply with my mother, who knew all too well the opportunity cost of a stunted education.

Those conversations left Gigi convinced that, in another life, one with resources and support, my mother might have been a doctor herself. Gigi was also convinced that my mother never gave up hope for romance. One time, the doctor, who is divorced, vented about dating and how hard it was to meet a man, when my mother replied, tongue-in-cheek, "I know what you mean." I was always learning new things about my mother through the many and varied people who sat with her in our breakfast nook. But you had to pick my jaw up from the floor when I heard that one.

Mom hated to have me—or anyone else—mothering her, but I did worry about her when I traveled, so it was a great comfort to know that she was never lonely. And here's proof that no matter how old you get or how far you climb, you never outgrow your mother: She also worried when I was away. She worried about *me*. Especially during the 2008 campaign, which proved to be a long and grueling fight. I was a sixty-one-year-old adult running for president, and every time I called her from a trip, Mom would sweetly pepper me with the same questions she'd been asking my entire life: Are you getting enough sleep? Are you eating right? On rare nights off, I would get home late and find that Mom had put flowers on my nightstand or left on my bed a book she thought I would enjoy or a news article she wanted me to read, usually one about the importance of sleep. The first time she joined me on the road for a campaign in which I was the candidate, not Bill, was in Iowa in late December 2007. She couldn't believe the huge, enthusiastic crowds that turned out for her daughter. I later learned that she told Chelsea how proud she was of me but was afraid to say it to me because she didn't want to add to the pressure I was under. That's how Mom was. She trusted me to just *know* how she felt. And I did.

I've had a yellow room in every house I've lived in. My first bedroom in Park Ridge was painted yellow, and I always associated it with sunshine and light. A yellow room makes me happy. At the little house Bill had bought in Fayetteville, Arkansas, in 1975 to convince me to marry him, it was my mother and Patty who painted the kitchen yellow as they helped us get the place ready for our wedding on very short notice. As my mother and I chose colors for Whitehaven exactly thirty years later, we picked a lemony yellow for the western-facing living room where the light of a setting sun would dance across her piano as she played.

It was a cloudy and busy Monday for me on October 31, 2011, with back-to-back meetings at the State Department and in the White House Situation Room. By the time I stopped home for a quick dinner with Mom before an evening address to the American-Turkish Council (now the U.S.-Turkey Business Council) and then an overnight flight to London, my mother was in a chipper mood. We ate at the breakfast table, and my brother Tony stopped in to give her photos of his daughter, Fiona, in her "Spider-Girl Vampire" Halloween costume. On his way out, he teasingly swiped Mom's copy of the latest issue of *Time*, with me on the cover, knowing it would get her goat. And then he gave the magazine right back to her with a kiss goodbye. She was standing in the foyer when I, soon after, headed out myself. "You look so beautiful tonight," she said, stopping me in my tracks. Some inkling in that moment made me offer to come back after my speech to see her before going to the plane. But she considered the time and demurred: "I'll be watching *Dancing with the Stars* then."

They were the last words she said to me. That night, as she headed up the stairs to watch her show (she was always too headstrong to use the elevator that came with the house), she fell, hit her head, and never regained consciousness. I got the call on my way to Andrews Air Force Base and immediately diverted to the hospital. She died very early the next morning with Tony, Megan, Bill, Chelsea, and me at her side. She was ninety-two years old.

Like all former U.S. presidents, Bill—and a coterie of government civil servants—worked years ago to put in place plans for his someday funeral. America has long honored its presidents with elaborate state funerals that involve a lot of moving parts. All of that requires detailed planning. My mother had no plans at all for marking the end of her life. She was too busy living it. And so our celebration of her life was just how she lived—at home, without ceremony, protocol, or pretense. Family and friends of all ages from all over the country gathered among the sunflowers in the garden that she loved, telling stories, laughing, remembering, hugging, and indulging in margaritas and Mexican food from her favorite local restaurant, Cactus Cantina.

There was music, too. Of course. That, and the margaritas, my mother would have insisted upon. But in our yellow living room, her piano sat silent. The last song she played, "It Goes Like It Goes," was still sitting on the music rack. It's from the soundtrack to *Norma Rae*, a 1979 film about a factory worker without much formal education fighting to unionize the plant for safer working conditions, better wages, and health care. It wasn't hard to imagine why my mother was drawn to the movie or the song. "Time it rolls right on," read the lyrics on my mother's sheet music, "And maybe what's good gets a little bit better / And maybe what's bad gets gone."

My mother's journey was done. But her spirit was as unsinkable as ever. In 2013, Gigi established the Rodham Institute at the George Washington University School of Medicine and Health Sciences to do just what she and my mom had talked about: level the unacceptable health inequities in the nation's capital through programs to keep disadvantaged students in school and increase the number of under-represented minorities in health care positions in underserved communities. I was touched that Gigi named this passion project of hers after my mother. Relocated to Georgetown University Medical Center in 2023, the institute has made impressive progress, starting with its Health Education Leadership Program (HELP), which, in ten years of serving D.C.-area high school students, has seen 100 percent of its participants graduate high school and 97 percent continue on to college. How my mother would have loved that.

I should sell Whitehaven. I know that. Bill and I got close to putting it on the market in 2019, but then didn't. Practically, there's little reason to keep a second house. Chappaqua, so close to Chelsea, Marc, and my grandchildren, is home now. That's where the sleepover bedtime stories happen and the poolside cannonball splash contests rage.

My mother has been gone almost thirteen years. I still think of her every day. My dad, too. I imagine how much delight my grandchildren would give them both. I wish I could walk my mother through our back yard in Chappaqua, asking for her advice. And I would relish hearing my father's views, maybe even rantings, about our politics today. When I'm back at Whitehaven, I look around—the sheet music still on the piano, the stained glass on the bathroom ceiling, her book of Mary Oliver poetry on a table beside the ceramic teapot that was a gift from Nelson Mandela—and I think, *I cannot sell this house.* I just don't know what I would do with all the things in it that are such important remembrances of her. I like seeing them right where she put them. I like them being here, right where she was.

When I got home from the hospital on that awful November day when I kissed Mom goodbye for the last time, I went up those blasted stairs at Whitehaven to my mother's room to just sit on her bed for a minute or two, steady myself for the life ahead without her. On her nightstand and another table were the two latest books she'd been reading: *The Mind's Eye* by Oliver Sacks and *Breakfast with Socrates* by Robert Rowland Smith. I chuckled to myself. She had said to me not long before, "You should read these when I'm done." I didn't think I had time to read them in addition to my State Department briefings. "No," I replied. "But Chelsea would love them."

I am not ready to give up my mother. Or this old house she called home. I don't think I ever will. And her books? They're right where she left them.

REMAINING AWAKE
THROUGH A COUP

One Sunday night when I was a teenager growing up in the suburbs of Chicago, Reverend Don Jones, the youth minister at our Methodist church, took a group of us to hear Dr. Martin Luther King Jr. speak downtown at Orchestra Hall. His speech that day was titled "Remaining Awake through a Revolution." It was a theme Dr. King touched on often as he preached across the country. He challenged his audiences—including middle-class white people like me—to fend off apathy and complacency and stay engaged in the great social changes unfolding around us.

His words made a lasting impression on me. I came back to them again and again when I was in college and law school, as the promise of the early 1960s curdled with the assassinations of Dr. King and Senator Robert F. Kennedy, the backlash to the civil rights movement, and the horror of the Vietnam War. When I felt myself slipping into despair—like after the killing of four unarmed college students by Ohio National Guardsmen at Kent State University in 1970—I thought back to Dr. King's message. I couldn't just shut down and stop caring or paying attention, as tempting as that was. For my mental health, I had to keep my eyes open and my mind fixed on the prospect of a better future. That didn't always work, but more often than not, it gave me the emotional boost I needed. And it helped teach me the persistence that's so essential in a life of politics and activism.

Dr. King's theme that day in Chicago was the old story by Washington Irving about Rip Van Winkle, who slept for twenty years and awoke to find America transformed around him. Dr. King noted that when Rip went to sleep, there was a picture of King George III hanging outside his local tavern, but when he woke up, it had been replaced by the unfamiliar face of George Washington. So much had changed that Rip felt like a stranger in a strange land. "There is nothing more tragic than to sleep through a revolution," Dr. King said.

Lately, I've been reflecting on that bit of wisdom, because so many Americans are once again feeling exhausted or resigned or have just plain tuned out the enormous changes remaking our country. We are heading toward an election that could transform America and undermine—or even end—democracy as we know it, yet many are struggling to stay awake to the dangers. To paraphrase Dr. King, it would be such a tragedy to sleep through a coup!

This isn't hyperbole. After the 2020 election, Donald Trump and his allies plotted to overturn the results and stop the peaceful transfer of power, culminating in the violent insurrection at the U.S. Capitol on January 6, 2021. They failed, but it was a narrow escape. If a few things had gone differently—if a handful of state election officials had buckled under pressure, if Vice President Mike Pence had been less committed to his constitutional duties, if brave Capitol Police officers had failed to protect members of Congress from the rampaging mob—the coup might have succeeded. And make no mistake, Trump and his allies will try again to seize power, whether they win the upcoming election or not. That's not speculation; it's what Trump himself has promised.

A 2023 report from the indispensable Brennan Center for Justice detailed how Trumpists are planning a "more coordinated and sophisticated election denial campaign" this time around and how "efforts to undermine electoral systems have proliferated and expanded." Trump has promised to pardon the January 6 insurrectionists and now celebrates them as heroes, laying the groundwork for future violence. Unbelievably, he has said, "Now, if I don't get elected, it's going to be a bloodbath for the whole—that's gonna be the least of it. It's going to be a bloodbath for the country. That'll be the least of it." His campaign later claimed he was talking about the car industry, but you can read what he said for yourself and judge it against his long history of inciting violence. When asked in an April interview with *Time* magazine whether he would reject violence over the 2024 election, Trump said, "If we don't win, you know, it depends. It always depends on the fairness of an election."

The defeat in 2022 of prominent election deniers like Kari Lake in Arizona and Doug Mastriano in Pennsylvania may have given many Americans a false sense of relief, even complacency. But a study from the organization Informing Democracy identified hundreds of local officials across six battleground states who have taken anti-democratic actions, such as refusing to certify vote totals, and many of them are set to administer or influence the 2024 elections. They're county clerks and municipal election commissioners, state legislators and members of canvassing boards. They're people you've probably never heard of who play vital roles in making our electoral system work. Like Peggy Judd, a middle-aged white woman from Cochise County, Arizona, who participated in the January 6 "Stop the Steal" rally and reportedly promotes Trump's Big Lie about the 2020 election and QAnon conspiracy theories. Judd is not just some Facebook gadfly. She is an elected member of the Cochise County Board of Supervisors. And in 2022, she refused to certify the results of the midterm elections until she was finally compelled to do so by a judge.

In late February 2024, a mob of Trumpist election deniers rushed the stage at a meeting of the board of supervisors in Maricopa County, Arizona, forcing officials to flee. "This is an act of insurrection," declared one woman, who leads a group whose website boasts a painting of Trump on a horse and costumed as a founding father. These fanatics are not trying to hide their intentions.

We need to stay awake to this threat. Please pay attention to Trump's incendiary rhetoric on the campaign trail. Go back and watch the riveting hearings conducted by the Select Committee to Investigate the January 6th Attack on the United States Capitol. Listen to the warnings of former Trump officials, like his defense secretary Mark Esper, who says Trump is "a threat to democracy." Or John Kelly, a retired four-star general in the Marine Corps who served as Trump's White House chief of staff and secretary of Homeland Security. He describes Trump as "a person that has nothing but contempt for our democratic institutions, our Constitution, and the rule of law." Read Liz Cheney's book. She rightly calls Trump an "existential threat."

Check out what respected historians are saying. The presidential historian Douglas Brinkley told *Time* that a second Trump term could bring "the end of our democracy" and "the birth of a new kind of authoritarian presidential order." The Princeton historian Sean Wilentz told the *Washington Post*, "I think it would be the end of the republic." Harvard's Steven Levitsky, co-author of *How Democracies Die*, predicted, "He's going to come in like an authoritarian autocrat on steroids."

I know some people hear warnings like this and think, *How bad could it really get? I won't be deported. I don't need an abortion. My voting rights won't be taken away. Maybe I'll have to read some mean tweets, but at least I'll get a tax cut.* Others say, *During his first term his malevolence was constrained by his incompetence, so we really don't need to be too worried. Someone will stop him before he causes any real damage. Cooler heads will prevail!*

These are dangerous delusions.

To understand why, and to see what could happen, let's take a page from Rip Van Winkle and imagine the America you'd find if you suddenly awoke a few years into a second Trump presidency. It's not hard to picture. All we have to do is take Trump both seriously and literally. He and his advisors have been telling us exactly who they are and what they want to do. We just have to pay attention. So shake off the cobwebs, rub the sleep from your eyes, and let's see what's happened to our country . . .

Welcome to Trump's America. If you live in a major city, the first thing you'll probably notice are the soldiers patrolling the streets outside your window. Are we at war? Have we been invaded by a foreign adversary? The answer is no. Here's what you missed while you were sleeping: On January 20, 2025, President Trump's first day back in office, he ordered the U.S. military to enforce "law and order" in cities with large minority populations like Chicago, New York, and D.C. that he called "crime dens." Peaceful protests began in many places, but they were harshly put down with aggressive rules of engagement that came straight from the Oval Office. Video of a few isolated incidents of protests turning violent played on a nonstop loop on Fox News and were boosted by an army of bots on X, the right-wing social media platform formerly known as Twitter. Trump cited this "carnage" to justify mass arrests and made the military deployment permanent "until we figure out what's going on."

Since you've been asleep since 2024, this might be a bit of a shock. After all, the military isn't supposed to do domestic law enforcement. The founders had seen how British troops abused their power and wanted to make sure nothing like that happened in the United States. Federal law is very clear about this . . . *except*: What Donald Trump knows, and you should, too, is that there's a loophole called the Insurrection Act. It was written way back in 1792 and not updated since 1871, and allows the president to deploy the military domestically in extraordinary circumstances like a rebellion. This obscure law has rarely been invoked, but it's how President Eisenhower, President Kennedy, and President Johnson were able to use federal troops to protect Black children desegregating schools in the South.

In an ugly reversal of that history, during his first term Trump talked about using the Insurrection Act to crush racial justice protests in American cities after the murder of George Floyd—and he later said he regretted being talked out of it. His legal advisor Jeffrey Clark, indicted alongside Trump in the Georgia election racketeering case, also pushed for using the Insurrection Act to prevent the transfer of power after the 2020 election and keep Trump in office with military force. Campaigning for president in 2024, Trump vowed to use the military to crack down on protests and crime much more aggressively. "The next time, I'm not waiting," he promised. This is all real—look it up. So, Rip Van Reader, there really should be no surprise that you're waking up under martial law.

That's not all you missed. The new president found it convenient to have troops in the streets when he ordered the mass deportation of all undocumented immigrants in the country, following through on plans his advisors had touted for years. Rounding up millions of people—many of whom had been in the country for decades, with families, jobs, and homes—was a logistical and humanitarian nightmare because there was no master list and because the immigration status records were sometimes wrong. It also swept up huge numbers of legal immigrants who spoke another language or looked "foreign."

The Department of Homeland Security was initially overwhelmed by the task, and Trump ordered the Army to step in. Some people asked if this was legal, and Trump just repeated what he told *Time* in April 2024: He can use military force because "these aren't civilians. These are people that aren't legally in our country."

The new Trump administration also revived his notorious family separation policy, tearing toddlers away from their parents and bragging that abject displays of cruelty would encourage others to "get in line." Families hid in fear. Businesses had to shut down because their workers were all gone. Communities were ripped apart. Exactly as planned.

Trump also severely restricted legal immigration and reinstituted a sweeping ban on Muslims entering the United States from a long list of countries. He ordered federal agencies to stop issuing passports or Social Security cards to the American-born children of undocumented immigrants, defying the Constitution's clear guarantee of citizenship to everyone born on United States soil. Martial law meant that protests against these draconian actions were muted. And no one could say Trump had kept his plans a secret. He was just keeping his promises.

Soon, massive, sweltering camps were established in the Texas and Arizona deserts to hold immigrants while the new administration tried to bully Mexico and other countries into accepting them. Those diplomatic negotiations were tricky, especially when Trump ordered airstrikes inside Mexico targeting alleged drug labs and cartel leaders. According to Esper, Trump's former secretary of defense, Trump actually explored this kind of military action against Mexico during his first term but was ultimately dissuaded. In 2023, the idea gained momentum among Republicans in Congress and on the campaign trail. Trump asked advisors for "battle plans" to be ready to attack if he became commander in chief again. (Seriously, this is all too real!)

So when Trump returned to power he eagerly pulled the trigger. He promised a "beautiful," quick military action, but things didn't go smoothly. When a cruise missile hit a Mexican hospital that was treating patients, not manufacturing fentanyl, it caused an uproar across Latin America. Then a team of U.S. special operations forces got into a firefight with Mexican troops outside Ciudad Juárez and there were casualties on both sides. Congressional Republicans demanded Trump formally declare war and tensions soared.

The new administration suddenly had its hands full of foreign policy crises. Trump also made good on his long-standing desire to effectively withdraw from NATO, the North Atlantic Treaty Organization, even though Congress passed a law in late 2023 to try to prevent any president from abandoning it. But Trump got around this by completely defunding the alliance rather than technically leaving it.

NATO, which had been a bulwark of peace and security since the end of World War II, could no longer defend its own members, and without American support, Ukraine was overrun by the Russian army. Trump has long thought of America's alliances as protection rackets that serve mostly to extort payments from weaker countries. During the 2024 campaign, Trump said he would encourage the Russians to "do whatever the hell they want" to NATO allies who refused to pay up. Once back in power, he just followed through.

The emboldened Russian dictator Vladimir Putin began massing troops on the borders of Estonia, Latvia, Lithuania, Poland, and former Soviet states that he had long coveted. As Europe braced for a wider war without American backing, the price of energy and grain shot up around the world.

Meanwhile, China took note of the clear signal that the United States would no longer guarantee the security of its allies and stepped up preparations to invade Taiwan. As he did throughout his first term on all things China, Trump vacillated between obsequious appeasement and unhinged bluster. Instead of Joe Biden's sober, principled foreign policy, America now had an erratic commander in chief careening from one flash point to the next.

It's a lot to catch up on, I know. But soldiers and roving deportation squads in the streets will only be the most visible signs that something profound has changed about our democracy in just a few short years. As you try to get your bearings, pay attention also to what you won't see.

The women's health clinic down the block is closed. There was a lot of talk during the 2024 campaign about national abortion bans, but in the end, Trump didn't even have to sign a new federal law. He simply instructed the Food and Drug Administration to withdraw approval for all abortion-related medications, so now safe and affordable drugs like mifepristone and misoprostol, long used for miscarriage and abortion care, are nowhere to be found. Some states have started invasively monitoring women's pregnancies to ensure they're carried to term, just as Communist Romania used to do. Hard to believe? In April 2024, Trump said matter-of-factly, "I think they might do that." Then he ordered the Justice Department to overturn decades of precedent and start interpreting another obscure old law—the 1873 Comstock Act, which prohibits mailing any "article or thing designed, adapted, or intended for producing abortion, or for any indecent or immoral use"—as banning all abortions across the country. There were legal challenges, but unsurprisingly, the ultra-right-wing majority on the Supreme Court that ended *Roe v. Wade* and protected Trump during the 2024 presidential campaign continued to aid and abet his agenda. Women and doctors were soon prosecuted and imprisoned. Those who could afford it flew to Canada or Europe, but new state laws criminalized crossing state lines for the purpose of seeking an abortion.

Unwanted births skyrocketed. Tens of thousands of survivors of rape and incest were forced to give birth to the children of their attackers. Women were regularly turned away from hospitals because they weren't close enough to death to qualify for an abortion. Doctors were driven out of hostile states because laws made it impossible to provide the health care they were trained to provide, and now many parts of the country have no practicing OB-GYNs and hospitals without maternity care. As a result, our already bleak maternal mortality crisis grew worse. Babies were left in dumpsters. On the first anniversary of his executive order, Trump threw a lavish party at the White House for Federalist Society donors and anti-abortion activists to celebrate their success.

That isn't the only change in American health care you'll discover. With the help of the Republican Congress that swept into power on his coattails, Trump finally succeeded in repealing the Affordable Care Act, kicking more than twenty-one million Americans off health insurance and fulfilling a long-standing personal goal. Republican moderates who had stopped him before, like Senator John McCain, were long gone, replaced by MAGA loyalists. Then, surrounded by beaming pharmaceutical CEOs in a White House ceremony, Trump also repealed rules put in place by President Biden to lower the prices of drugs like insulin and allow Medicare to negotiate better prices for seniors.

Now, you might be wondering: What about the filibuster? It's hard to imagine Republicans with sixty votes, even in this nightmare scenario. But Trump has said for years that he wants Senate Republicans to eliminate the filibuster once and for all using a simple majority vote. Do you really think if he's president again he won't be able to bully fifty-one senators into doing that? And even if he didn't, don't underestimate how much he can do with executive power alone, especially without the usual guardrails. For example, if he removes key civil servants and installs dedicated Trumpers to manage the Affordable Care Act's websites and insurance plans, how long do you think it will last? Even if the law allows our government to negotiate lower drug prices for Medicare recipients, who will show up to meet with Big Pharma if they're ordered not to by the president? I could go on, but you get the picture. Trump and his co-conspirators can stop doing the work and issue orders to ignore laws they reject. Who's going to stop them?

Back to our story. As the price of lifesaving medicine shot up, so did the prices of groceries and other everyday staples. In his first week back in office, Trump kept his campaign promise to impose an across-the-board 10 percent tariff on all imported goods—and 60 percent on goods made in China. A global trade war quickly ensued, crushing American exports. During the 2024 presidential campaign, economists at Moody's predicted Trump's economic plans would destroy 675,000 jobs, reduce gross domestic product, and plunge the country into a recession and "stagflation," the dreaded combination of low growth and high inflation that plagued the United States in the 1970s. Former Treasury secretary Larry Summers, a prominent Biden critic who was one of the few economists to accurately predict the post-pandemic spike in inflation, said, "There has never been a presidential platform so self-evidently inflationary as the one put forward by President Trump." Experts at the nonpartisan Peterson Institute for International Economics estimated Trump's tariffs would mean, in effect, a $1,700 tax increase each year for the average American family—or more. That all came true.

A severe labor shortage caused by Trump's massive immigrant deportation campaign forced businesses to raise prices and cut back on production. Construction projects ground to a halt. Nursing homes and childcare centers closed. Farmers had no choice but to let produce rot in the fields. Prices for groceries and other goods rose. Inflation, wrestled down under President Biden, spiked again.

Wages did not keep up, especially as Trump-appointed officials and judges busted unions and crushed strikes. The new president pushed through another massive tax cut for corporations and the super-wealthy, sending inflation and the budget deficit even higher. (So, yes, even if you don't need an abortion and aren't going to be deported, this should matter to you. Unless you're a billionaire. Honestly, *even if* you're a billionaire.)

Is this making your head hurt? Well, the burning you feel in your eyes and throat is probably from the smog blanketing the sky. In his second term, Trump accelerated the climate crisis and removed restrictions on polluters, making it easier for them to dump toxic chemicals into our air and water. Just as he promised oil executives during the campaign if they donated $1 billion to his cause, Trump reversed Biden's climate rules and ended most incentives for green energy and electric vehicles (except for money he could steer toward supporters like Elon Musk). Half-built factories turned into ghost towns. Federal scientists were muzzled or fired, but outside academics and UN researchers issued increasingly dire warnings that a global climate catastrophe was becoming unavoidable.

Trump's financial backers got what they paid for. They long ago decided that democracy was bad for business. Corporations couldn't abuse workers and pillage the environment so long as the rest of us had a say. That's why the right-wing billionaire Peter Thiel wrote in 2009, "I no longer believe that freedom and democracy are compatible." It's a twisted idea of freedom that prizes unchecked corporate power above all else.

Like everything else, this should come as no surprise. Trump may have originally campaigned as a populist, but in his first term, he governed as a plutocrat eager to line his own pockets and those of his wealthy friends. That policy agenda goes hand in hand with his authoritarian impulses. In the 1930s, Franklin Roosevelt rightly called out the "economic royalists" who, "thirsting for power, reached out for control over Government itself" and tried to create "a new despotism." Too much concentrated economic power is antithetical to democracy, and that's why generations of Americans fought for commonsense rules for the economy—everything from anti-monopoly laws and limits on child labor to the minimum wage and the right to unionize—all of which Trump and his allies seek to roll back in a second term.

And this is just the beginning. We haven't touched on the favors a back-in-power Trump can now do for the foreign dictators he admires and the oligarchs whose money has flowed, and is flowing, through his family's companies. The opportunities for corruption are staggering.

At this point, you might be asking: How could Trump get away with all this? In his first term many of his worst impulses were tamed by Congress, the courts, and his own advisors. Wouldn't that happen again in a second term? The answer is no, no, and no.

Republican moderates—or Republicans willing to protect the Constitution instead of protecting Trump—were already a dying breed when you fell asleep. Many key leaders who opposed Trump in his first term were gone or would be soon, from McCain and Mitt Romney in the Senate to Liz Cheney and Adam Kinzinger in the House. Even Mitch McConnell bent the knee and slunk away. By the time of the second Trump term, Republicans were a total rubber stamp for whatever their Dear Leader desired.

Holding out hope for relief from the courts is another pipe dream. Do you think the Supreme Court majority that struck down *Roe*, gutted the Voting Rights Act, made it much harder for government agencies, scientists, and other experts to stop polluters and check corporate power, refused to enforce the Fourteenth Amendment's prohibition on insurrectionists holding high office, and invented sweeping new legal immunity protections for Trump was suddenly going to hold him accountable? If anything, the decision in July 2024 to grant immunity to official acts gave a green light for Trump's future criminal acts. It was beyond reckless. As Justice Sonia Sotomayor wrote in her dissent, if he "orders the Navy's Seal Team 6 to assassinate a political rival? Immune. Organizes a military coup to hold onto power? Immune. Takes a bribe in exchange for a pardon? Immune. Immune, immune, immune." The conservative legal icon and retired federal judge J. Michael Luttig called the ruling an "abominable decision." He wrote, "The Supreme Court held today that the President of the United States—and the former president in particular—is above the law, and the only person in America who is above the law."

What about the "adults in the room" in the White House and the Pentagon who sometimes managed to redirect Trump's wildest moves during the first term? Gone. Weeded out in the transition by loyalty tests and a rigorous screening process to ensure no one but hard-core MAGA loyalists get close to power. Or in prison. Trump had promised a campaign of retribution, and he meant it. Remember how he suggested that General Mark Milley, chairman of the Joint Chiefs of Staff during Trump's first term, should be prosecuted and potentially executed for treason? And that his former attorney general Bill Barr should be investigated for lack of loyalty? When you start locking up former generals and Justice Department officials, dissent disappears quickly.

There were mass resignations, but that just cleared the way for more MAGA appointees. These loyalists aren't the bumbling clowns of the first term, either. They're more experienced and disciplined this time, with a clearer understanding of how to manipulate the levers of power and muscle through their agenda. During the campaign, they even wrote out detailed plans called "Project 2025," which described exactly what they intended to do—from dismantling the Department of Education and gutting the EPA and climate protections, to ending the independence of the Justice Department. An analysis from the nonprofit Democracy Forward found that this agenda, which was designed to avoid congressional approval, would strip overtime protections for 4.3 million hardworking Americans, reduce food assistance for 40 million people in need, cost hundreds of thousands of jobs, roll back civil rights, and much more. It was a blueprint for a less free, less fair, less prosperous America.

Many of those Trump put into government had their own scores to settle and pet ideological projects. After Trump's Schedule F executive order ended the historic independence of the federal civil service and allowed the president to summarily fire huge swaths of experienced federal workers, there was virtually no one left in the government willing or able to question increasingly authoritarian policies, or with the competence and experience needed to make crucial decisions. All of a sudden, injecting bleach to treat a virus seemed like a splendid idea.

When it comes to his policies, "cruelty is the point," as the writer Adam Serwer memorably put it. Well, incompetence is also the point. If Republicans make our government dysfunctional, that only bolsters their argument that the "deep state" is the problem and the only solution is a leader who uses dictatorial power to get things done. The message resonates with frustrated voters who want to blow up a broken system. Tails he wins, heads we lose.

While you're thinking about all this, don't forget that Trump also promised to weaponize the Justice Department against his political enemies—especially me, President Obama, and "the entire Biden crime family." I take this seriously, and so should you. After all, "Lock her up" wasn't just a campaign slogan. When Trump became president, he tried to do it. According to the report from Special Counsel Robert Mueller, in 2017 Trump called Attorney General Jeff Sessions at home and told him to order the Justice Department to prosecute me. He made the same request to White House counsel Don McGahn in 2018. Of course there were no crimes to prosecute and no case was ever brought. But Trump's State Department did launch two additional investigations into my emails after the FBI had already determined there was no case. In both 2017 and 2019, the State Department reached the same conclusion: "None of the emails in this review were marked as classified," they reported. By contrast, we now know that when Trump left office, he took highly classified secrets and left them strewn around Mar-a-Lago like party favors. For Trump, the rule of law is meaningless. He only understands the rule of the jungle. So I have no doubt that if given the chance again, he'd abuse his power to come after me, Biden, and anyone who has had the temerity to stand up to him.

I know it's tempting to dismiss everything I've said here as hysterical. I wish the imagined future I've sketched out were just a liberal fever dream, some kind of dystopian MSNBC fan fiction. But it's not. I didn't even mention the fact that Trump has repeatedly said he would be a "dictator on day one" or his previous calls to "terminate" the Constitution. That felt too on the nose for this exercise. But if we take Trump's plans and promises at face value, and if we are realistic about the lack of guardrails, then this dark future becomes chillingly real. And the only way to stop it is by defeating Trump this November so soundly that he can't steal or bully his way into power. That means we all have to be wide awake, highly engaged, and absolutely tireless in our efforts.

Easier said than done, right?

After the 2016 election, I worried that many of the people who poured their hopes into my campaign—especially young people all over the country—would be so discouraged and deflated that they would disengage from politics altogether. Instead, a mighty resistance emerged, from the grassroots up, that mobilized to challenge the Trump administration's abuses. Thousands took to the streets. Hundreds of new organizations sprang up. People ran for office for the first time. And in 2020, a pro-democracy coalition overwhelmed MAGA and sent Joe Biden and Kamala Harris to the White House.

But I understand how difficult it can be to sustain this kind of engagement over years and years of unrelenting political warfare, especially if it seems like there's no end in sight. Exhausting us is part of the authoritarian playbook. They unleash a torrent of lies not because they think we'll believe all of them, but because they hope we'll eventually be so overwhelmed that we'll give up on the idea of truth and justice completely. They tell us the game is rigged so we won't bother playing. They sling as much mud as they can and say that everyone is corrupt because they want us to get disgusted and walk away.

Exceptional political talents sometimes come along like shooting stars, cutting through the noise and capturing our imaginations. Governor Ann Richards did it in Texas. Bill Clinton did it in 1992. Barack Obama did it in 2008. But most of the time, politics is less like an inspiring episode of *The West Wing* and more like "a slow boring of hard boards," as Max Weber put it. Progress only comes through persistence and usually in fits and starts. It can be demoralizing.

Most Americans are not political junkies. They don't want to have to think about the fate of democracy every day. They have jobs to do, kids to raise, aging parents to support, meals to cook, and houses to clean. At the end of a long day, if you turn on the news or scroll through social media and all you see is an unrelenting drumbeat of bad news, conflict, and propaganda—it's enough to make anyone give up and tune out.

We can't do that. Not this time.

Being informed is crucial, but stepping away from the news when it's got you down is an important part of staying in the fight over the long term. Big Tech's algorithms are designed to keep us hooked

24/7, but that's not a healthy way to consume news and will only lead to burnout.

Here's my advice for when you start to feel overwhelmed or out of gas: First, put down your phone and go outside. Take a walk. You don't have to tramp around in the woods for hours like I do. It might be enough to just walk around the block. Take a deep breath and think about the people you love and the hopes you have for the future. Perhaps you're looking forward to going to college next year, or getting married, or finding a new job. Then look around at everyone else in the neighborhood. Think about *their* hopes and dreams. Remember we're all in it together. This is why we have to stick together. It's why we can't give up. Because the stakes matter for you and for all of us.

Take care of yourself. Maybe don't listen to a gut-wrenching interview from a war zone or with a rape survivor denied an abortion on your morning commute. Save it for later so it doesn't set the tone for your whole day. Try creating digital firewalls for yourself. That could mean putting your laptop or phone on "do not disturb" while you're at the park with your kids or cooking dinner, so you're not seeing push notifications and breaking news pop up incessantly. But don't give up on the news entirely. Be a savvy media consumer. Find journalists you trust who will give you the straight story and pay attention to what they report.

The prospect of a Trumpy future should scare you. We have to stop it. But the prospect of a better future should also motivate you. If Democrats have the chance, there's so much progress we can make. Abortion rights and voting rights can be restored and written into law. We can build on the boom in clean energy, electric vehicles, and advanced manufacturing that Biden began. We'll see real results— with more good jobs, rising incomes, and a healthier environment. You won't have to worry about a madman with his finger on the button or a crook with his hand in your pocket. Instead of chaos and narcissism, we can have competence and compassion.

Here's another piece of advice: Get busy. As the wise and wry congresswoman from Colorado Pat Schroeder used to say, "You can't wring your hands and roll up your sleeves at the same time." There are millions of Americans working to defend our democracy every day, in ways big and small. They're volunteering, organizing, donating, even running for office themselves. And history tells us that when our nation faces the greatest perils is when our people find their greatest strengths. So I'm not giving up, and I hope you won't, either.

We can't allow ourselves to be exhausted. Instead, we should channel the strength of Rosa Parks, who dismissed the idea that the only reason she sat down in the front of that bus in Montgomery, Alabama, was because she was tired. "The only tired I was, was tired of giving in," she said.

There's a wonderful phrase in a letter that the dissident playwright and first freely elected president of Czechoslovakia Václav Havel sent to his wife, Olga, from prison:

> Everything meaningful in life is distinguished by a certain transcendence of individual human existence—beyond the limits of mere "self-care"—toward other people, toward society, toward the world. . . . Only by looking outward, by caring for things that, in terms of pure survival, you needn't bother with at all . . . and by *throwing yourself over and over again into the tumult of the world*, with the intention of making your voice count—only thus will you really become a person. (emphasis mine)

I love that. We're all tired. It's been a long few years. It's easy to feel powerless or like our efforts and our voices don't matter. They do. We can't stop throwing ourselves over and over again into the tumult of the world. It's the only way to prevent the bleak future we fear and build the better country we deserve.

REBELS WITH A CAUSE

Her eyes were red from tears but flashed with resolve. It was February 2024, and Yulia Navalnaya had just learned that her husband, Alexei Navalny, the Russian opposition leader and pro-democracy activist, had died in an arctic penal colony. We were at the Hotel Bayerischer Hof in Munich, Germany, at a conference on international security attended by world leaders, diplomats, activists, and academics.

"I thought: Should I stand here before you or should I go back to my children?" Yulia said. "And then I thought: What would Alexei have done in my place? And I'm sure that he would have been standing here on this stage."

Like everyone, Yulia assumed Navalny had been murdered by Vladimir Putin's thugs. For years, Navalny had been a persistent thorn in Putin's side, exposing the corruption of Russia's political elite and speaking out against authoritarian repression. He was poisoned in 2020 by Russian agents and nearly died. Yet he recovered, returned to Russia, and was promptly arrested. Navalny knew the risks but refused to bow to intimidation. It was no secret what happened to prominent critics of the regime. They fell out of windows or were shot in the elevator of their apartment building. Their tea was poisoned with radioactive isotopes. Their planes mysteriously exploded in midair. Sometimes they just dropped dead with no explanation offered. Now Navalny was dead, too, and so was one of the best hopes for change in Russia.

"I want to call on the world community, everyone in this room and people around the world[,] to come together to defeat this evil, defeat this horrible regime that is now in Russia," Yulia said, keeping her composure through the grief and anger.

After she left the stage, I took her hand and told her how sorry I was for her loss. I was in awe of her strength.

Over the years, I had gotten to know Yulia and her daughter, Dasha, as well as a number of Navalny's colleagues at the Anti-Corruption Foundation, which does so much to expose abuses by Putin's regime. As Navalny languished in a Russian jail cell, I encouraged the Biden administration to push for his release and explore possible prisoner swaps. I was impressed by Yulia and her devotion to both her family and the cause of Russian democracy. A former banker with a degree in international economics, she is fiercely intelligent and politically savvy. Before Navalny's death she often preferred to stay in the background. He was the charismatic leader rallying opposition to Putin; she was the rock giving him strength and sure footing. Now, Yulia was grappling with whether to step forward and pick up Navalny's public role.

It was a painful decision I had seen too many other women face over the years. I'll never forget visiting Violeta Chamorro, Nicaragua's first woman president, and seeing the bullet-riddled car in which her journalist husband had been assassinated by the regime of dictator Anastasio Somoza. She kept it on the front lawn of her house in Managua as a reminder of the sacrifices she and her country had made for democracy.

In Munich, as Yulia reeled from the news of Navalny's death, she huddled with another woman who had been unexpectedly thrust into the spotlight: Sviatlana Tsikhanouskaya from Belarus. Sviatlana considers herself an "accidental politician." She never intended to run for office or become the face of the opposition to dictator Aleksandr Lukashenko, a key Putin ally. As for Yulia, it was Sviatlana's husband, the activist and journalist Siarhei Tsikhanouski, who was the public figure. In 2020, as Siarhei prepared to run for president, he was arrested and held incommunicado. Without even being able to talk to her husband, Sviatlana stepped in and ran in his place. She didn't think it would be more than a gesture of love to Siarhei.

"I didn't have a political background," Sviatlana explained to me. "I was an ordinary housewife, but it became so important for me." Lukashenko underestimated Sviatlana and didn't bother to block her candidacy. She joined with two other women leaders, Veronika Tsepkalo and Maria Kolesnikova, to mobilize a unified opposition movement. Sviatlana did it all while juggling the demands of being a de facto single parent to her two young children.

To everyone's surprise, Belarusians responded enthusiastically. They bravely joined rallies and protests—rare and risky in a country ruled with an iron fist. In July 2020, more than sixty-three thousand gathered in Minsk in what was the largest rally in Belarus's history. "I don't need power, but my husband is behind bars. I had to hide my children," Sviatlana told the throng. "I'm sick of putting up with it, keeping quiet, and being afraid."

With Sviatlana's support surging, Lukashenko's regime got serious about rigging the election. In the end, he declared himself the winner with 80 percent of the vote. Independent observers say Sviatlana was the real winner, but she was forced into exile, and her husband was sentenced to nearly twenty years in prison. Protesters filled the streets but were met with mass arrests and a widespread crackdown.

Sviatlana refused to fade into obscurity. She now travels the world urging leaders to hold Lukashenko accountable for his crimes and support freedom in Belarus. She coordinates the country's pro-democracy movement and does everything she can to shine a spotlight on the plight of the many political prisoners held in Belarus, including her husband. She has had no contact with him and doesn't know if he's alive or dead. The Belarusian regime denies the International Red Cross's requests to visit him and the other prisoners arrested for running the political protests. It's a form of personal torture that she channels into her work.

After meeting with Yulia in Munich, Sviatlana told the press, "We understood each other without any words."

In the days that followed, Yulia showed the same kind of steely determination. She addressed the European Parliament and urged the continent's leaders to treat Putin like the criminal he is.

"You aren't dealing with a politician but with a bloody mobster," she said. Because "Putin is the leader of an organized criminal gang," Yulia explained, the world needed to think like a Mafia prosecutor: "Not diplomatic notes, but investigations into the financial machinations. Not statements of concern, but a search for mafia associates in your countries, for the discreet lawyers and financiers who are helping Putin and his friends to hide money."

"There has been so little time to think, to plan, to process," she told a reporter in early April. "But we have to keep working, to keep moving forward." In July, Russia ordered Yulia's arrest in absentia, meaning that if she ever returns to her country, she'll be imprisoned just as her husband was—a clear sign that her voice and advocacy pose a threat to Putin's corrupt regime.

I have been working with courageous women like Yulia and Sviatlana for thirty years. Eleanor Roosevelt said, "A woman is like a tea bag: You never know how strong she is until she's in hot water." Time and again, I've seen women activists in difficult and dangerous circumstances prove her right. Exposing corruption and human rights abuses, defying dictators, fighting for democracy—this is dangerous work. Yet all over the world, I've met women who answer repression with astonishing resilience and determination. I still don't know how they find the courage, but their example gives me hope and inspiration.

"The world has finally woken up to the fact that we're powerful," Leymah Gbowee told me recently at a conference on democracy at Wellesley College.

Leymah won the Nobel Peace Prize for her efforts to bring peace and democracy to Liberia after a long period of war and dictatorship. Between 1989 and 2003, about 250,000 Liberians were killed and millions fled their homes. Soldiers, many of them little more than children, raped and assaulted women with impunity. In 2003, women like Leymah started saying to one another, "Enough is enough." She began organizing nonviolent protests. Thousands of women from all walks of life, Christians and Muslims together, flooded the streets, marching, singing, and praying. Dressed all in white, they sat in a fish market in the hot sun under a banner that read THE WOMEN OF LIBERIA WANT PEACE NOW.

Soldiers threatened to flog them, imprison them, shoot them in the head. The women stayed put. "We used our pains, broken bodies and scarred emotions to confront the injustices and terror of our nation," Leymah recalled later.

On behalf of the protesters, Leymah went to see Liberia's corrupt and violent dictator, Charles Taylor. No one knew if she'd come out alive. But she managed to persuade him to start peace negotiations with rebel warlords.

Leymah and other women traveled to Ghana to support the talks. When word came that the men were deadlocked and giving up, the women linked arms and blocked the doors and windows so the negotiators couldn't leave. Security forces moved in. Leymah stood her ground and threatened to strip naked there in the hall, shaming the men. They stopped in their tracks. The negotiations restarted, a peace agreement was signed, Taylor fled, and Liberians elected Ellen Johnson Sirleaf as the first woman president in Africa. The peace has held ever since, even as other conflicts and coups have swept across the region. The whole story is captured in a remarkable documentary, *Pray the Devil Back to Hell*, which I highly recommend.

Leymah once told me that back in 2003, while she was organizing protests in markets and soccer fields, someone gave her a copy of my memoir *Living History*, and she was struck by a quote from

Harriet Tubman that had inspired me. As Tubman guided escaped slaves to freedom, she would say: "If you are tired, keep going; if you are scared, keep going; if you are hungry, keep going; if you want to taste freedom, keep going." Leymah loved that and shared it with her friends in Liberia. If they wanted to stop a war and oust a dictator, they needed to keep going.

That's exactly what they did. The women of Liberia refused "to be silenced in the face of AK-47 and RPGs," as Leymah recalled when accepting the Nobel Peace Prize. "We walked when we had no transportation, we fasted when water was unaffordable, we held hands in the face of danger, we spoke truth to power when everyone else was being diplomatic, we stood under the rain and the sun with our children to tell the world the stories of the other side of the conflict."

I've heard that same determination from women activists and dissidents all over the world. *One foot in front of the other, no matter what comes. Keep going.* When I wonder if I can find the strength to overcome some obstacle in my own life, when I'm not sure how to get back up after I've been knocked down, I think about women like Leymah. Their stories put my problems in perspective. Their wisdom helps me see more clearly. Their courage is contagious.

I set out to be a voice for women who are silenced by repression. Yet in ways I could not have predicted, they helped me find my voice.

It started in early 1995, a time when I felt lost both personally and professionally. The heady early days of the Clinton administration, when so much seemed possible, were over. I had waged and lost a long battle to pass legislation that would provide affordable, quality health care for all Americans. In part because of my failure, Democrats had been decimated in the 1994 midterm elections, and right-wing Republicans now controlled Congress. I felt I had let down Bill, our team, and the millions of Americans who had put their faith in us. I thought about withdrawing from active political and policy work, which I hoped would remove a distraction for the administration and deprive Republicans of political ammunition.

Against that backdrop, in March 1995, I took my first extended trip overseas as First Lady without the president. With fifteen-year-old Chelsea by my side, I visited five countries across South Asia over twelve days. It was my first serious experience in the developing world, including countries where women had few rights and faced widespread persecution. I would never be the same.

A highlight of the trip came at a women's luncheon in New Delhi, India. The principal of a secondary school shared a poem written for me by one of her students, Anasuya Sengupta. It was called "Silence." All these years later, I still can't get it out of my head. It begins like this:

> *Too many women in too many countries*
> *speak the same language of silence.*

Wow. It was like a bolt of lightning cutting through the clouds in my head. I had been feeling sorry for myself, too worried about politics and the press. This felt real. It felt like the work I was called to do. Then there was this:

> *When a woman fights for power,*
> *as all women would like to,*
> *quietly or loudly,*
> *it is questioned.*
> *And yet, there must be freedom—*
> *if we are to speak.*
> *And yes, there must be power—*
> *if we are to be heard.*
> *And when we have both*
> *(freedom and power)*
> *let us not be misunderstood.*
> *We seek only to give words*

to those who cannot speak
(too many women
in too many countries).

I rewrote the speech I was preparing to give the next day. Now I knew what I wanted to say. I quoted from the poem and, a few months later, brought it with me to China for the United Nations' Fourth World Conference on Women in Beijing, where I declared that "human rights are women's rights and women's rights are human rights." The Chinese authorities had banned thousands of NGO representatives from attending the main conference and forced them to gather an hour away in the Huairou district. So of course I went to see them. A raucous crowd of women activists from around the world sang, yelled, clapped, and cheered as I walked on-stage. They loved Anasuya's poem as much as I did.

Her words and the spirit of the women I met on my travels gave me a new sense of purpose. I committed to use whatever power and platform I had to lift up women who were fighting for peace and democracy, who were doing the hard work of building power and defending human rights. That would be my mission.

I met Rigoberta Menchú during another challenging time in my life. In November 1998, Republicans in Congress were preparing to impeach my husband. Personally, I was heartbroken. Politically, though, I was furious—and absolutely convinced that the best thing for the country was for Bill to remain as president. It was during this painful, confusing period that I set out on a trip through Central America, which had recently been devastated by Hurricane Mitch.

Guatemala is a country so beautiful that, as the indigenous poet Humberto Ak'abal put it, "if you climb up an ancient cypress tree and creep among its branches . . . you will see the earth is not so far from heaven." Yet for nearly four decades, it had been torn apart by coups and a bloody civil war between the right-wing military-controlled government and leftist guerrillas. Hundreds of thousands of people were killed, and there were widespread atrocities and human rights abuses, especially against the indigenous population. I was proud that Bill formally apologized for the role the United States had played over the years in supporting the Guatemalan military's abuses.

In 1996, a peace agreement ended the fighting, and the country began the hard work of rebuilding democracy and reconciling old foes. Even with the guns silent, however, justice and accountability were proving elusive. The country's power structure was not yet ready to give up its culture of impunity and embrace accountability. No high-ranking military officers or political leaders had been held responsible for human rights abuses during the civil war. A Historical Clarification Commission was slowly compiling a report but was not going to name names.

Bishop Juan José Gerardi, a revered champion of human rights in Guatemala, led a separate investigation under the auspices of the Catholic Church that he hoped would spur prosecutions of war criminals. But in April 1998, just two days after publishing his findings, the bishop was brutally beaten to death with a concrete block. The government seemed paralyzed and unable to respond. Human rights activists feared the murder signaled a return to the bad old days of massacres and disappearances.

This was the backdrop for my visit. I came to offer aid in the wake of a deadly hurricane but also to encourage Guatemala's leaders to deliver on the promise of peace. At the U.S. ambassador's house in Guatemala City, I met with former dissidents now working to promote reconciliation and accountability.

One of them was Rigoberta Menchú, who had won the Nobel Peace Prize in 1992 at the age of thirty-three for her work exposing genocide against indigenous Guatemalans during the war. I remembered Chelsea reading Rigoberta's 1983 memoir when she was in fifth grade in Little Rock. Rigoberta's story of turning tragedy into activism made a lasting impression on Chelsea. It was easy to see why. In her book, Rigoberta described growing up in extreme poverty and how both her parents, her two brothers, and other members of their family were killed by the repressive military dictatorship. Rigoberta continued to fight for the rights of indigenous communities, land reforms, and democracy even after being exiled from Guatemala in the early '80s.

Now Rigoberta was back and determined to bring to justice human rights abusers from the old regime, despite the official stonewalling. She had recently gone to court to protest biased judges putting their fingers on the scales in the trial of twenty-five soldiers accused of massacring indigenous villagers in 1995. The prosecutor who had been brave enough to bring the unprecedented case also complained of political interference and resigned. It was a debacle.

When we met, Rigoberta told me about her efforts and the entrenched obstacles she and other human rights activists faced. She asked me to mention her work when I visited the Guatemalan Congress. My voice could give her cause momentum—and perhaps protect her from retribution. After all, it was just months since Bishop Gerardi had been killed.

Her words stunned me. The idea that a mention from me could be that meaningful—that it could potentially be the difference between life and death—was hard to process. I had been First Lady for nearly six years. I flew on Air Force One, dined with kings and queens, and was constantly surrounded by armed guards. Yet none of that drove home for me the gravity of the role I occupied in the world like that conversation in Guatemala. I could feel the responsibility pressing down on my shoulders. At the same time, I was lifted up. Here was a woman who had endured so much, had persevered through unimaginable hardship, and she was totally undaunted. Yes, I had problems. But if she could stay focused on the all-important fight for human rights, then so could I. And if I could use what power I had to help, then that's what I would do.

The next day, I talked with lawmakers about Rigoberta and the hard work of truth and reconciliation. "You also have the opportunity to teach the world that you cannot have a lasting peace without strengthening the rule of law and ensuring justice and security for all citizens of your nation," I told the Guatemalan Congress, adding, "There is no greater tribute to Bishop Gerardi than to see justice done, not only in his case but in every case, and impunity rejected throughout the country."

Rigoberta's words stayed with me. Over the years that followed, I had similar conversations with other women on the dangerous front lines of democracy. In 1999, the Belarusian human rights activist Vera Stremkovskaya asked to take a photo with me. Her work exposing the abuses of the Lukashenko regime (the same dictator that Sviatlana Tsikhanouskaya is still opposing today) had put a target on her back. She hoped that a picture with me—physical proof that the international community had its eye on her—might provide some measure of protection. "That picture will be my bulletproof vest," she said.

Alexei Navalny's death tragically demonstrated that even intense global scrutiny cannot deter every reprisal, but it is true that most authoritarian regimes prefer to commit their crimes behind a veil of secrecy. They "disappear" dissidents and silence critics when they think no one's paying attention, when the world isn't watching and there will be no consequences. That's one reason I've tried to put a spotlight on as many heroic women as I can.

Before a speech at Tina Brown's Women in the World Summit in 2012, I was thrilled to be introduced by Meryl Streep, one of my favorite actresses of all time. She talked about meeting some of those women, and I was absolutely bowled over by what she said: "Women from all over the world said the same thing," Meryl reported: "I'm alive because [Hillary] came to my village, put her arm around me, and had a photograph taken together. I'm alive because she went on our local TV and talked about my work, and now they're afraid to kill me. I'm alive because she came to my country and she talked to our leaders, because I heard her speak, because I read about her."

I often don't know how much I've actually helped, but I do know that I've been humbled by the brave women who have risked their lives to meet with me, tell me their stories, and urge me to keep up the fight. Like the Iraqi women who waited for hours to talk with me in Baghdad in 2005, ignoring the dangers that came with being out after curfew because they wanted me to know that their country was falling apart and U.S. policy was failing. I also know that my life is richer and my spirit is stronger because of all the women I've met and worked with over the years. Whatever inspiration I've managed to give them, they've given me so much more in return.

The day after I embraced Yulia Navalnaya in Munich, I sat down with Sviatlana Tsikhanouskaya and three other remarkable women dissidents for a discussion about resistance and resilience: The crusading Filipino journalist Maria Ressa won the Nobel Peace Prize for her work exposing corruption and campaigning for freedom of the press. Zin Mar Aung is a leader of Myanmar's democratic government-in-exile and is part of the rebellion opposing her country's military junta. I first met Zin Mar Aung when I visited Myanmar, formerly called Burma, in 2011, at the start of a brief experiment with freedom and democracy that was tragically cut short by the military in 2021. I had also met and been impressed by the exiled Iranian journalist and activist Masih Alinejad, who is part of the movement resisting the Islamic Republic's brutal repression of women and whose voice the regime has tried to silence. The panel was called "Rebels with a Cause."

I was glad that world leaders in Munich would hear from these women, because while their stories are different, they share powerful insights about what it takes to defend democracy and defeat dictatorship. We were all still absorbing the tragic news of Navalny's death in Russia, and the reality that all these women—and so many more around the world—live under the constant threat of violence was inescapable.

"My husband has been in prison for four years, and in the last year he's been kept incommunicado. I don't know if he is alive," Sviatlana said. "Even his lawyer is not able to visit him. Letters are not delivered. My children ask me every day when they are going to see their daddy."

"My family is on the run. All of my family's property has been seized by the military junta," said Zin Mar Aung. "It's like this for everyone who has participated in the civil disobedience movement against military rule. Many suffer more than me. But the only thing I would like to underscore with you is resilience. Resilience is the symbol of our revolution."

These were not idle words. In 1998, Zin Mar Aung was a university student protesting against the ruling junta. She was arrested after reading a pro-democracy poem at a rally in Yangon (formerly Rangoon). She was imprisoned for eleven years, nine in solitary confinement, and not even allowed to read books. She emerged unbroken and even more determined to continue the struggle for democracy. Zin Mar Aung started a new organization to help other women who had been political prisoners rebuild their lives and advocated for the rights of women and ethnic minorities. When the country started opening up, Zin Mar Aung ran for parliament. The experiment with democracy was tenuous but exciting. On my first visit, in November 2011, there were just flickers of progress. By late 2012, when I visited with President Obama, Yangon felt like a different city. Crowds jammed the streets as we drove by. Children waved American flags. People were starting to believe they could be free, that they could finally live in a "normal" country. I wish it had lasted.

"Half of Myanmar's population is under the age of thirty," Zin Mar Aung said. "They saw a promising future for themselves, during our so-called democratic transition. And they are determined not to let the military take that future away from them."

In Myanmar, nonviolent protests have given way to an armed rebellion. Zin Mar Aung does not carry a gun herself. She's the foreign minister for the democratic government-in-exile. But she is clear-eyed about the need for armed resistance. "We faced the choice to either succumb to Min Aung Hlaing's ugly dictatorship or to defend ourselves and our belief in a better future," Zin Mar Aung explained. She later added, "Dictators don't understand the language of nonviolence. The only thing that they understand is force."

That's a tough statement but one born out of brutal experience. I'm not ready to give up on the idea of nonviolence, but I understand where she's coming from. Sometimes, you really do have to fight for freedom.

I marvel at the resilience of all these women and how much they've had to overcome. "In order to keep doing my job, I had to be okay with going to jail for over a century," Maria said. She posed this question to the audience: "What are you willing to sacrifice for the truth, for the facts, for your own individual battle for integrity, for your values?"

That spirit is how Maria has persevered as a journalist in the face of decades of intimidation and harassment in the Philippines. She came of age as the People Power Revolution was toppling the corrupt regime of Ferdinand Marcos. Working for CNN, Maria exposed efforts to sabotage the Philippines' fragile democracy, including multiple coup attempts. She co-founded her own news organization, called Rappler, and provided indispensable coverage of President Rodrigo Duterte's reign of terror after he came to power in 2016. Duterte claimed to be cracking down on illicit drugs but acted like a dictator, and thousands of bodies piled up in mass graves. Maria was repeatedly threatened, arrested twice, and accused of "cyber-libel"— in other words, she was telling the truth about a violent would-be autocrat. Today, Duterte is gone, but he's been replaced by Marcos's son as president and his own daughter as vice president. As Maria put it during our conversation in Munich, "We've moved from hell to purgatory."

Hell is also how I'd describe life in Iran for many women. "In Iran, women [are] facing rape in prison. They're being gassed, they're being blinded, just because of demanding freedom, equality, dignity," Masih told us. She was exiled in 2009 and has been forced to dodge kidnapping and assassination attempts by Iran's agents. They can't stand that she dares speak out against the theocratic regime's brutal treatment of women, including by collecting and distributing videos shared by thousands of women on the ground in Iran.

In 2022, the Iranian morality police arrested a twenty-two-year-old woman, Mahsa Amini, for allegedly wearing her headscarf improperly. She was beaten and pushed into a police van, and her family was told she was being taken to a women's "re-education" class at a nearby detention center. Just thirty minutes later, she was taken to a hospital in Tehran with clear signs of beating and torture. She fell into a coma and died three days later at the hospital. Protests broke out almost immediately. Women marched in the streets with their hair uncovered and took videos of themselves setting hijabs on fire. They chanted "Woman, Life, Freedom." The regime responded with assault rifles and submachine guns. Many women were arrested and subjected to sexual violence and torture. From New York, Masih supported the protest movement by publishing video evidence and forcing the world to pay attention to the crimes of the Islamic Republic.

As we spoke in Munich, Masih asked a young woman named Kosar Eftekhari to stand up. Kosar had been shot in the face by Iran's morality police because she dared to remove her hijab during a protest. She was blinded in one eye. Like other women in the resistance, she reached out to Masih to help share her story.

"She sent videos to me saying, 'Masih, tell the rest of the world that this regime can take my eye, they can take our life, but not our hope,'" Masih explained. "That's why I brought her here." She looked at the world leaders gathered in the room. "We don't want to cry, we want you to help us to make our oppressors cry. I feel the pain of my sisters on stage. Sviatlana, my brother was in prison. And millions of Iranians are still in prison—a bigger prison called Iran. Zin Mar Aung, I feel your pain when you say that the people of Myanmar are even braver than you. We feel guilty talking about ourselves. Although we feel pain and suffering from being away from our families. We don't even know what they're going to do with our families. I don't even know when I'm going to hug my family."

I could feel the solidarity among these women. They came from different backgrounds and spoke different languages, but all of them shared the same struggle. And it's our struggle, too. As Zin Mar Aung said, democracies must "unite and be one voice against authoritarianism" or we risk losing our freedoms, too.

As the poem says, "Too many women in too many countries speak the same language of silence." But not these women. They are shouting from the rooftops—and we need to listen.

It can be hard in the hustle and bustle of our daily lives to hold on to that clarity of purpose. Conflicts on the other side of the world can feel awfully far away when you have your hands full just getting through the day. Casualty figures from distant battlefields, reports of human rights abuses in unfamiliar places, the stories of women you'll never meet enduring persecution you'll never face—we care, but we forget.

In Munich, Maria quoted the Czech novelist Milan Kundera, who said, "The struggle of man against power is the struggle of memory against forgetting." We must remember. We have to stay in the fight.

As I look back on my career, I owe so much to the courageous women I've met and learned from. I'll never forget what they've taught me about the world, about the human spirit, and about myself.

DO ALL THE GOOD

My grandson Aidan bounded up the steps of the sanctuary of the church my daughter's family attends, then clutched his mother's hand as Chelsea read from the pulpit. It was the morning of Christmas Eve 2023, and the church was decked out for the holiday. Behind Chelsea and Aidan, the choir's red robes matched a bank of poinsettias. Beside them were four lit Advent candles representing hope, love, joy, and peace. A fifth candle, the Christ candle, was waiting expectantly.

"The images of violence and destruction in the world are often before our minds and before our eyes. It seems that nothing changes as the years pass," Chelsea began. "And then we hear the words—" Just then Charlotte climbed up the steps to join her mother and brother. Chelsea paused and added with a smile, "And we hear the footsteps of small children," and then continued, "—the words of the prophet Isaiah who shows a radically different path to liberation, peace, love, and justice."

What a joyful day to be a grandmother. And how blessed I felt to be watching from the pews. For me, faith and family have always been entwined. I am a Methodist both by birth and by choice. I was born into a Methodist family—parents, grandparents, great-grandparents, going all the way back to the coalfields of Wales and Newcastle, where the church's founder, John Wesley, preached to miners, farmers, and factory workers. My mother taught Sunday school at our church in Park Ridge, Illinois. She said it was because she wanted to make sure my brothers showed up. But as I grew up I came to understand how faith had sustained her through a difficult life and why it was so important to her that we kids share in it. She made sure the church was a significant part of our lives. We went to Methodist Youth Fellowship on Sunday nights, church activities on Wednesday nights, and summer Bible school. I was even on the altar guild, cleaning and preparing before services.

As I looked at Charlotte holding her mother's hand, for a moment I was a little girl again watching my mother read us Bible stories, watching my father praying by his bed. He was gruff—a former foot-ball player, a Navy man, a proud self-made businessman—but there he was, humble on his knees before God every night. It made a big impression on me.

"Hope comes with a mighty vision of the end of violence and op-pression through the birth of this tiny human being," Chelsea contin-ued. "The prophet reminds us the world cannot be changed by power and might, but through a helpless baby, innocent and vulnerable."

How can it be that my baby is now a wonderful mother herself? It feels like just ten minutes ago that I held "this tiny human being" in my arms for the first time. *We hear the footsteps of small children.* I wished my mom could have been there beside me in the pew, watch-ing Chelsea guiding and teaching her children just as Mom once guided and taught me and my brothers.

I thought back to another wintery Sunday morning. It was not long after Bill's first inauguration in 1993, and there had been a major snowstorm in Washington. At least ten inches piled up in the streets, and much of the city shut down. We were going a little stir-crazy in the White House, which didn't yet feel like home, so I said, "Let's go to church." After all, we had gone to church as a family, both to Bill's Immanuel Baptist Church and to First United Methodist Church in Little Rock. (Once, during the "children's moment" at First United, all the kids were asked what they wanted to get us moms for Mother's Day, and Chelsea said, "Life insurance." After the congregation began to laugh, she said she thought it meant I would live forever.) I knew that Chelsea, almost a teenager, missed her home and her friends in

Little Rock. She missed First United, too. She didn't think she would find any place as special in this new city, where it seemed there were cameras and crowds everywhere. But I thought it was worth a shot. So the three of us set out on foot into the deep snow and a biting wind, followed by some bewildered Secret Service agents, to walk eight blocks from the White House to Foundry United Methodist Church.

It was the start of a wonderful chapter in our lives. At Foundry, we discovered a community where we could worship, study, contemplate, be of service, get good pastoral advice from its pastor, Reverend Philip Wogaman, and step outside the hurly-burly of life in the White House. When we were there, we were not the First Family; we were just our family. We cherished that time. I particularly valued how the congregation embraced Chelsea and how she in turn embraced the church.

Now, all these years later, Chelsea and her husband, Marc, who is Jewish, have decided to raise their children in both traditions, so they go to both Sunday school and Hebrew school and celebrate both Christian and Jewish holidays.

"God help us to make this dream our dream every day," Chelsea read. "This morning we light the Christ candle, remembering Jesus, born in a humble stable long ago, yet born in us. A child is born today." Then she lifted Aidan up so he could reach the microphone.

"A child is born to us," he said.

I've never been one to wear my faith on my sleeve. I inherited a certain midwestern reticence about that (and a few other things, as you might have noticed). For me, faith has never been something to brag about or exploit, even though you see that a lot in politics. But that doesn't mean it's not important to me. Quite the opposite: My faith has sustained me, informed me, saved me, chided me, and challenged me. I don't know who I would be or where I would have ended up without it.

My parents raised me and my brothers in the Methodist tradition of "faith in action." At church, we were taught to be "doers of the word, and not hearers only." That meant rolling up our sleeves and being of service. And not grudgingly. We had to be, as Saint Paul put it, generous and diligent and cheerful in our service.

I understand and respect that some people believe that faith is about one's personal salvation and a direct relationship with God and should not be sullied by the life of the streets, by the challenges of those who are the lost, the last, and the least. But I was taught to believe that is precisely where our faith is most needed. There's an old saying often attributed to Saint Francis of Assisi: "Preach the Gospel always and if necessary, use words."

My faith gave me both the great gift of personal salvation and the great obligation of social gospel, to serve and give back to others. I spent a lot of time when I was growing up trying to work out for myself the balance between those things. I have always appreciated that in Methodism, we are invited to reason and work through what faith means to us and how we can live it in our daily lives. I'm someone who needs to believe with both my head and my heart. The balance I came to early on is rooted in James in the New Testament: "What does it profit, my brethren, if someone says he has faith but does not have works? Can faith save him? If a brother or sister is naked and destitute of daily food, and one of you says to them, 'Depart in peace, be warmed and filled,' but you do not give them the things which are needed for the body, what does it profit? . . . For as the body without the spirit is dead, so faith without works is dead also." I need both; nurturing my personal faith gives me the energy and strength to go out in the world and try to do good.

The youth minister at our church in Park Ridge, Reverend Don Jones, had a profound effect on my spiritual and intellectual development. He and my mother made sure I internalized the famous Methodist credo attributed to John Wesley: "Do all the good you can, by all the means you can, in all the ways you can, in all the places you can, at all the times you can, to all the people you can, as long as ever you can." Those words inspired generations of Methodists—including a lot of fantastic, fearless Methodist women—to take their faith out of the pews and into the streets, volunteering in hospitals, schools, and slums. For me, growing up in a comfortable middle-class suburb, it provided a sense of purpose and direction.

At different times in my life, different parts of the credo have loomed larger in my mind. When I was young and trying to decide what to do with my life, "do all the good" provided a guide. In 1970, as an intern for Marian Wright Edelman, I attended Senate hearings on the mistreatment of migrant farmworkers by large corporations and ran into several classmates from Yale Law School who had summer jobs at fancy white-shoe law firms. They told me they were learning how to buff up a corporate client's dented reputation. For a moment I imagined what it would be like to spend my career doing that kind of work. Then I thought, *Do all the good.* I told them the best way for their clients to improve their image would be to treat their workers better.

Instead of corporate law, I decided in law school to focus on how the law could better protect children and families. I started consulting with the medical staff at Yale New Haven Hospital about child abuse, a problem that in the early 1970s was just starting to be acknowledged. I accompanied doctors on their rounds and saw children whose parents had beaten or burned them, left them alone for days in squalid apartments, or failed or refused to seek necessary medical care. One father who brought in his badly injured three-year-old claimed that he had beaten the boy to "get the devil out of him." I was horrified. Could I stomach being a children's advocate in a society that allows kids to be abused and exploited like this? *Do all the good.*

That's what propelled me to a life of service, doing all the good I could in all the ways I could. As Marian often said, "Service is the rent we pay for living."

Later, when I became First Lady, senator, and secretary of state, my horizons were wider, and there were more ways to do good and in more places. I traveled the world, speaking out for human rights and women's rights, working to make peace and fight poverty. As secretary, I visited 112 countries. People would ask me: *Why are you spending your time worrying about an LGBTQ+ activist in Uganda or helping women in India get cleaner cookstoves? Why are you going to places like little Togo, in West Africa, where no secretary of state had ever been before?*

In all the ways you can, in all the places you can.

These days, I find myself thinking more and more about the end of Wesley's famous phrase: do all the good you can . . . *as long as ever you can.* I may no longer be a high government official. I can't write legislation or sign treaties. But I can still try to do a lot of good. You've read about some of it in this book. Teaching young people. Helping Afghan women escape persecution. Working with women bearing the brunt of the climate crisis. Supporting candidates and causes on the front lines of democracy. Trying every day to be a generous friend and a devoted mother, grandmother, aunt, and wife. I have no intention of slowing down. There's no retirement from doing good, no statute of limitations on our call to service.

In Galatians 6:9, we are told: "Let us not grow weary while doing good, for in due season we shall reap if we do not lose heart." My faith is a big part of how I shake off weariness and stave off despair; it keeps me engaged and in the fight. And throughout my life, it's sustained me in difficult times. Faith is what I look to for guidance, for wisdom, for the strength to forgive, to ask for forgiveness, to pick myself up and start over again when I have fallen short.

I've often taken comfort in the wisdom of the mid-twentieth-century theologian Paul Tillich. I remember sitting in my church's basement in Park Ridge as Don Jones read aloud from Tillich about grace: "Grace strikes us when we are in great pain and restlessness. . . .

Sometimes at that moment a wave of light breaks into our darkness, and it is as though a voice were saying: 'You are accepted.'" Years later, when my marriage was in crisis, I called Don. He said to read Tillich. I read it again after the 2016 election. Tillich says grace is reconciliation—it's "being able to look frankly into the eyes of another"; it's "understanding each other's words"—"not merely the literal meaning of the words, but also that which lies behind them, even when they are harsh or angry." He says grace happens. Or it does not happen. Be patient, be strong, keep going, and let grace come when it can.

I try to practice what the Dutch priest Henri Nouwen calls the "discipline of gratitude." That means making the choice to not just be grateful for the good things in life—that's easy—but also to be grateful for the hard things, too. To be grateful even for our flaws. Nouwen writes:

> I can choose to be grateful even when my emotions and feelings are still steeped in hurt and resentment. . . . I can choose to speak about goodness and beauty, even when my inner eye still looks for someone to accuse or something to call ugly. I can choose to listen to the voices that forgive and to look at the faces that smile, even while I still hear words of revenge and see grimaces of hatred.

Forgiveness—to forgive and to ask for forgiveness—is tough. It is not easy to let go of wounds, slights, and disappointments. It is human nature to look for people to blame—and sometimes they deserve it. It is human nature to blame ourselves. Sometimes we deserve it, too. In Arkansas, I used to teach a Sunday school lesson about forgiving ourselves. We all carry these enormous burdens around. Blame. Anger. Shame. And I've found one of the great gifts of faith is being able to let them go. It doesn't mean that you forget. It doesn't mean that you don't have to make amends. But if you begin to forgive yourself, then you can begin to forgive others.

Saint Paul reminds us that we all see through a glass darkly because of our limitations and imperfections. It's humbling. It's also comforting. Perfection is out of reach. It's because of our limitations and imperfections that we must reach out beyond ourselves, to God and to one another. Faith—the assurance of things hoped for and the conviction of things unseen—always requires a leap.

A few years after we started attending services at Foundry, it became what was called a "reconciling congregation," meaning it publicly welcomed all people regardless of gender or sexual identity. This only added to our joy in being part of the Foundry community. It felt in keeping with Foundry's commitment to "love God, love each other, change the world."

Unfortunately, not everyone felt the same way. There were—and are—a lot of Methodists around the country and across the world who took a hard-line approach on gender issues. In 1972, as part of a broader conservative backlash to the social movements of the 1960s, the General Conference of the United Methodist Church, which periodically gathers representatives from congregations around the world to make important decisions about church governance, voted to add anti-gay language to the *Book of Discipline*, Methodism's rule book, including "We do not condone the practice of homosexuality and consider it incompatible with Christian teaching" and "We do not recommend marriage between two persons of the same sex." In 1984, the General Conference also banned gay clergy. A prohibition on using church funds to "promote acceptance of homosexuality" meant that congregations were barred from even supporting suicide prevention efforts for LGBTQ+ youth.

Foundry was part of a progressive movement within the United Methodist Church to push back on these moves and embrace a more inclusive, welcoming church. Over the years there were big debates whenever Methodists got together, with passionate disagreements about the right path forward. Similar debates were playing out in other mainline Protestant denominations as well.

I was glad to be part of a reconciling congregation because I saw it as a natural extension of the mission to heal, love, and serve. I respected that people of goodwill and good faith could see these questions differently, but I kept coming back to the fact that we're called to humility, mercy, and radical inclusion. The book of Micah tells us "to do justice, to love kindness, and to walk humbly with your God." And in Hebrews we are told, "Let us not neglect meeting together—as some have made a habit—but let us encourage one another." Jesus befriended prostitutes and cleansed lepers. So I just couldn't see how we could close the church doors to people seeking fellowship. We may look and love differently, but "we have different gifts, according to the grace given to each of us."

It pained me to see the United Methodist Church riven by disagreement. For me, faith has always been deeply personal but also communal. The institution matters. I want a strong, vibrant, *united* Methodist Church. But over the past several years, it's been united in name only. As progressive voices within the church gained momentum—and as gay rights became more widely accepted in society—anti-gay traditionalists dug in. Conservative American congregations threatened to secede and join traditionalist congregations in Africa and elsewhere to form a separate church. There was ugly precedent for this kind of schism. In the run-up to the Civil War, the Methodist Church in America split between the North and South over the issue of slavery. It took until 1939 to come back together.

In 2019, a closely divided General Conference reaffirmed bans on gay clergy and same-sex marriages and actually increased penalties for violations. The conference also approved a process to allow congregations to leave the United Methodist Church. Despite their victories, many conservative congregations opted to take advantage of this provision. About a quarter of American congregations ultimately departed.

Secession prompted difficult legal and financial questions concerning church property, which technically belonged to the United Methodist Church rather than local congregations. Given how high passions were running on all sides, this proved difficult to resolve. I suggested to Tom Bickerton, then the bishop in New York, that he should talk with my friend Ken Feinberg, a lawyer and mediator who had served as special master for the 9/11 Victim Compensation Fund and other delicate negotiations. Ken agreed to work with a committee of Methodist leaders free of charge and help them come to an equitable resolution. I was pleased but not surprised to hear that Ken managed the process with his characteristic deftness, and in early 2020, the committee proposed a Protocol of Reconciliation & Grace through Separation. "He kept us at the table when walking away seemed imminent," Bishop LaTrelle Easterling said. "He defused tense moments with just the right balance of humor and hard truths."

Before Ken's protocol could be voted on by the General Conference, the COVID-19 pandemic intervened. It was not until the spring of 2024 that Methodists from around the world gathered again to grapple with the future of the church. This time, with many of the most conservative members absent because their churches had already left the denomination, the conference moved in a different direction. Delegates voted overwhelmingly to eliminate the anti-gay provisions added in the '70s and '80s. They blessed a new organizational structure that would give different regions more flexibility to set policies in line with local values and interests. The conference also declared that no one would be excluded based on their "race, color, gender, national origin, ability, age, marital status, or economic condition." Altogether, it was a tremendous sea change representing a more inclusive, tolerant church.

I followed the developments at the General Conference closely and rejoiced at the outcome. I felt that we Methodists were finally living up to our responsibility to "incline our ears to wisdom and apply our hearts to understanding." I am proud that my grandchildren will know a church that welcomes all, loves all, and serves all.

A few days later, Bill and I joined Chelsea for a Sunday afternoon service at Park Avenue United Methodist Church. It was a celebration of the retirement of Reverend Cathy Gilliard, who led the church for more than thirteen years, and drew a wide range of distinguished clergy. We listened as they spoke about Reverend Gilliard and also the momentous decisions of the General Conference. Reverend Stephen Bauman of Christ Church UMC in New York said it was the most important General Conference in half a century and "a glimpse of what lies ahead."

His words echoed the theme of the sermon that day, delivered by Reverend Willie James Jennings from Yale Divinity School, who had taught Reverend Gilliard at Duke University Divinity School during her mid-career shift to ministry. He spoke about experiencing "glimpses of God." It can be easy to fall into despair in this broken world, Reverend Jennings said. We see so much hate and violence; we face so many crises. It's not hard to see why many people today lack hope. But God through Christ and the Holy Spirit promises something better, Reverend Jennings reminded us. Just as God lifted the veil from Moses's eyes for a brief moment in Exodus 33, Jesus's life in the New Testament is a series of glimpses into a promised future of peace, healing, and inclusion.

As the choir sang an energetic rendition of "Goodness of God," I sat thinking about "glimpses of what lies ahead," for the world and for us. I have reached a place in my life where many are content to "sit under their own vine and under their own fig tree," and I love playing the proud matriarch surrounded by grandchildren. Yet I feel the pull of an active faith and the push to "do all the good" as keenly today as ever before. There's no time to sit still or grow weary.

Faith remains for me a great gift and a great challenge. I hope it always will.

STRONGER TOGETHER

Most mornings find Bill and me lingering in bed, on our phones playing Spelling Bee. That's the *New York Times'* online game where you rearrange seven letters to form as many words as possible. After a few minutes, Bill will sidle over to compare lists. "Have you found 'pizzazz'?" he'll ask. "Oooh, 'pizzazz'!" I'll say. After a few more minutes, he'll call out, "Queen Bee!" That's the highest score, when you find every possible word. "Still working on it," I'll reply, wondering, even after a half century at his side, how he does it so fast. We've been together a little longer than we've been in politics, both of us going to work for George McGovern's 1972 campaign against Richard Nixon a year after we met at Yale Law School in the spring of 1971. The firestorms of national politics—the relentless pace, sky-high stakes, scrutiny, and criticism—can as easily destroy a marriage as forge an indestructible bond. Well, we're still here, living, laughing, loving, and pursuing our life's work—together.

Like all marriages, ours took work. Lots of work. Unlike most, ours existed on a bright spotlighted stage. You know the public stories but not the private ones, not the everyday joys and setbacks. Not the special challenges of public life. Being a political spouse is an act of sublimation. You can say "two for the price of one," but there can only be one Queen Bee at a time. Especially if your partner is president of the United States, the pecking order is always clear. That was the life I chose and I never regretted it. And to his credit, when it was my turn to take center stage and reach for the presidency, Bill embraced his role in the wings with enthusiasm. He was my biggest booster and most trusted advisor. Nobody believed in me more or worked harder to help me win. When I lost, nobody felt the blow more deeply. He still does. As he has been polishing up his latest memoir, *Citizen*, I can see him losing sleep every time he revisits the chapter on 2016 and has to relive those events.

But he lost much more than sleep. Even today, I am angry and carry a lot of guilt about what my run for president cost Bill.

Let me rewind. In February 1998, I went to the World Economic Forum in Davos, Switzerland, and delivered a speech to an audience of powerful CEOs, philanthropists, and politicians. I wanted them to think more expansively about what it takes to build a healthy society—and how they could help do it.

For too long, American politics had been stuck in a reductive binary. On the Left, there was still a belief that big government programs were the answer to nearly every problem. On the Right, conservatives demonized government and claimed that unregulated markets were a magic solution to just about everything. Bill won two presidential elections and presided over a historic economic boom by pioneering a third way. He said government and business needed to work together. I went to Davos to highlight another important dimension of this approach.

I argued that a healthy society is like a three-legged stool. An open and dynamic market economy is one leg. An effective and accountable democratic government is a second leg. And the third, too often overlooked in political and policy debates, is a vibrant civil society. "It is the stuff of life," I said. "It is the family, it is the religious belief and spirituality that guide us. It is the voluntary association of which we are a member. It is the art and culture that makes our spirits soar." Instead of pitting government against business or trying to solve problems in silos, we needed all three legs of the stool.

"We are not stable if we are only on one leg, no matter how strong the economy might be, no matter how strong a government might be. We are also not stable if we rest merely on two legs of the stool," I said. "Rather we need to see the independence and connection among the economy, the government and the civil society." I wanted the powerful men and women (but mostly men) in Davos to think more deeply about how they could work with and empower activists and non-governmental organizations, community organizers and labor leaders, artists, academics, and scientists. We could unlock so much potential if we just got the right people around the table to think creatively about solving complex problems.

That metaphor of the sturdy three-legged stool has stuck with me in the decades since. And as secretary of state, I made it a priority to defend and promote civil society all over the world.

The other highlight of that visit to the Swiss Alps was the fantastic skiing. With Secret Service agents following gamely behind, I spent three and a half glorious hours flying down the snowy alpine slopes. There were no trees, just wide-open trail, stunning views, and a lovely cup of hot chocolate waiting at the bottom. It's been way too long since I last put on a pair of skis. The fear of falling crept up on me with age, but I still treasure the carefree memory.

When I got home, I told Bill about my trip and suggested he think about going to Davos himself at some point. Two years later, he did, becoming the first sitting U.S. president to attend the conference. Bill was energized by the conversations he had at the World Economic Forum and became a regular attendee once he was out of the White House and had launched the Clinton Foundation. But something was missing. "All these people leave Davos every year full of energy. They want to do something, they don't know what to do," Bill told me over dinner one winter evening in the early 2000s, when he had just returned from Switzerland. "They're all asking: What's my assignment?"

I could see a plan was forming. I know that look. I've seen it a million times. When he latches on to an idea—especially an opportunity to solve an old problem with new thinking—he can barely sit still until he sets it in motion. I love watching Bill's brain work. It's so different from mine. Though he rarely plays the saxophone anymore, he's still a jazz musician at heart, leaping from idea to idea with brilliant improvisation. I am more practical and linear. When we go for walks, Bill prefers to wander. In our town of Chappaqua, he stops to talk with people, compliment good-looking dogs, and engage in long conversations about politics inside Starbucks or the Village Market or on the street. If he's alone walking, he'll tell me later about whom he met and what was on their minds. I enjoy that as well, but I usually prefer to go to the Rockefeller State Park Preserve and walk for an hour as quickly as I can. When I get home, I will have gotten my heart rate up but won't have as much to share, unless I saw a coyote or an eagle.

Thinking out loud over dinner, Bill said there was too much talk but too little action at Davos and other places where the global elite gathered. Too many CEOs saw these gatherings as a chance to network and do business deals instead of as an opportunity to make concrete commitments to take on urgent global challenges. And even when they did, like Marc Benioff's commitment to the One Trillion Trees Initiative, they are the exception, not the rule. There had to be a better way to harness all the energy, leadership, and resources of the private sector and civil society and channel them into measurable concrete actions.

In September 2005, Bill and the Clinton Foundation launched the Clinton Global Initiative (CGI) to coincide with the annual meeting of the UN General Assembly every September in New York. Everyone who attended CGI's annual meeting—world leaders, business executives, philanthropists, activists—would be expected to make a commitment to take a specific action to help solve an important global problem.

It was a simple yet transformative idea that would reinvent philanthropy for the twenty-first century. By 2023, CGI's commitment-keeping had improved the lives and livelihoods of more than five hundred million people in 180 countries, with more than ten thousand groups, companies, governments, and individuals making four thousand commitments to action on everything from solar panels to clean water to the gift of hearing aids to deaf children. Nearly one million doses of lifesaving naloxone have been distributed to schools and community organizations through the Overdose Response Network.

CGI members raised $500 million to support small businesses, farms, schools, and hospitals in Haiti after the devastating earthquake in 2010. They sent five hundred tons of medical supplies and equipment to West Africa to help fight the Ebola epidemic in 2014. They helped support more than one hundred thousand new STEM (science, technology, engineering, and mathematics) teachers in the United States and brought together unions and pension funds to create America's largest private infrastructure bank. Water.org, the nonprofit that Matt Damon and Gary White founded at CGI, has increased access to safe drinking water for sixty-three million people around the world. In 2023, the CGI Ukraine Action Network launched partnerships to channel desperately needed resources to humanitarian groups on the ground amid Russia's continuing onslaught. The list goes on and on.

I love going to CGI meetings and watching plans and partnerships come together in real time. For example, in 2014, I helped organize a coalition of educators, community leaders, workforce training organizations, and businesses from across the country focused on the challenge of youth unemployment. Nearly six million young Americans between the ages of sixteen and twenty-four were out of school and out of work. For those who hadn't graduated from college or even high school in the years following the Great Recession, most doors just wouldn't open, no matter how hard they knocked. So, job training was crucial. But too many state workforce development systems and nonprofit training programs weren't connected directly with local employers, and as a result young people often weren't learning the skills that businesses were actually looking for. This was a coordination problem that seemed solvable. At our CGI America conference in Denver, nonprofits and employers from a wide range of industries—from high tech to hospitality, from financial services to retail to manufacturing—made specific and measurable commitments to do better. They pledged to connect young people to training, jobs, and mentoring opportunities.

Those partnerships, and the CGI model more broadly, were the three-legged stool in action. Business and labor leaders, nonprofits, and government officials all working together, bringing their unique experience and expertise to bear in solving common problems. Too often over the years, I've seen well-meaning people and organizations take on big challenges but circumscribe whom they will work with based on ideology. They won't work with business, or with government, or with people they disagree with politically. That's fine if you care more about looking pure than delivering results. But I know from experience that bringing together all three legs of the stool is often the only way to get things done. And that's what I care about. Networks of creative cooperation can solve problems better, faster, and at a lower cost than any one sector can alone. There's a reason my slogan in 2016 was "Stronger Together." By drawing on diverse talents and perspectives, we can achieve more than any of us can do alone—and more than we can do by working just with people like ourselves. This isn't "let's hold hands and feel better about ourselves"; it's "let's roll up our sleeves and work together to make positive differences in other people's lives." Talking together is nice; working together is better. That's the idea at the heart of CGI and its "community of doers."

Bill had another big idea. I could hear it in his voice, all the way from Rome. It was April 2005, and Bill was attending the funeral of Pope John Paul II at the Vatican, but his mind was far from the marble and gold of Saint Peter's Basilica. He was thinking about health clinics in sub-Saharan Africa, where about twenty-five million people were living with HIV/AIDS, including two million children, but the price of lifesaving drug treatments remained largely out of reach.

Wherever we are in the world, Bill and I always make a point of checking in at the end of the day, just to hear each other's voice. He'll be in a motorcade in Malawi or a meeting in Malaysia and turn to his aides and ask, "What time is it where Hillary is? I don't want to miss her." The phone will ring, and I'll hear his voice from halfway across the globe. For a moment, I'm back in New Haven, and this tall, handsome young man is holding my hand as we wander through the Yale University Art Gallery on our first date. I'm back in the living room of the little red-brick house in Fayetteville, saying "I do," as Arkansas sunlight pours through the bay window. Bill and I have been married since 1975, and there's still no one I want to talk to more than him. About politics, public policy, and our foundation projects, yes. But also about the streaming series we're watching or the books we trade back and forth. Or the funny new game Aidan and Jasper invented or how Charlotte might like to celebrate her birthday. Tales from our adventures in grandparenting are an especially hot topic. If one of us sees Chelsea, Marc, and the kids when the other is traveling, a thorough report is expected. Bill and I have built a full life together. Sharing that life now—all the little moments that bring a smile—is a gift only the passage of time can give.

On that phone call from Rome, I listened intently as Bill shared the thoughts racing through his head. He had just flown across the Atlantic on Air Force One with President George W. Bush so they could pay their respects at the pope's funeral. Bill is always restless on long flights. I like to sleep, but he keeps everyone up playing cards, telling stories, or chewing over some complex policy question. On this flight, he had used his time with Bush to talk about an issue near to both their hearts: HIV/AIDS.

At the 2002 International AIDS Conference in Barcelona, Nelson Mandela had talked with Bill about the urgent need to increase the availability of HIV/AIDS drugs in Africa and across the world. Bill had recently established the Clinton Foundation and immediately decided this should be a priority for the new organization. He began negotiating agreements with drugmakers and governments to lower medicine prices dramatically and raising the money to pay for it. The Clinton Foundation created the Clinton HIV/AIDS Initiative (now the Clinton Health Access Initiative, or CHAI) and sent experts to improve quality and increase production at generic drug factories in India and elsewhere. Around the same time, Bush also decided to make the fight against HIV/AIDS his administration's signature global health initiative. He launched the President's Emergency Plan for AIDS Relief (PEPFAR), one of the most impressive and effective examples of American global leadership in decades. But there was a problem: PEPFAR funded only expensive brand-name medications. Even with Big Pharma's discount, low-income countries couldn't afford to treat everybody, and PEPFAR's partners, mostly in Africa, couldn't use U.S. aid to buy cheaper generic drugs, keeping prices up and access down.

During the flight to Rome, President Bush asked Bill about the foundation's AIDS work. Bill was full of compliments for PEPFAR— it really is an amazing program—but he also said, "You know, you're wasting a lot of money paying way too much for drugs I can get you for much less." At the time, the Food and Drug Administration was testing only a few generic AIDS drugs, while there were many more available. Bush was worried that those generics were not as good as the more expensive brand names.

"So," Bill said, "I know you really want to save lives. This is the compassionate part of your commitment to compassionate conservatism. I know it's real."

"It is," Bush replied.

Bill proposed that if CHAI could marshal the evidence and win FDA approval for more generic drugs, Bush would then allow them to be bought with PEPFAR funds. Bush was skeptical but agreed.

On the ground in Rome, Bill's mind was racing with plans for how to get this done and what it would mean for millions of people around the world. I told him I thought it sounded fantastic—and important. *Go for it,* I said.

In the end, the FDA found nearly all the generic drugs—twenty-two out of twenty-four—to be safe and effective. President Bush was as good as his word, even though he probably took some heat from his backers in the pharmaceutical industry. CHAI then collaborated with drug manufacturers on the supply side and PEPFAR partner governments on the demand side to transition the market for HIV/AIDS treatments to a high-volume, low-cost model. It worked. Some twenty-one million people worldwide now have access to cheaper HIV/AIDS, tuberculosis, and malaria medications through CHAI. And not just *a little* cheaper. The initial price of medicine came down from $500 a year per person for generic drugs and $1,500 per person in the PEPFAR countries to $60 a person. PEPFAR quickly expanded the program from seven to fifteen countries, treating more than twice as many people for the same amount of money.

Bill and I have always been drawn to practical, everyday problems that impact people's daily lives—from dirty cookstoves that cause respiratory diseases to sugary sodas in schools that cause obesity—and pragmatic solutions that may be unglamorous but deliver meaningful results. That does not mean shying away from the hardest fights or transformative solutions, but it does mean a relentless focus on what can be done to actually make people's lives better as opposed to scoring rhetorical points, virtue signaling, or hoping for a "revolution" that may never arrive. This is how we both approached our time in government, and it's the spirit still driving the Clinton Foundation today.

Every marriage involves sacrifice. Building a shared life together means giving up some measure of independence. It means making your partner's cares and concerns your own—sometimes at the expense of your own. Partnership takes work. It can extract painful costs, but it also brings joy and emotional nourishment. Something lost, something gained.

Bill and I have been partners since day one. In law school, we teamed up in the Barristers' Union for moot court competitions. We'd stay up late researching cases and crafting arguments. Occasionally, he'd get distracted and launch into a story about his home in Arkansas, or the novel he'd just read, or a brilliant piece of music he couldn't get out of his head. I'd gently redirect us back to the law books spread out on the table. We made it to the finals of the competition, presenting the arguments we'd honed together to retired Supreme Court justice Abe Fortas.

I knew that marrying Bill would be like hitching a ride on a comet. Was I brave enough to take the leap? He thought that marrying me would be like planting an oak. It would root him and give him strength and resilience. He was certain it was the right choice.

We became partners in life, in parenthood, and in politics, too. A lot of people didn't understand that. Or chose not to. They were convinced our marriage was purely transactional. "It doesn't seem like a family—more like a merger," one Republican operative told the New York Times in 1992. I thought that said more about their own relationships than about ours. Was it so strange to share each other's passions and fuel each other's aspirations? I've always thought "love" was a verb as well as a noun, and that's proven true for us.

Bill has been my greatest champion since the moment we met. He never once asked me to put my career on hold for his. He never resented that I made more money than him or that my work and independence (keeping the name Rodham, for example) sometimes caused him political problems. He never once suggested that I bow to the critics and trim my sails. He always dared me to dream bigger. From the beginning, we've been in it together.

My run for president in 2016 exacted a toll that neither one of us saw coming. It still pains me. The Clinton Foundation was like Bill's second child. He poured his enormous energy and enthusiasm into building it. He got so much pleasure and satisfaction from seeing its impact on the world. All those people finally able to afford treatment for HIV/AIDS. Thousands of farmers in Malawi, Rwanda, and Tanzania going from subsistence to prosperity. More than thirty million American kids leading healthier lives because of the deal Bill struck to get sugary sodas out of school vending machines. The work kept him young. The results kept him happy. I could not have been prouder. And I loved that Chelsea joined him in this labor of love. She brought her expertise in public health and sharp management skills to help the foundation grow and professionalize. It was a family operation in the best possible way.

I expected that when I ran for president all our work over the years would be scrutinized and that right-wing media and political operatives would go on a fishing expedition looking for any hint of scandal. But the smear campaign that targeted the Clinton Foundation surprised even me. It didn't matter that independent watchdogs gave the Clinton Foundation top marks as a well-run philanthropy. CharityWatch gave it an A. Charity Navigator gave it four stars. GuideStar rated it platinum. None of that stopped the brutal partisan attacks or the gullible coverage in the press.

In retrospect, this was a clear case of the "vast right-wing conspiracy" in action. It was driven by a fake-news factory misleadingly called the Government Accountability Institute, which was founded by Trump advisor Steve Bannon and funded by the right-wing billionaire Robert Mercer—the same duo behind the toxic far-right propaganda outlet Breitbart and Cambridge Analytica, which became infamous for using illicitly obtained Facebook data to target voters for Trump. The head of the Government Accountability Institute was a Bannon associate by the name of Peter Schweizer, and he concocted a web of lies about the Clinton Foundation in an effort to hobble my campaign. In 2015, Schweizer published a garbage book called *Clinton Cash* that peddled a wild conspiracy theory about how I had supposedly arranged the sale of American uranium to Russia in exchange for millions of dollars in contributions to the Clinton Foundation. It was a lie, pure and simple, but many in the press took it seriously—including, shamefully, the *New York Times*. Eventually, the *Times* and the *Washington Post* realized the uranium story was a lie and tried to undo the damage of their initial stories. But the damage was already done to the foundation and board member Frank Giustra, which hurt a lot. The stupidity dominoes kept falling. FBI agents read the book and decided to open an investigation that the Justice Department later described as based solely on "unvetted hearsay information." Of course, word of the investigation then leaked and became fodder for more partisan attacks. None of it came to anything at all. But the Trump administration kept the investigation open until the final days of his term, despite prosecutors determining much earlier that it was baseless. For his part, Schweizer shifted his focus to spreading conspiracy theories about Joe Biden and his son Hunter.

All these lies caused a lot of damage. It hurt my campaign, just as intended. It also tarnished the Clinton Foundation, which, as a nonpartisan charity, was not equipped to fight back. The bogus uranium story and all the right-wing huffing and puffing created a stink during the campaign that no amount of nonpartisan fact-checking could wash off. As the founder of CharityWatch said, "If Hillary Clinton wasn't running for president, the Clinton Foundation would be seen as one of the great humanitarian charities of our generation." Instead, it became a punching bag. Donations dried up. Staff had to be let go. CGI shut down. Impactful programs had to cut back or end altogether. Needy and vulnerable people all over the world paid the price.

Bill put on a good face, but I could tell how much it hurt. I felt terrible. I knew that if I had not decided to run for president, none of this would have happened. Marriage takes sacrifice, and politics isn't for the faint of heart, but this was too much.

It's a remarkable thing to be married for nearly fifty years. Some couples bicker more as they get older. Others find that a little hearing loss with age—or the late Ruth Bader Ginsburg's marriage advice to practice "selective deafness"—can go a long way. You can't start a fight over your spouse's impatient sigh or muttered sarcasm if you don't hear it. Other couples grow so close they start finishing each other's sentences. My parents often sat in silence, which saddened me. For Bill and me, the conversation we started all those years ago in the law library is still going strong. It's comfortable, comforting, and energizing all at the same time, this person beside me whom I know so well. I never get tired of hearing what's on his mind (except when he can't let go of a grievance that's too late to fix—he says that's the Irish in him). And he seems just as interested in what I have to say. On my regular Zoom calls with girlfriends, he'll sometimes settle onto the couch beside me to join the chitchat or just listen, soaking up the easy banter of lifelong connection and the joy it brings us both. It's no secret that Bill and I had dark days in our marriage in the past. But the past softens with time, and what's left is the truth: I'm married to my best friend.

During the pandemic, when our frenetic travel schedules came to a sudden stop, we spent more days and nights together than we had in decades. We put together puzzles of all sizes and degrees of difficulty with our family. Chelsea and Bill were, by far, the most prolific. My favorites were the Zen puzzles with wooden pieces. For a time during COVID, Chelsea, Marc, and the kids moved in next door so we could all be together in a "pod." Bill and I loved it. Many mornings before eight a.m. our grandchildren came over to play or eat breakfast. It was sacred time. No Zooms, no calls. Just family. At home we're not Mr. President and Madam Secretary, we are Pop Pop and Grandma. There's nothing better. We spent our secluded days playing countless games of hide-and-seek or Tiger, which consisted of Bill or me pretending to be a tiger pursuing Charlotte and Aidan. We spent long summer afternoons in our pool, introducing Jasper to the water and watching his brother and sister gain confidence as swimmers. Water fights and dunking contests kept us all laughing. We even produced our backyard version of *The Wizard of Oz*. I searched online for a much-abridged children's version of the script, ordered costumes, and convinced everybody to participate. Charlotte played Dorothy with her family Yorkie, named Soren, playing Toto. Aidan was the Scarecrow; Bill, the Lion; Chelsea, Glinda the Good Witch; Marc, the Wizard; and little Jasper, a flying monkey. Other friends in our pod played the Tin Man and the Wicked Witch. I was (no surprise) the director. It went off without a hitch but closed after only one performance.

Bill's mind is quicker than ever, but it takes him a little longer to get out of bed in the morning. He's always been a night owl, but now I hear him moving around at all hours. I wish he slept more. In 2021, we had a scare. Bill was traveling in Southern California and came down with a bad infection that turned into sepsis. At the hospital, Bill was in the intensive care unit for five long days while doctors figured out what was wrong and started treatment. He was delirious with fever for two of the scariest days and couldn't recognize people he'd known for years. Chelsea and I immediately flew out to be with him. On the flight, I wondered what condition I'd find Bill in. His aide had sounded worried on the phone. When you're our age, the thought is always in the back of your mind that you have fewer tomorrows than yesterdays. One day time runs out. But not this time, thanks to the miracle of antibiotics. When I walked into the hospital room, he gave me a big smile, and I could finally breathe. Bill went right to work trying to reassure me that he was going to be just fine. He even got me to laugh about his two days of delirium, which I was

surprised to learn from his doctors occur in 80 percent of ICU patients. "Were you as scared as I was?" I asked him. In that aw-shucks
way he's always had about him, he laid his hand on my shoulder and
confessed that he was too sick to know he should be scared, adding,
"I should probably be scared now that the young men who were with
me took notes on all the crazy things I said!"

I've always loved Bill's hands. He has narrow wrists and tapered
fingers. For half a century they've closed comfortably around my
smaller hand. Sometimes now, when he's tired, his hand has a slight
tremor. The doctors say it's just normal aging, nothing to worry
about. One more little legacy of a long life well lived.

I still think he's the most handsome man in every room. We
recently both got dressed up to attend a formal state dinner at the
White House honoring the Japanese prime minister, with a musical
performance by Paul Simon. Bill looked stunning in his tuxedo, every
inch the debonair former leader of the free world. As we entered the
White House through the East Colonnade, filled with cherry blossoms and enormous Japanese fans, Bill grinned and pointed to the
portrait hanging on the wall. It was me, painted by Simmie Knox in
2002. How young I was then! *What a strange, magical life we've lived
together,* I thought. Bill squeezed my hand, and we went into the
party.

When Bill was an undergraduate at Georgetown, he had a professor named Carroll Quigley who made a lasting impression on him.
Professor Quigley used to say that the most important gift Western
civilization has brought to the world is the idea that "the future can
be better than the past, and each individual has a personal, moral obligation to make it so." As Bill explained it to me a few years later, he
took that as his life's mission: focus on the future. Or as Fleetwood
Mac sang: "Don't stop thinking about tomorrow."

As we get older, we find ourselves thinking more about how we can help build a future we'll never see. One of my favorite proverbs is from the Greeks: "A civilization flourishes when people plant trees under whose shade they will never sit."

Today, Bill is busier at the Clinton Foundation than ever before. He and Chelsea painstakingly bound up the organization's wounds and breathed new life into its programs. Thanks to their leadership and the staff, led by Kevin Thurm, the foundation has not just survived, it's thrived. CGI is back and new partnerships are launching.

After 2016, I was initially reluctant to get too involved for fear of inviting more partisan attacks and undercutting the progress they were making. But Bill and Chelsea are persistent, persuasive advocates. They say there's too much important work to do, and we can't let fear hold us back. They're right, of course. So I dived back in.

The challenges facing future generations will look different from the ones Bill and I spent our careers tackling. But the principle of putting people first is just as critical in an era when the world is fracturing, the planet is rapidly warming, artificial intelligence is changing everything, and democracy is hanging by a thread. Our world will need new leaders who understand how to solve problems, feel a responsibility to address them, and are ready to take action. We will need what the Clinton Foundation does best: collaborative, catalytic leadership that mobilizes partnerships to make a difference in people's lives. More than ever, we still need all three legs of the stool working together.

Three decades ago, Bill reinvented the Democratic Party by putting solutions ahead of ideology. Two decades ago, he reinvented philanthropy by centering partnerships and action. The Clinton Foundation's model for solving problems and building partnerships has the potential to inspire a new generation of leaders, organizers, and philanthropists to help people build better lives for themselves, their families, and their communities.

Progress is hard. You have to work at it, day in and day out, for a long time. We may not live to see the full impact of our work. No generation ever does. But if you believe in the promise of the future and feel a responsibility for building it, you have to try. That's how Bill and I see the next ten years of our life: putting down a firm foundation that can benefit and be built on by those who follow.

KEEP MARCHING

Since 2016, a lot of people have wondered how I'm spending my time. Long walks in the woods followed by a glass of chardonnay? Yes to the walks, but not so much wine these days. Quietly retiring was never an option. Yes, I have grandchildren to enjoy, piles of books to read, places I still want to travel to, work to do with the Clinton Foundation, and a husband who's good company. True enough. But I'm still committed to "doing all the good." I need to dive into projects, not settle into a rocking chair.

In this book, you've read about some of the ways I've kept busy, from teaching at Columbia University to helping Afghan women escape the Taliban. Because I'm so concerned about the future of our democracy, I also spend time on my political action committee Onward Together, which helps fund and support candidates and organizations dedicated to our democracy. We've supported organizations that fought against Trump's Muslim ban and family separation at the southern border, helped recruit and train women and people of color to run for office, mobilized voters, fought for abortion ballot referenda in red states, combated disinformation, and so much more. Since 2017, we've raised about $66 million for candidates, causes, and organizations of all kinds standing up for a fairer, more inclusive, democratic America.

I've also tried new things that my previous life never had room for, like teaming up with my friend and mystery writer Louise Penny to write a thriller during the pandemic. Together we penned *State of Terror*, about a female secretary of state racing to outmaneuver international terrorists and homegrown traitors hell-bent on turning the United States into a Russian satellite state. When a publisher approached us about collaborating, I was excited but nervous. I had never written fiction before, and I didn't want to disappoint Louise or jeopardize our friendship if the writing partnership bombed. Turns out Louise was also concerned. She confessed that her first drafts can be "really soft and smelly," and she was reluctant to let me see that. She was being too hard on herself. I soon saw for myself that her first drafts are brilliance in progress. The partnership went so well that now Louise and I are collaborating as executive producers on a screen adaptation.

In 2021, I agreed to become the American advisor to the Imperiale, an international art prize awarded by the Imperial family of Japan on behalf of the Japan Art Association in the fields of painting, sculpture, architecture, music, theater, and film. David Rockefeller Jr. asked me to join and it's been a delight to attend the ceremony in Tokyo with him and his wife, Susan. My friend Susie Buell attended with me in 2022 and she bonded with acclaimed artist and prize recipient Ai Weiwei. The next year my friends Lisa Perry and Ann Tannenbaum, who are both well-known art collectors, were my guests. The highlight of 2023 was the wonderful reception for the American awardees hosted by Dr. Biden at the White House.

I also ventured into what I worried would be the lion's den for an interview with the infamous shock jock Howard Stern. He'd been trying for years to put me in the hot seat on his show, but it always seemed a little too far outside my comfort zone—and I didn't feel comfortable with the comments that too often objectified and demeaned women. Turns out Howard has mellowed (and maybe so have I). Despite my initial trepidation, it was a lot of fun. We spent more than two hours talking about everything from Trump's inauguration ("some weird shit," to quote George W. Bush) to my relationship with Bill. I enjoyed the candid back-and-forth. The audience seemed to agree—of all the press I've done in recent years, people have talked to me about that interview more than any other. It made me wonder about opportunities I may have missed over the years to reach different audiences who otherwise might not have heard my message. My caution with the press is well-earned, having endured more than my share of hit jobs and silly gotcha questions, but I've also learned that an arm's-length approach carries its own risks.

And, perhaps most surprisingly (to me), I agreed to cooperate on a documentary about my life produced by Propagate and directed by Nanette Burstein, which resulted in a four-part series on Hulu called, predictably, *Hillary*. No subject was off-limits, and I've heard from lots of viewers how much they learned about me from it, and how much they understood about the challenges facing any woman who dares to run for president.

One important through line for me since 2016 has been finding new and impactful ways to tell women's stories and lift up women's history. This won't come as a surprise to anyone who knows me. I'll never forget when I was a young girl and discovered a library book of Greek myths that featured strong female figures like Athena, the goddess of wisdom and war, and Artemis, the goddess of the hunt and wild animals. Their examples gave me so much courage that I asked my mom if I could get a bow and arrow like the hunter Artemis. She wisely refused, despite my best argument that the Roman name for Artemis, Diana, was like my middle name, Diane.

I was thrilled when Oxford University established the world's first chair in women's history—and humbled when they named it after me. I hope it will not be the last such position. Creating this endowed chair at one of the most revered universities in the world sends the message that women's history is worthy of study, not just the notable but also the marginalized and forgotten, and that no one can write us out of history again.

I'm also excited about the work getting underway at the new Hillary Rodham Clinton Center for Citizenship, Leadership, and Democracy at my alma mater Wellesley College and at the Hillary

Rodham Clinton School of Law at Swansea University in Wales, with a focus on the human rights of children. And I'm delighted to serve as the first woman chancellor at Queen's University Belfast in Northern Ireland, where Bill and I have worked so hard over the years to support peace and reconciliation.

Chelsea and I wrote a book together for the first time, *The Book of Gutsy Women*, about the women who motivate us—women with the courage to stand up to the status quo, ask hard questions, and get the job done. I loved hearing stories from readers, particularly little girls, about how they connected to the civil rights activist Dorothy Height, or the LGBTQ+ trailblazer Edie Windsor, who took her fight for marriage equality to the Supreme Court, or the figure skater Michelle Kwan, who kept pushing forward, no matter what.

We turned the book into a docuseries called *Gutsy* on Apple TV+ with the production company we've created, HiddenLight. Chelsea and I traveled all over the country (and to Paris) on adventures with bold, brave women. We walked the halls of Little Rock Central High School with Carlotta Walls LaNier and Minnijean Brown-Trickey, who were among the Little Rock Nine students to bravely desegregate the school in 1957. We learned magic tricks from Meriam Al-Sultan, who told us she left a controlling marriage in Saudi Arabia with her daughter, Judy, to pursue their dreams in America. We walked with the activist and academic Kimberlé Crenshaw through the Metropolitan Museum of Art's replica of the African American settlement called Seneca Village that had existed in the middle of Manhattan until it was seized and destroyed to create Central Park.

Producing and starring in my first television series was deeply meaningful, but I wanted HiddenLight Productions to be more than my personal platform. I wanted it to amplify untold and important stories from brave women around the world, particularly in their own voices. That's why I was delighted to produce *In Her Hands*, the Emmy Award–winning Netflix documentary detailing the story of Zarifa Ghafari, one of Afghanistan's few female mayors discussed earlier in the book, and *Lyra*, an award-winning film about the re-markable young gay journalist Lyra McKee, who was murdered in Northern Ireland in 2019 after a life fearlessly committed to truth and justice. We're now working on a documentary about how losing *Roe v. Wade* has impacted women across America and the very real harms of abortion bans.

In my podcast called *You and Me Both* I talk with inspiring people making and shaping history, literature, entertainment, politics, and so much more. After decades of being interviewed, I enjoyed being the one asking the questions. Like anything, it took practice. Now, with fifty-two episodes and counting, I've hit my stride. It's been thrilling to learn a new way of telling stories, particularly for and about women.

Another project that was deeply personal to me was trying to turn my friend Elaine Weiss's 2018 book, *The Woman's Hour*, a riveting account of the women who fought for ratification of the Nineteenth Amendment, into a film. The story is a page-turner. Real-life drama with historic consequences. I thought, *Who better to be attached to this project? I know women's history—I'm a part of that history—and I believe strongly in the importance of teaching it.* I shopped the idea to one studio after another, who were not as enthralled as I was, with the help of my friend Steven Spielberg. *Women's history? A constitutional amendment? Not sure how to make that sell.* Elaine eventually got an offer and started working on a show, only for it to be canceled during COVID. That was a big disappointment.

I believe passionately in the importance of this story, because too many Americans now want to deny or erase our nation's complicated history. They think somehow learning about the struggles of America takes away from the dreams and ideals of America. But the opposite is true. We need to understand women's history (and *all* our history) to better secure our rights and fight for the ones we've lost or have yet to gain. How much more effective could we be in future battles—for abortion rights, for paid family leave, for childcare, for liberty and justice for all—if we better understood what it took just to get us started?

While Elaine was writing *The Woman's Hour*, Shaina Taub, a young woman in New York who was similarly inspired by the suffrage movement, was hard at work giving the story a different home: the stage. Shaina's inspiration would ultimately allow me to help bring this pivotal chapter in women's history to a whole new audience and realize a dream so secret I didn't even know I had dreamed it. I would become a Broadway producer.

It probably won't surprise you that one of my favorite musicals is Lin-Manuel Miranda's *Hamilton*. I've seen it four times in New York and once in Puerto Rico with Lin's parents, Luis and Luz Miranda, who are longtime friends. I devoured it when it started streaming on television during the pandemic. There's a wonderful moment when the free-thinking, fast-talking Angelica Schuyler quotes the radical idea at the heart of America's new Declaration of Independence, "That all men are created equal," but then adds an even more radical twist: "When I meet Thomas Jefferson, I'm 'a compel him to include women in the sequel."

Whenever I hear that line, I think about Elizabeth Cady Stanton, the woman who actually did it. In July 1848, seventy-two years after Jefferson wrote the original Declaration of Independence, Stanton drafted the sequel for the first great conference on women's rights, held in Seneca Falls, New York. Sixty-eight women and thirty-two men signed Stanton's Declaration of Sentiments, which updated Jefferson's text and asserted, "We hold these truths to be self-evident; that all men *and women* are created equal" (emphasis mine, but inspiration hers).

Stanton was just thirty-two years old, but she had grown up reading her father's law books (he was a New York judge), and she was convinced that for American democracy to succeed, it had to include women. She had already managed to persuade the state legislature to allow married women to own property, make contracts, and have legal custody of their children. Now Stanton set her sights on the most fundamental right in a democracy: the right to vote.

The idea that women should be able to vote was highly controversial even among the activists gathered in Seneca Falls, including Stanton's own husband. But she pointed back to Jefferson's argument that legitimate governments derive "their just powers from the consent of the governed." How could American democracy be legitimate if it denied women the right to consent? If it forced women to submit to laws and leaders they had no say in choosing? The only way to live up to our founding ideals was to rewrite our founding documents and expand the "we" in "we the People."

The power of this idea sparked a suffrage movement that spread across the country. For decades, women (and men) organized, marched, picketed, went to jail, and refused to sit down or shut up until finally, in 1920, the Nineteenth Amendment to the Constitution granted women the right to vote. It took decades more to enact the Voting Rights Act and protect the rights of Black women (and men), which remain under threat to this day.

At Seneca Falls, Stanton was following in the footsteps of abolitionists who often quoted the Declaration of Independence to encourage Americans to live up to the nation's promise of equality by ending slavery. Many Americans knew the words by heart; "Life, Liberty, and the pursuit of Happiness" had been drilled into them in school, over the dinner table, or in the town square. That meant that nearly everyone who heard the new phrasing in the Declaration of Sentiments—"all men and women are created equal"—would recognize the change immediately.

Stanton understood this would be controversial. And sure enough, one newspaper called the convention and its declaration "the most shocking and unnatural incident ever recorded in the history of womanity." But by rooting her demand for equality in a familiar, widely revered frame, Stanton hoped to make a radical reform sound like a natural, patriotic step forward.

As First Lady, I initiated a program called Save America's Treasures to recognize and restore cultural and historic landmarks and artifacts around our country. To kick off the program, I went on July 16, 1998, to the Women's Rights National Historical Park in Seneca Falls to mark the 150th anniversary of the campaign for women's suffrage. A crowd of sixteen thousand people gathered, and I urged them to be guided into the future by the vision and wisdom of those who signed the Declaration of Sentiments: "The future, like the past and present, will not and cannot be perfect. Our daughters and granddaughters will face new challenges, which we today cannot even imagine. But each of us can help prepare for that future by doing what we can to speak out for justice and equality, for women's rights and human rights, to be on the right side of history, no matter the risk or cost."

On August 26, 2020, while the pandemic raged and the presidential campaign between Joe Biden and Donald Trump was heating up, I gathered in Central Park with a small, socially distanced crowd on the hundredth anniversary of the Nineteenth Amendment. We were there to unveil the city's first sculpture depicting real women in Central Park (the others of unreal "women" are Alice in Wonderland and Mother Goose). Men, it's worth noting, have 145 statues erected to them in New York City.

This long-overdue statue stands fourteen feet tall and depicts three women who devoted their lives to winning the right to vote but never lived to cast a legal ballot themselves. Gathered around a small table are Susan B. Anthony, who was arrested in 1872 for the crime of "voting while female" and for whom the Nineteenth Amendment is named; Elizabeth Cady Stanton, who never forgot that she and her fellow suffragists were fighting not for themselves alone but for the generations that would follow; and Sojourner Truth, who told the Ohio Woman's Rights Convention in 1851, "If the first woman God ever made was strong enough to turn the world upside down all alone, these women together ought to be able to turn it back, and get it right side up again!"

When I was in the Senate, the civil rights pioneer Dorothy Height and a group of other civil rights leaders from the National Congress of Black Women came to see me about putting a statue of Sojourner Truth in the U.S. Capitol Building alongside other national heroes (mostly white men, of course). It took us years, but we finally got Sojourner's bust put up when I was secretary of state, the first sculpture honoring an African American woman to be represented there. I was so pleased to see her likeness again in Central Park.

Looking up at the three determined faces whose life's work made so much of my own possible, I wondered what they'd say about the struggles and setbacks we now face—about the loss of constitutional rights for women and the disappointment of getting so close to shattering the highest, hardest glass ceiling. I imagine it would be something like what the monument's sculptor, Meredith Bergmann, said after the unveiling ceremony: "Our rights were not gained by one dramatic action but from long shared struggle."

To honor that struggle, each of us wore a purple, white, and gold sash—the official colors of the suffrage movement. Over my decades-long political career, I've often reached for those colors during symbolic moments. I wore a white pantsuit and gold jewelry during my final debate with Trump and when I accepted the 2016 Democratic nomination for president—the first time in American history when a woman secured the backing of a major party. I also had planned to wear yet another suffragist-white pantsuit on election night to claim victory as the first female president of the United States. Instead, I wore it to Trump's inauguration. On the rainy November morning when I delivered my concession speech, I wore a suit with purple lapels (and Bill wore a purple tie) that I had intended to wear on my first trip to Washington, D.C., as president-elect. It was a nod to bipartisanship and to the women whose shoulders I stood on.

Wrapped in those suffragist colors on that sunny morning in Central Park four years later, I thought about the many milestones that their long struggle had made possible. My mother was born before women had the right to vote, and she lived long enough to cast her ballot for me in the 2008 primaries. In my own lifetime, women couldn't have a credit card in our name. We couldn't have a bank account. We couldn't access birth control unless we were married. Couldn't access legal abortion. Couldn't sue for sexual harassment. There were schools we couldn't go to, jobs we couldn't apply for. We could get fired for getting pregnant. We've made so much progress because the suffragists pushed for women's voices to be heard. And yet their stories are rarely told. Growing up, I didn't learn about suffragists in school. There were no lessons on great American women in my history classes. When I got to college, the women's liberation movement was just beginning, and there were wonderfully smart women like Gloria Steinem and Betty Friedan writing about politics and gender equality. But I wouldn't learn much about the Declaration of Sentiments, about the women on the pedestal in Central Park and the determination of the suffrage movement, until years later.

"Our charge now," I told the crowd as we stood in the shadows of Sojourner Truth, Elizabeth Cady Stanton, and Susan B. Anthony, "is to take the stories of the women in this statue and carry them forward into our schools, into the media, onto social media, and into our lives." Those weren't empty words. They were a mission statement.

I wasn't the only one to feel this mission in my bones. In 2016, Shaina Taub was a young volunteer on my campaign when she began writing a musical about the final push for the passage and ratification of the Nineteenth Amendment. The suffrage movement had all the makings of a dramatic stage production: parades and pageantry, a decades-long bitter political fight, and a cast of daring, dynamic women who refused to back down.

There was Carrie Chapman Catt, president of the National American Woman Suffrage Association and Susan B. Anthony's anointed heir. For nearly three decades Carrie faithfully followed the strategy laid out by her foremothers: a state-by-state approach to put the question of women's suffrage to (male) voters. There were few victories. There was plucky upstart Alice Paul, a New Jersey Quaker who founded the rival National Woman's Party to pursue more provocative tactics: dramatic parades, picketing the president, publishing letters from prison where she and her fellow "suffs" were force-fed raw eggs for hunger striking—all for the goal of a constitutional amendment granting women the right to vote. There was Ida B. Wells, the fearless Black journalist and anti-lynching activist, and her good friend Mary Church Terrell, the daughter of formerly enslaved parents and co-founder of the NAACP.

Together these suffragists defied entrenched cultural norms, applied political pressure, endured sexist abuse and harassment, formed unlikely coalitions to push the movement forward, quarreled with anti-suffragists and each other—all so women could have an equal voice in government. Their victory wasn't perfect, nor were their strategies. Both the moderate Carrie and militant Alice, whose activism began during the abolition movement, made compromises with racist southern suffragists and at times excluded Black women from fully participating in their activities. In the later years of the movement, they also refused to work together. In the dramatic final push for the amendment's ratification, Carrie and Alice were too stubborn to unify their separate campaigns. And even their victory, important though it was, still largely excluded Black women.

Shaina didn't shy away from recounting the painful parts of the suffrage movement. But she almost didn't finish the musical. On that gray November day in 2016 when I conceded the race to Trump (in suffragist purple), Shaina sobbed while listening to my speech and considered giving up on her project. I'm so grateful she didn't, because when I saw *Suffs* in its first iteration at the nonprofit Public Theater in New York City in 2022, I couldn't imagine a better time to bring the story of the suffrage movement to life. A month after *Suffs* opened off-Broadway at the Public, the Supreme Court's decision to overturn *Roe v. Wade* leaked, alerting women across America that our reproductive autonomy would soon be revoked—and in effect our equal citizenship. Suddenly, the story of fearless women fighting for a better future didn't feel like ancient history. It felt like a blueprint.

Suffs was so successful that its sold-out downtown run was extended three times. A year later, the lead producers, Jill Furman and Rachel Sussman, announced it was moving uptown to Broadway. To my immense surprise, a letter arrived in June 2023 from Shaina inviting me to come with them. Would I join the team as a co-producer? she asked.

Did I know what being a co-producer entailed? Not quite. But I love a challenge. And I love Broadway. Between 2017 and March 2020, when the bright lights of Broadway were dimmed by the pandemic, I saw nearly fifty shows, often with my friends like the late and greatly missed Liz Robbins or Brooke Neidich, and Annette de La Renta, Barry Diller, and Anna Wintour, whose love of theater matches mine, by my side. There is nothing like sinking into a seat, feeling the excitement and the anticipation as the lights go down, and being transported out of our troubling world for at least a little while. School plays, summer stages, Broadway shows—I love them all. One of my longtime aides, Rob Russo, has a second life as a Broadway critic and producer and always has his finger on the pulse of what's new and can't-miss. His recommendations never steer me wrong.

I watched shows that were silly and just good fun (like Disney's *Frozen*, which I took Charlotte to see for her fifth birthday). Others were a gut punch of humor and heart (like Phoebe Waller-Bridge's off-Broadway hit *Fleabag* and Jez Butterworth's *The Ferryman*, about a family navigating the Troubles in Northern Ireland). Others got me thinking about the zigzag of American history—two steps forward and one step back on the road to a more perfect union. Heidi Schreck's brilliant play *What the Constitution Means to Me* asked deep questions about our founding document's failure to protect women from violence and discrimination. And Selina Fillinger's *POTUS; or, Behind Every Great Dumbass Are Seven Women Trying to Keep Him Alive* . . . well, let's just say it gave me a lot to laugh about (and I got two standing ovations just for showing up!).

But I never imagined I could be more than a fan. In high school, a classmate who was in the spring musical, *Bye Bye Birdie*, told me the director was looking for students to join the show's chorus. I'd been in the director's drama class and he was friendly, so I volunteered. "I'll tell you what, Hillary," the director said to me, "you can be in the production as long as you don't actually sing. Just mouth the words." It was an early lesson in the importance of direct feedback.

Now, with Shaina's invitation, I offered suggestions on the script she was revising, learned some theater lingo (like *sitzprobe*, German for "seated rehearsal," where performers sing sans costumes or props for the first time with a live orchestra in a studio—what a thrill!), watched a video of the newly revised version, attended the first rehearsal for Broadway, and gave my notes to Shaina and our amazing director, Leigh Silverman. I could relate to the persistent professional process the actors were engaged in. All the rehearsing, critiquing, and revising was kind of like preparing for a presidential debate (only with more joy and no Trump).

I also learned that many of us involved in the production shared a similar story of finding our way to the suffragists on our own. Few learned about Carrie Chapman Catt or Alice Paul in school (fewer still had been taught about Ida B. Wells or Mary Church Terrell). I learned that Rachel Sussman had wanted to write a paper on the suffrage movement for her high school history class, but her textbook had just a scant paragraph of details. So she picked up the suffragist Doris Stevens's firsthand memoir, *Jailed for Freedom*, and was so moved she gave it to Shaina years later and shared her big idea: *What about a musical about these women?* Shaina stayed up all night reading the book and sent Rachel an email in the morning: "We have to do this." Shaina wrote the book, the music, and the lyrics— and stars in the show as Alice Paul (she's only the second woman in Broadway history to do all four).

After months of rehearsing and a few weeks of preview performances, in April 2024, it was time to roll out the purple carpet for the opening night of *Suffs*. I couldn't contain my joy. With my hands over my heart and holding back tears, I listened and watched as the cast and orchestra electrified the room with one of the most thrilling stories of American history. *Suffs* would later earn six Tony Award nominations, including Best Musical. On the night of the awards show, I had the honor of introducing the company to perform the final song, "Keep Marching," and I celebrated with them backstage after Shaina won the Tony for Best Book of a Musical and Best Original Score. I couldn't be more proud.

The suffrage movement has a lot to teach us about the power of effective advocacy movements, especially right now as our democracy hangs in the balance, women's reproductive rights are being rolled back, and a radical Supreme Court has signaled rights like birth control and same-sex marriage may be next. The suffragists teach us that movements don't always work in perfect harmony. There are disagreements and difficult trade-offs, and sometimes progress seems impossibly slow. But the suffragists never gave up. They never gave in to fear of defeat. And in the end, it took all their dogged determination to convince an ambivalent-at-best president, a deeply sexist Congress, and racist southern state legislatures to correct the mistake of our founding fathers and give women the vote.

But that's not the end of the story. In fact, it's a call to action.

What the suffragists' example shows us (and what the "suffs" sing in the rousing finale) is that "progress is possible, not guaranteed." Change doesn't happen on its own. Equality will not be given to us. Throughout American history—from our founding to the Civil War and Reconstruction to the movements for women's rights, civil rights, and LGBTQ+ rights—change happened because people devoted their lives to it. Many were born and died bumping up against the hard walls of injustice. As Elaine Weiss writes, "The women who launched the movement were dead by the time it was completed; the women who secured its final success weren't born when it began." But no one gave up. They kept marching. They fought hard to make the dream of equality a reality. If they could do it, so can we. As the Talmud says and Shaina wrote into her script: "You are not obligated to complete the work, but neither are you free to abandon it."

I hope I'm alive to see the United States elect a female president. I hope I'm alive to see my daughter and grandchildren enjoy more rights than they were born with, not fewer. I know I won't live to see the world achieve true gender equality. At the current rate of progress, it will take 286 years to close global gender gaps in legal protection and remove discriminatory laws against women, 140 years for equal representation in positions of power, and at least 40 years to achieve gender parity in national parliaments. I also know it doesn't have to take that long and that progress is possible. That's what the suffragists believed. That's what I want my grandkids and future generations to know. Just before the curtain falls at the end of *Suffs*, the final score reminds us what the strong women who shaped our nation knew to be true and what we must carry "forward, into light":

> *I won't live to see the future that I fight for,*
> *Maybe no one gets to reach that perfect day.*
> *If the work is never over,*
> *Then how do you keep marching anyway?*
> *Do you carry your banner as far as you can?*
> *Rewriting the world with your imperfect pen?*
> *Till the next stubborn girl picks it up in a picket line over and*
> *   over again?*

And you join in the chorus of centuries chanting to her.
The path will be twisted and risky and slow,
But keep marching, keep marching.
Will you fail or prevail? Well, you may never know,
But keep marching, keep marching.
'Cause your ancestors are all the proof you need
That progress is possible, not guaranteed.
It will only be made if we keep marching, keep marching on.

ACKNOWLEDGMENTS

It takes a village to publish a book. Particularly this one, which depended on the help, support, and memories of many friends, advisors, and colleagues.

First, my deepest gratitude to my longtime colleague Dan Schwerin, who's been by my side since he joined my Senate staff through two presidential campaigns and the State Department helping me put my thoughts and feelings into words. He and I started thinking about a book back in 2021, trading ideas and drafts, but I couldn't decide what exactly I wanted it to be. It took a while for my ideas to gel, and once they did I told Dan I was ready to go and we dove into the joy of collaborating.

This time we were joined by one of his colleagues at Evergreen Strategy Group, Caty Gordon, who had previously worked at the Clinton Foundation and who began writing for me in 2021. Caty is not only an accomplished researcher and wordsmith but a true delight to work with on any project. She rose to the demands of this one with skill and grace.

I knew that I wanted to bring a new perspective into this book, so I reached out to Sandra Sobieraj Westfall, a longtime journalist for the Associated Press and *People* magazine, who covered the White House in the 1990s and stuck with my story through all the years since. I respected her straightforward approach to reporting and how she took care to bring out the authentic character of the people she wrote about. When I asked Sandra earlier this year if she would participate in my latest book, she happily agreed and we began a stimulating and productive collaboration. She worked closely with me on a few of the more personal chapters, interviewing my old friends, mining my memories of being First Lady, and eliciting thoughts on my parents. Sandra has been a valuable addition to the team.

The talented Noëlle Elmore and Lily Weber, also of Evergreen Strategy Group, provided invaluable insights, research, and thinking for this book, and I thank them both.

Special thanks to Huma Abedin, Nick Merrill, and Lona Valmoro, who have advised me through this adventure and so many others. I am once again grateful for all of their help.

And appreciation to Joyce Aboussie, Carol Biondi, Allida Black, Patsy Henderson Bowles, Susie Buell, Lisa Caputo, Kiki McLean Clark, Kelly Craighead, Patti Criner, Ann Drake, Karen Dunn, Gigi El-Bayoumi, Karen Finney, Tina Flournoy, Aileen Getty, Cheryl Harbor, Rosemarie Howe, Bonnie Ward Klehr, Jen Klein, Tamera Luzzatto, Capricia Marshall, Virginia McGregor, Judith McHale, Donna McLarty, Kiki McLean, Cheryl Mills, Minyon Moore, Lissa Muscatine, Liz Naftali, Brooke Neidich, Alyse Nelson, Ann O'Leary, Judy Osgood, Maria Otero, Louise Penny, Carol Pensky, Lisa Perry, Jan Piercy, Amy Rau, Annette de la Renta, Julissa Reynoso, Kathleen Rogers, Lynn Rothschild, Evan Ryan, Regina Scully, Patti Solis Doyle, Aprill Springfield, Sukie Stanley, Ann Stock, Neera Tanden, Ann Tenenbaum, Melanne Verveer, Rachel Vogelstein, Maggie Williams, and Anna Wintour, and in memory of Diane Blair, Betsy Ebeling, Jill Iscol, Hardye Moel, Liz Robbins, and Ellen Tauscher.

Not long after I finished the chapter on friendship ("One Is Silver and the Other's Gold"), I attended my fifty-fifth reunion at Wellesley College. Reconnecting with my classmates there, I was forcefully reminded of how many more stories of friendship I could have shared in these pages if only I had unlimited space. To *all* the friends I hold dear, you know who you are, and I'm so fortunate to have you in my life.

A heartfelt thanks to everyone who provided wise advice, or helped review pages and check facts, including Arman Abrishamchian, Dan Baer, Rachel Chen, Raj Chetty, Lucy Coady, Jon Davidson, Pete Davis, Shelby Deibler, E. J. Dionne, Alex Djerassi, Karen Dunn, Al From, Michael Fuchs, Kita Kanakadandila, Jim Kloppenberg, Alexander Konwal, Bree Henshaw, Abby Hiller, Shannon Lausch, Brian Lazzaro, Bari Luri, Clare Smith Marash, Peyton Marshak, Mike Martinez, Mike McFaul, Yascha Mounk, Alison Myers, Reema Nanavaty, Jennifer Nix, Chinyere Okonkwo, Sarah Oppenheimer, Luis Patiño, Lauren Peterson, Maggie Polachek, Ai-jen Poo, Ella Price, Bob Putnam, Philippe Reines, Megan Rooney, Rob Russo, Georgina Seal, Ella Serrano, Bill Shillady, Anna Smilie, Vas Srivastava, Elizabeth Stigler, Chelsea Tabachnik, Lona Valmoro, Roxana Wang, Shanna Weathersby, Glenn Whaley, and Sean Wilentz.

I am lucky to work with the best in the publishing business at Simon & Schuster, especially Chief Executive Officer Jonathan Karp, who is always available to talk, and my wise editor Priscilla Painton, as well as Janet Byrne, Paul Dippolito, Jon Evans, Lauren Gomez, Kayley Hoffman, Irene Kheradi, Johanna Li, Beth Maglione, Dominick Montalto, Amanda Mulholland, Linda Sawicki, Jackie Seow, and Nancy Tan. And how lucky am I that my friend Annie Leibovitz put her brilliance and vision to work photographing the book's cover portrait? Thanks to her and Karen Mulligan for their collaboration and support, as always. Thanks also to my attorneys and friends Bob Barnett and David Kendall, whose professional advice I've relied upon for all of my books—and so much else, along with their team at Williams & Connolly, including Michael O'Connor and Emily Alden.

This book would not have been possible without the many colleagues who have been involved with my adventures and endeavors since 2016.

Thank you to the team, past and present, at Onward Together—Charlie Baker, Kris Balderston, Dennis Cheng, Howard Dean, Justin Klein, Jenna Lowenstein, Judith McHale, Kelly Mehlenbacher, Minyon Moore, Jess O'Connell, Laura Olin, Adam Parkhomenko, Lauren Peterson, Amy Rao, Emmy Ruiz, Reshma Saujani, Ellen Tauscher, Jessica Wen, and Liz Zaretsky.

I'm grateful to Dean Keren Yarhi-Milo and everyone at Columbia University's School of International and Public Affairs for the opportunity to dive back into teaching, including Daniel Aho, Michael Becker, Lionel Beehner, Katie Day Benvenuto, Lee C. Bollinger, Nancy Cieri, Caroline Donovan, Lauren Hoffman, Susan Glancy, Felicia Goodman, Susan Lee, Hazel May, Lincoln Mitchell, Marianna Pecoraro, Nicole Peisajovich, Heather Penatzer, Laura Samotin, Alex Sanford, Christina Shelby, Simran Singh, Paola Solimena, Adam Stepan, Elyse Surette-DiMuzio, Rachel Szala, and Naomi J. Weinberger. Thanks also to Alena Yarmosky, Chelsea Kohler, Renee Betterson, Jack Craven, and the team at Evergreen Strategy Group for your support.

Thank you to the HiddenLight production team, especially Sam Branson and Johnny Webb, and Taylor Anderson, Rayhan Arif, Vicki Bax, Rob Blok, Alex Cavalier, Liz Collier, Ragaa Cheba, Cherry Dorrett, Claire Featherstone, Katharine Fish, Amy Flanagan, Ben Gordon, Didem Gormus, Nicky Huggett, Eleanor Keeffe, Roma Khanna, Toby McCathie, David Pearce, Brenda Robinson, Antonia Sanders, Siobhan Sinnerton, Michaela Whittle, and Millie Wilkinson.

Thanks as well to our partners at Apple TV+ who brought *Gutsy* to life, especially Molly Thompson and Colleen Grogan. And to the team who brought my podcast *You and Me Both* to listeners: Forrest Gray, Bree Henshaw, Lindsay Hoffman, Sara Horowitz, Brianna Johnson, Zach McNees, Laura Olin, Lauren Peterson, Binita Raman, Kathleen Russo, Rob Russo, Opal Vadhan, and Julie Subrin, and our colleagues at iHeartRadio, especially Bob Pitman and John Sykes.

I'm thrilled to thank the cast and crew of *Suffs* for making my

Broadway dreams come true, particularly its creator Shaina Taub; lead producers Rachel Sussman and Jill Furman; director Leigh Silverman; Oskar Eustis of the Public Theater; Rob Russo, my personal translator of all things Broadway; Huma Abedin, who made the *Suffs* journey with me; and Grady Keefe, who advances my trips to the theater and stays to watch with me. Thanks also to the press team of Amy Jacobs, Marta Gryb, and Nicole Suder at Rubenstein; Morgan Steward and Miranda Gohh on the producing team; Susie Bryant from general management; company manager Jenny Peek; stage manager Lisa Iacucci; music director Andrea Grody and her entire music department; our designers and creative team; the marketing team; the scenic and costume shops; and everyone backstage and front of house at the Music Box Theatre on Broadway. And, of course, to Alice Paul, Carrie Chapman Catt, Ida B. Wells, Mary Church Terrell, Inez Milholland, Doris Stevens, Lucy Burns, Ruza Wenclawska, Alva Belmont, Mollie Hay, and all the original "Suffs" who believed in a future for women and girls that many never got to see, but that was made possible only because of their vision, sacrifice, and hard work.

Thanks also to the amazing leaders and staff at the Clinton Foundation, the Clinton Global Initiative, and the Clinton Presidential Center for their groundbreaking and life-changing work in this country and around the world. I'm honored to be a board member and colleague.

Thanks to the leadership of Swansea University's Hillary Rodham Clinton School of Law; Oxford University's Hillary Rodham Clinton Chair in Women's History; Wellesley College's Hillary Rodham Clinton Center for Citizenship, Leadership, and Democracy; and Queens University Belfast for appointing me their first female chancellor.

My heart was in my throat the entire month of August 2021 as we evacuated roughly one thousand Afghan women and their family members from Kabul as it fell back into the hands of the Taliban.

I will always be grateful for the courage, commitment, and creativity of Huma Abedin, Belquis Ahmadi, Noha Alkamcha, Linton Bell, Teresa Casale, Nelson Castro, Zoya Craig, Carter Farmer, Kat Fotovat, Saba Ghori, Heather Harms, Tanya Henderson, Olivia Holt-Ivry, Lina Tori Jan, Jess Keller, Amed Khan, Jen Klein, Magda Kushi, Nick Merrill, Horia Mosadiq, Alyse Nelson, Jacqueline O'Neill, Julissa Reynoso, Zainab Salbi, Roy Shaposhnik, Allie Smith, Melanne Verveer, Matt Welborn, and Aleksandra Zaytseva. Thank you to Diane von Furstenberg, the Maverick Collective, and everyone who donated to the Vital Voices Emergency Fund for Afghan Women, from major philanthropies to little girls who sold their toys to support our efforts. Thank you to the governments of Albania, Bahrain, Canada, Germany, Greece, Kuwait, Pakistan, Qatar, Rwanda, Turkey, Ukraine, the United Arab Emirates, and the United States for helping to evacuate and resettle Afghan women. The women of Afghanistan are in my heart, now and always.

Finally, thanks as always to Bill, my first reader and invaluable editor, for his suggestions and encouragement. A huge thanks to Chelsea, my partner in so many of the experiences I recount, from writing *Gutsy*, starting our production company HiddenLight, working together at the foundation and CGI, and providing me with necessary constructive criticism and advice. And, of course, boundless gratitude to her and Marc for Charlotte, Aidan, and Jasper, who've made me the happiest grandma to walk this earth. To quote *Suffs*, "the future demands that we fight for it now," and I'm fighting for yours.

INDEX